2⁵⁰

(6²⁵ New)

Heavy ink scoring

THE NEW TESTAMENT WORLD

THE NEW TESTAMENT WORLD

A Brief Sketch of the History and Conditions
which Composed the Background
of the New Testament

THIRD EDITION, REVISED

H. E. DANA

BROADMAN PRESS
NASHVILLE, TENNESSEE

Broadman Press
Nashville, Tennessee
Twelfth Printing

421-032

Printed in the United States of America
2.AT6313

LOVINGLY INSCRIBED TO

ELIZABETH

AND

ELSIE MARIE

INTRODUCTION

The historical method of approach to the New Testament inevitably raises some insistent questions in the mind of the evangelical Christian student. First of all, since the New Testament is the divine truth of redemption, he wishes to know why we need concern ourselves with ordinary factors of human history. And how may earthly conditions be employed in an effort to understand a heavenly message? What reason and justification have we for an historical approach to a divine revelation? Whereas the particular design of this work is to serve the devout evangelical student, we feel it incumbent upon us to answer these questions as a preliminary step to the discussion.

The reason for the historical approach lies in the undeniable and inevitable human element in the New Testament. This human element is as essential to its efficiency in man's spiritual experience as its divine element. It was impossible for God to speak to man and be understood without involving in his message this human element. Even if the New Testament were a collection of divine oracles, independent of any connection with human experience, these oracles would necessarily be expressed in human language. But, on the contrary, an inductive study of the books of the New Testament proves that they were not oracular messages given from heaven without any earthly medium, but actually arose from real human conditions and were affected by normal human influences. The human element is simply a fact which unmistakably presents itself on the pages of the New Testament as they lie before us.

But we also believe that the human element alone fails to explain this Book. We believe that recognition of the divine element also is necessary to account for it in a rationally satisfactory way. One meets as grave difficulties who attempts to explain the New Testament by the human element exclusively as are encountered in the effort to understand it as exclusively divine. Both must be accepted if we are to satisfy the demands of all the facts.

So the New Testament is subject to an historical approach, but the historical approach does not forestall the approach of religious faith. We need to perceive both the justification and the limitations of the historical method.

The human element in the New Testament exhibits itself in certain clearly defined features. For instance, we find there the unmistakable imprint of human individuality. The various authors present different styles, different psychological traits, different groups of characteristic conceptions, and different modes of expression. No one can study closely the writings of Paul and John without being impressed with the difference between the two. Paul's style is in the main rugged and complicated, while John's is simple and smooth. This is of course to be detected most clearly in the Greek text, but even the English text exhibits it to some extent. Paul views Christian teaching as a system of logically related principles which he calls "the gospel"; while John sees in it a group of concrete, mystical ideas which he calls "the truth." With Paul the problem of human redemption is in the antithesis of the law and grace, works and faith, merit and justification. With John the antithesis is of life and death, light and darkness. In Mark we find the loose and broken style of the typical vernacular, while Luke's writings present a literary finish which compares favorably with some of the best Greek literature of his day. These differences are plain and undeniable phenomena, which appear on the text of the New Testament, and can only be accounted for as the free and normal play of individual capacities and faculties.

The New Testament carries clear traces of the life out of which it came. It was written by Jews—with the probable exception of the Third Gospel and Acts—and is distinctly a Jewish book. For many centuries it was claimed that the language of the New Testament was a special Holy Ghost speech, divinely provided as a vehicle of redemptive revelation. This idea arose because of the fact that the language of the New Testament is not like the ancient Attic or classical Greek. But within the past century it has been learned that the New Testament was composed in the ordinary colloquial Greek of the world of its day. The New Testament reflects certain Palestinian customs and ideas, without a knowledge of which it is impossible to interpret it in places. It is simply a fact presented by the New Testament itself that it is intimately connected with the life from which it was produced.

Every book or discourse of the New Testament has some sort of connection with a definite historical situation. With the exception of a few instances, we may discern with a high degree of certainty what these situations were. Men in the midst of their life's experiences, in order to meet problems and demands thrust upon them by their own environment, wrote or spoke their impassioned messages. To know these historical situations augments to an immeasurable degree the understanding and appreciation of the particular book or passage under consideration.

The New Testament cannot be adequately interpreted if approached as a collection of independent oracles handed down from heaven, without any reference to the human experience and environment amid which it was written. It is, indeed, the divine revelation of redemption, but this revelation did not arise as a product independent of historical relations. God was pleased to reveal his redemption in and through history, and we are not able rightly to comprehend that revelation until we approach it from the historical side. The New Testament is God's redemptive truth mediated to men through human experience and human consciousness. When viewed in this light it is best understood and yields its richest treasures.

The important point is to discern the real bearing of the environmental conditions upon the thought expressed in the New Testament. The historical setting was not the original source of the thought and teaching. The high hopes, exalted conceptions, and holy ideals which constitute the distinctive character of apostolic life came from contact with Jesus and the experiences which grew out of his resurrection and the advent of the Holy Spirit. Had it not been for these fundamental facts of experience, the forces of historical environment could never have provided such transcendent results. Therefore, historical environment constituted the external frame-work of the gospel: its inner heart was the product of an experience in Christ.

We are to use the historical approach in understanding the forms of expression, the conditions reflected, and the reasons for the directions of thought and life in the New Testament. That is, the writers used terminology, phraseology, and figures of speech current in their time; they took for granted ideas or facts which they knew were already familiar to their readers; they wrote because of the demands of certain existing circumstances; they were engaged in applying the gospel message to situations confronting them. The student must have some knowledge of these features of the life behind the New Testament before he can adequately understand its message. Such is the process involved in the historical approach.

The historical approach, however, is not without some important limitations. Just as important as apprehending what is the true historical method, is to be cautious of those points at which one may abuse the historical method. Lack of caution, and abuse actuated by prejudice, have done serious damage in the employment of the historical approach, and won for it an unjust disfavor from evangelical quarters. There are essential limitations which the historical student in fairness should respect.

1. The historical method does not require that we reduce the New Testament to what we may regard as natural, or scientifically explicable. Its proper motive is to elucidate records of the past, not to repudiate them. The historical approach is to be sharply distinguished from the naturalistic or rationalistic approach. It is an abuse of the historical method to use it as a means of conforming the New Testament to a certain type of mind, an attitude of skepticism toward the supernatural. One who wishes to exploit such a type of mind has an inalienable right to do so, but should not do so in the name of the historical method, and rule out of the court of historical inquiry all who do not subscribe to this attitude. It is not necessary as a prerequisite to the historical method that we abandon our confidence in the New Testament as a redemptive interposition of God into the current of human history. The historical method deals with the phenomena of human development in the New Testament period; religious faith ascribes to that history a redemptive significance. Such religious faith is not to be discountenanced unless it seeks to force the history into conformity with its own presuppositions.

2. The historical method does not require us to regard a religious interpretation of events as the invention or perversion of tradition. Because the New Testament writers had an intense religious interest in what they recorded or discussed, and clothed their accounts of events in the impressions of reflection and experience, does not disqualify them as dependable historians. On the contrary, it heightens the value of their records. Just suppose the historians of the Apostolic Age as giving us a New Testament which were nothing more than naked annals, a disinterested chronicle of events, divested of all the marvelous impact upon their own conscience and experience and its eternal aspect as it arises from the crucible of their impassioned souls, and then imagine

if you can how much appeal it would make to the religious mind of a generation nineteen centuries removed from those events. It is that religious interest of the New Testament which gives it its timeless character and its value to subsequent generations. It is not the facts of first century Christian history in which we are primarily interested, but the functional factors of first century Christian experience. Therefore, the competent historical student finds substantial value in the reflected reaction of first century Christian consciousness to the events of the period, and contemplates the religious interest and interpretation as an essential part of the history, and not a worthless veneer which is to be detected and discarded in the effort to arrive at the "genuine historical residuum." The historical residuum would be worthless without the "traditional accretions" which have gathered about it as a result of the religious interest and reactions of apostolic Christianity.

3. The historical method does not require that we reject the New Testament as a valid norm for Christian belief and experience. Here the historical approach is to be distinguished from a certain philosophical attitude. There is a large school of modern philosophy which regards truth as relative and fluid rather than stable and absolute, and upon this hypothesis no revelation of truth could be given in history which would be a final norm for subsequent generations. But this is primarily a question of philosophy, not one of history. The purpose of the historical method is to discern the facts and interpret their operation in first century Christian experience; it is not its province to prescribe what those facts and their significance are to mean to the views and conscience of the twentieth century individual. It does not therefore disqualify one as an historical student because he sees in the New Testament a standard for his own religious experience.

When these limitations are recognized and respected, the historical method has its value for the evangelical student, and need not be rejected as in any sense a menace to the most devout Christian faith.

The fact that the New Testament is clearly interwoven with the great currents of human history, rather than becoming a hindrance to faith or reverence, should be an aid to both. It should be profoundly inspiring to realize that God is as certainly immanent in history as he is in the Bible. It is but a different kind of immanence. His immanence in history is the course of ordinary providence. His immanence in the Bible is by special revelation. History is indeed "His story." It is a record of God's direction of human progress. History is the vast landscape of divine redemption, and the New Testament is the glory-crowned mountain peak which lends radiant grace and beauty to the whole. All the contours of antecedent and subsequent history converge in the commanding vantage ground of its transcendent heights. Every element contributed to its literary contents by anterior and contemporaneous history exhibits human life elevated and illuminated by the glorious meaning of God's redemptive plan. Viewed in this way, the New Testament as a product and factor of human history is seen to be all the more the handiwork of God. The same God who, on the divine side, was inspiring the individual writers, was also at work on the human side providing an adequate historical situation in which his kingdom might be founded. Under the glow of this holy light the first Christian century presents a significance which is, and is destined to remain, without parallel in the annals of mankind.

CONTENTS

CHAPTER I

THE ENVIRONMENT OF THE NEW TESTAMENT

We would begin this chapter with the observation of T. R. Glover, "that the Church came into being in a world with great features and great needs and a great inheritance, and that it conquered the world because it appealed to a great race on its highest level".[1] Let those who will, assume that this wonderful world, to which Christianity so easily adapted itself, was an accident issuing from fortuitous developments, but as for us, we interpret it in the light of Christian faith as a divine provision for the effective establishment of Christ's kingdom on earth.

The world in which Christianity first planted its roots was a plastic and cosmopolitan world. It was composed of the heritage of three great races, Oriental, Greek, and Roman. The three had practically blended into one, but each had made its distinct contribution. The Oriental had brought a vast bequest of philosophy and religion. His heritage was found by Christianity buried deep in the heart of both the Jewish and Gentile world, but potent still in the life of the time. The world which Christianity confronted was quite evidently a Greek world, because Greek culture had permeated it, and the Greek language was in almost universal use, so that Paul wrote Romans in Greek to a church which was at the heart of the Latin races, and Roman emperors used Greek as the language of their official seals. It was a Roman world because it was under the political control of Rome. This Græco-Roman world extended around the shores of the Mediterranean from the province of Africa to Gaul, and embraced the highest civilization of that age, and one of the highest of human history. To thoroughly understand and appreciate the progress of primitive Christianity we

[1]*The World of the New Testament*, p. 231.

need to perceive the factors and the relations of this entire Græco-Roman world. But the foundation was laid in a world that was generally Oriental and particularly Jewish.

The Oriental Substratum

Without any doubt the Oriental element was a substratum in the first century world. It was basal and original. Greek culture and custom had flowed in upon the Asiatic mind through the gateways opened by Alexander, but the Asiatic mind had remained there, with its intense mysticism, with its concrete mode of thought, with its hoary religious systems and conceptions. The mystery-religions, which potently influenced the background of the New Testament, were largely Oriental in origin and genius. The philosophy of the first century exhibits many traces of Oriental thought. This is particularly true of the philosophy of the eastern Mediterranean world.

The Oriental was well in the background, but close scrutiny can detect his presence. He made to primitive Christianity a threefold contribution.

1. *A Point of Contact.* In its genetic character Christianity was Oriental. We have observed that the Jews were an Oriental race, possessing fundamentally an Oriental mind. The original and fundamental tenets of Christian teaching were historically Oriental. Hence when Christianity appealed to the Gentile world it found a religious psychology susceptible to its message. And the fact that Oriental influence had been so diffused through the first century world that Oriental religions were popular alike in Alexandria, Athens, and Rome, spread out the field of contact for Christianity through the greater part of the Roman Empire. This fact is of no slight significance in the interpretation of apostolic history.

2. *A Definition of Religious Conceptions.* The Oriental contribution to Christianity was made chiefly through Judaism. The contact of Judaism with Oriental thought

during the periods of Captivity and Restoration without doubt had its effect upon the development and definition of Jewish religious conceptions, and Jewish religious conceptions formed the major content of Christianity. The extent and exact substance of the contribution of Orientalism to Judaism cannot be definitely determined—doubtless will never be; the fact of such a contribution seems beyond dispute. This, however, should in no way prove a disturbing factor to our evangelical faith. If God was pleased to use contacts of Oriental thought in order to bring into clearer view some of the elements of his revelation, the original authority is none the less divine because such instrumentalities were used. We must accept the means God has used, rather than assuming the prerogative of dictating the means he should have used.

Persian and Babylonian theology had close parallels to Jewish theology. The immortality of the soul, the existence of the spirit-world, the eternal rewards of human conduct, and the resurrection of the dead, were ideas which the Jews held in common with many of their Oriental neighbors.

(1) Judaism was affected by *Babylonian influence*. The Hebrew race from remotely ancient times was in close contact with Babylonian civilization. This contact was especially intimate in the time of the Captivity. This fact is convincingly attested by many Jewish names which bear evidence of Mesopotamian origin.[2] The Babylonian influence certainly had its economic effects, producing among the Jews great wealth and power, and likely a rather highly organized commercial life. It produced its cultural effects, turning many Jewish thinkers and teachers to the astrology and philosophy of the Babylonians. We cannot well doubt that the influence exerted was likewise religious, affecting the theology of Judaism. The traces of such influence are, however, indistinct.

[2]See Daiches, *Jews in Babylonia*, pp. 11-29.

(2) Evidences are more definite and pronounced when we turn to the *Persian influence.* From Persian sources came a more distinct definition of eschatological conceptions: heaven and hell, the resurrection and triumph of the righteous. The forces and functions of the spirit world were more clearly defined in Jewish thought after contact with the Persian religious mind.[3] It is significant that apocalyptic interest and expression appear far more prominent in Judaism after the Persian period. Judaism found homogeneous contact with Persian thought in its angelology, and developed it far beyond the simple Old Testament conception. The word "paradise," applied frequently to heaven, was of Persian origin, as was also the word "Satan." The demonology of later Judaism was chiefly derived from Persian sources.

The response of Judaism to Babylonian and Persian influence was certainly an unconscious reaction. In the main the Jews maintained their distinctive life and doctrine with an unyielding tenacity. When the Restoration came, the fundamentals of Jewish religion came out of the Mesopotamian valley untouched. The results of Babylonian-Persian influence were chiefly in new modes of conception and in terminology.

3. *An Occasion of Conflict*. The contribution to the New Testament made by this Oriental substratum was more antithetic than syncretic. It brought out certain elements of Christian thought in bold relief by the conflict which it offered. The positive contribution came through Judaism; the negative contribution came through Hellenistic philosophy and Græco-Oriental religions. The separation of religion from morality, the dualistic conception of the universe, and the distorted notions of the powers of the spirit world, created confusion and complications which menaced the Christian message as it advanced in the Gentile world. In fact, from the second century on these Oriental elements were adulterating the Christian message, but the relation of

[3] Cf. Booth, *The World of Jesus*, p. 24.

apostolic Christianity to Orientalism was chiefly one of antagonism. That is why Dean Inge has referred to Christianity as being the least Oriental of the great religions.[4]

The Jewish Background

The world in which Christianity originated was ultimately Oriental, but particularly and immediately Jewish. It was Oriental because Judaism was racially and basally Oriental. However, there was a distinctiveness about Judaism which set it apart from the Oriental world in general, and which requires its treatment as a separate phase of ancient life. It was from Judaism that Christianity received by far its largest content on the historical side. Jesus was a Jew, Paul was a Jew, all the first Christians were Jews. Doctrine, practice, psychology, and experience in first century Christianity were predominantly Jewish, though advancing constantly in the Hellenistic direction. One therefore cannot begin to study the New Testament without the consideration of its Jewish background.

There is repeated reference to various sects, institutions, and customs which originated in preceding centuries of Jewish history, such as the Pharisees, the Sadducees, the Sanhedrin, the synagogue, and so forth. Well established and familiar modes of expression were used by Jesus, such as aphoristic utterances, didactic discourse, and parables. Current religious conceptions of standard Judaism are adopted or presupposed by the New Testament, such as God, revelation, immortality, judgment, angels, Messiah, and so forth. The prevailing conditions of Palestinian life are in the background of every verse of the Gospels. These and many other features require a knowledge of Jewish life and history for adequate interpretation.

The Græco-Roman Background

Jewish history, based upon its Oriental substratum, is the history out of which the New Testament came as a

[4]Cf. Glover, *op. cit.*, p. 29.

product. There is also a history into which the New Testament came as a factor. The Messianism of Jesus and his followers having been rejected by Judaism as such, the new religion was forced to make its appeal to the great world outside standard Judaism. This was first liberal minded Palestinian Judaism, then Hellenistic Judaism, and finally the Gentile. So the field of operation for apostolic Christianity was the vast Græco-Roman world. Evangelical Christian faith sees in this development the movement of redemptive providence.

We call the Gentile world of that day "Græco-Roman" because it was composed of two elements, Greek and Roman. The type of life produced by these two combined elements we call *Hellenism.*

1. Over the Oriental basis of the great eastern world had flowed the Greek civilization. It was introduced by Alexander the Great. To exaggerate the effect of Alexander's conquest upon the world of the New Testament would be difficult. But the great direct contribution he made was bringing forward as the servant of Christianity the Greek mind with its philosophic inquisitiveness and literary expression—that is, Greek thought and Greek language. As far as our human understanding can perceive, the religion of Jesus Christ could never have received adequate interpretation had it not come into possession of Greek thought and expression. The Son of God could best make his contact with the world through the religious heart of the Jew, but that contact could best be interpreted and expressed by the Greek mind. This Greek mind was found the minute Christianity touched the Gentile life of the day—yea, even before, for Hellenistic influence had affected Judaism far more than Judaism realized or confessed. The Romans gave the first century its political principles and administration, but the Greeks were the molders of its intellectual life. Greek influence dominated the culture of the entire civilized world. That world was politically

Roman, culturally Greek, socially pagan, religiously Græco-Oriental.

2. The Græco-Oriental world, created by Alexander, had been conquered and reorganized by Rome. But Rome changed only the outward form. The Roman contribution to the New Testament world was largely external. Whatever contribution it made to the essential content of thought and life was indirect. Essentially, the thought and life of the Mediterranean world remained Græco-Oriental. This was of course originally and especially true of the Asiatic regions, but it became increasingly true of the Western world, particularly in post-apostolic times. When Pompey marched his legions eastward he did not destroy the results of Alexander's conquest; he only succeeded in bringing peace and reorganization to the chaotic domains of Alexander, that the latter's great program of Hellenization might the more effectively proceed. Hellenism turned back on Rome with its culture and made of the Roman Empire a Græco-Roman world.

Continuing the metaphor which we have been using, the Oriental element persisted as the substratum and Greek as the surface stratum of the eastern Mediterranean world, and Rome shaped and modified the contours. To speak in more literal terms, Rome organized and administered the life already constituted when Alexander blended Greek culture and language with the social and religious life of Asia. But since the world in which Christianity originated was governed by imperial Rome, a knowledge of the character of Roman rule is a valuable and indispensable aid in New Testament interpretation.

By this survey we may discern that the environment of the New Testament was composed of two distinct aspects of first century life, which were intimately related, and yet quite distinct in their general character. These two primary phases of the New Testament world are known as *Judaism* and *Hellenism*. Judaism embraces the life, thought, and literary products of the Jews. It had its chief center in Jerusalem and its primary field of operation in Palestine. Hellenism comprehends the factors and conditions of the Gentile world with which the New Testament came in contact. We describe it as Hellenism because Greek influence was dominant in its intellectual, social, and religious life. Judaism had to do chiefly with the factors which produced the New Testament, while the Græco-Roman or Hellenistic environment had to do chiefly with the functions exercised by the New Testament and its effects upon the world of the day. However, each of them affected both the production and operation of the New Testament message. In the analysis of these factors we have found that the Jewish is basally Oriental, and the Hellenistic is composed of both Greek and Roman elements. Then the three contributions of historical environment to the New Testament were the Oriental through Judaism and the Greek and Roman through Hellenism.

The three greatest historical movements of the past centuries converged in New Testament life. The most sublime spectacle which human annals present is the way in which God converged these three currents of history at the immortal manger of Bethlehem, where a Jewish maiden, who was there under the requirements of Roman law, gave birth to a babe, the wonderful story of whose life was to be told in the Greek language. Ere those sages of the distant Orient had come from afar to render their homage to the new-born king, a scene far more entrancing had transpired, when Jew, Greek, and Roman stood unseen about that Bethlehem manger, gathered there by the silent urge of an irresistible providence, that each might contribute from his own resplendent heritage to the preparation of the historical stage of action for the ministry of the world's Redeemer. That group who first assembled at the holy manger brought not their gifts of gold and frankincense and myrrh, but laid at the feet of the Bethlehem babe offerings far richer and more enduring than the glittering material wealth of the Orient could ever hope to provide. The Jew laid out gifts from the wealth of his religious history and consciousness, the Greek brought an expressive language and a trained intellect, and the Roman presented an organized world.

PART ONE

JUDAISM

Gen. Ster. div.
phy. div.
Pol. div.

CHAPTER II

THE LAND OF JUDAISM

The geographical designation "Palestine" is adopted from the nomenclature of Roman administration, and not from original Jewish terminology. It is a corruption of "Philistia," and originally denoted only the southern seacoast portion of what is called Palestine. The Jew had no distinctive name for his country, but simply called it "the Land." To him it was the Land *par excellence*, the special gift of Jehovah to his chosen Israel.

It is not possible for the Gentile mind to appreciate fully the feeling of the Jew toward this Holy Land. To him it was the divine stage for the accomplishment of Jehovah's covenant plan for his people. The land of Judaism was really a part of the religion of Judaism, for it was in a peculiar and distinctive sense "Jahweh's Land."[1] It was the land of divine promise and blessing, the land of many sacred traditions and holy exploits, the land of the Holy City and Temple.

It need not be mentioned that in a single chapter we can give but a bare sketch of the geography of Palestine.[2]

General Features

There are certain matters relative to the land as a whole to which we may first turn our attention.

1. *Area.* The area of Palestine is about twelve to fourteen thousand square miles. Its breadth at the north is approximately one hundred ten miles, and at the south about seventy-five miles. Its length may be given as one hundred seventy-five miles. The student may easily visualize the extent of the little country by calling

[1]Cf. Fairweather, *Background of the Gospels*, p. 60.

[2]For a thorough treatment of Palestinian geography the student may consult G. A. Smith, *Historical Geography of the Holy Land;* for a more concise treatment a splendid handbook is offered in W. W. Smith, *Student's Historical Geography of the Holy Land.*

to mind a territory in his own vicinity of comparable dimensions.

2. *Boundaries.* The western boundary of Palestine is formed by the Mediterranean Sea. On the north are the towering peaks of the Lebanon and Antilebanon Mountains, which in New Testament times lay in the Roman province of Syria. To the east and south lay the shifting haunts of the Arabian Bedouins and the kingdom of the Nabateans. These neighbors had made ceaseless trouble for the Jews, and had never been completely conquered by the Romans.

In treating the geography of ancient Palestine, if we define its "boundaries" we are to bear in mind that the term does not denote definite territorial limits as in modern times. There was no such thing as a legally established boundary *line* limiting Palestine or dividing its several districts. We could not properly speak of the *line* between Judea and Samaria. The different districts were divided by an indefinite border land, a mile or several miles in width, and recognized as a sort of common ground. The "parts of Tyre and Sidon" (Matt. 15: 21) were the border land between Galilee and Phœnicia, occupied by both Jews and Gentiles, and the "parts of Cæsarea Philippi" (Matt. 16: 13) were the borders of Philip's domains. Indeed, for the Jew the character and nationality of the inhabitants meant much more than the mere matter of territorial limits. Much land within the geographical boundaries of Palestine was outside the national boundaries of Judaism. Judea, with Jerusalem at its center, was the real heart of "the Land." However, there was a wide border territory lying around Palestine which Judaism regarded as potentially and rightfully the land of Israel, though not actually so. This helps to explain the attitude of the church at Jerusalem toward Christianity in Antioch, and the effort of the Sanhedrin, through the agency of Saul, to eradicate Christianity from Damascus.

3. *Climate.* Palestine is situated in the great desert district of southwestern Asia, and consequently its climate is calculated to be very dry. However, its proximity to the Mediterranean Sea mitigates to a considerable extent this condition. The Palestinian year may be divided into the wet and dry season. The wet season begins in October, the dry season in April. Hence most of the farming must be done in the winter months, to take advantage of the rainfall, which averages only twenty to thirty inches annually. The moisture was slightly better than that in the New Testament period. As to temperature, the climate of Palestine is temperate. Jerusalem lies in a latitude just north of New Orleans and Houston. Snow is rare, even in Galilee, except in the most elevated portions. There are sudden changes in temperature, but not to great extremes. The mean temperature is sixty-five degrees, seldom rising above ninety in the summer, or falling below forty in the winter. Taking the country as a whole, from Galilee on the north to Idumea on the south, it experiences a wide variety in climate, due to variation in altitude and topography as well as difference in latitude.

4. *Cities.* There are several of the more important cities of Palestine with the location and character of which every New Testament student should be familiar.

Naturally the one which first attracts our attention is *Jerusalem.* It is located a short distance east of the latitudinal center of Judea, and almost due west of the upper end of the Dead Sea. It is some 2400 feet above sea-level, and thirty-four miles from the Mediterranean coast. The site of the city is near the crest of the central mountain range, and therefore quite irregular in topography. The central ridge of the mountain range passes just west of the city, while Mt. Olivet lies on the east. Thus the city lies in a triangular basin, bounded on three sides by mountain ridges. Of course between these mountains and the city there are valleys, which enclose the city on three sides, leaving it readily accessible only from the north. On the eastern side is the Kidron Valley, while to the west and south runs the Valley of Hinnon, or *Gehenna.* From remotely ancient times Jerusalem was surrounded by walls, the remains of which are still in existence. The walls were penetrated by several gates, the exact number and location of which are matters of debate. Within the walls the city was situated upon two ridges, the western, with Mt. Zion as its summit, being the higher, longer, and more massive; the lower being on the east side, the crest of which was Mt. Moriah, the Temple site.[3] Each of these ridges was cleft by a deep ravine; consequently, the physical formation of the city consisted of four principal elevations, Mt. Zion being the highest and in the southwestern corner, Mt. Moriah the second highest, over against Mt. Olivet. At the upper end of the triangular basin, to the north of the city walls, the two ridges merged into an ascending plateau.

Six miles south of Jerusalem was *Bethlehem,* the birthplace of our Lord. In New Testament times it was scarcely more than a village. About two miles east of Jerusalem was the town of *Bethany,* home of Lazarus and his sisters, devoted friends of our Lord. About fifteen miles northeast of Jerusalem, at the western edge of the Jordan valley, was the ancient city of *Jericho.*

We think next of *Nazareth,* the boyhood home of Jesus. It is located on the southern edge of the hills of lower Galilee, just above the Plain of Esdraelon. Through it passed one of the most frequented Roman roads, from Capernaum to the coast. On the same road, five miles northeast of Nazareth, was *Cana,* scene of Christ's first miracle (John 2: 1ff.).

Most of the active ministry of Jesus revolved about *Capernaum.* It was the port of entrance on the *Via Maris* to the domains of Herod Antipas. Through its toll station passed a vast import and export trade. Matthew's

[3]The names of these two hills are confused in the sources. It may be that the eastern or Temple mount was called both Moriah and Zion. The traditional view is accepted here, but see *per contra, Int. St. Bib. Ency.,* art., "Temple."

place as toll collector here was a lucrative and important position—but, doubtless, just because so profitable and prominent, all the more despised by the loyal Jews. The exact site of the city is in dispute, but in general we may say that it was located near the northern end of the Sea of Galilee, to the west of the Jordan. It was certainly a city of considerable size and importance.

In the vicinity of Capernaum were *Bethsaida* and *Chorazin*. Bethsaida was the southern suburb of Capernaum, situated just below the latter, on the Sea of Galilee. Chorazin likely nestled in the mountains north of Capernaum. They were not towns of any considerable size, but must have been quite influential as trading points. Toward the southern end of the Sea of Galilee were *Dalmanutha* and *Magdala*.

"The houses and streets of these places we must picture to ourselves as resembling those of Oriental ones of the present day, and not after the analogy of the Græco-Roman architecture."[4] But when we come to *Tiberias*, located about midway the western shore of the Sea of Galilee, we find a city constructed after the Greek and Roman fashion, and hence obnoxious to the Jews. Herod Antipas had built it as his capital, and named it in honor of the then reigning emperor. The town of *Tarichœa,* which lay near the shore of the Sea of Galilee south of Tiberias, was the principal center of the fishing trade. In this portion of the lake numbers of fishermen were constantly plying their nets, and from Tarichæa a large export fish trade was carried on.

Two cities on the coast are of interest to the New Testament student. *Cæsarea,* about sixty miles northwest of Jerusalem, was built by Herod and named for his Roman patron. It was a thoroughly Hellenistic city, and consequently despised by the Jews. North of west from Jerusalem, and about forty miles away, was *Joppa,* which was dominated by Jewish influence. These

[4]Hausrath. *Time of Jesus*. Vol. I, p. 5.

towns played an important part in early Christian history.

5. *Roads.* Palestine in New Testament times was threaded by a number of highways. Some of these the Romans paved, and remains of the pavement are in existence to the present day. However, there quite probably were not any paved roads in Palestine in the time of Christ. But at least the principal roads were maintained under Roman supervision.

There were four main highways. Two of them connected with Gaza, in the extreme southwest. One took a northeasterly course from Gaza, passing through Hebron and Bethlehem to Jerusalem, thence by way of Bethany and Jericho across the Jordan and up the eastern plateau to Damascus. From this a road branched off in the region of Decapolis, crossed the Jordan south of the Sea of Galilee, and led to Capernaum. It was this road about the eastern side of the Jordan which the Jews traveled from Jerusalem to Capernaum, in order to avoid going through despised Samaria. The second road from Gaza passed directly north along the coast through Jamnia, Joppa, Cæsarea and Ptolemais to Tyre. This was the principal Maritime Plain highway. Two branches of this road led from Lydda to Jerusalem, one by way of Beth-horon, and the other by Emmaus. The third road of importance was the direct route from Jerusalem to Capernaum, passing up the ridge of the central mountain range, by way of Shechem—the road which Jesus was traveling when he won the Samaritan woman. The greatest of all Palestinian highways was *Via Maris,* "the Way of the Sea." Doubtless Jesus played by its side as a boy. It came from Damascus, crossed the Jordan between the Sea of Galilee and Huleh, passed by Capernaum and Nazareth into the Plain of Esdraelon, and skirted the Galilean hills to Ptolemais. It was the most extensively used route from Damascus to the sea. It was maintained by the Roman Government, and a customs tax was charged for all commodities transported over it. At such "receipt of custom" Matthew was sitting when Jesus called him to discipleship.

There were, of course, a large number of subordinate roads branching off from these principal highways and connecting with every section of Palestine. These corresponded to what we would call lateral roads. Then there was a third class of thoroughfare, passable for those who were walking or riding, but rarely accessible by vehicular transportation. These may be called the bypaths. So we may classify the roads of first century Palestine as highways, lateral roads, and bypaths.

Physical Divisions

The topography of Palestine is defined by four distinct physical features. They are the Mediterranean coast, the Lebanon Mountains with their southern extension, the Jordan valley, and the Antilebanon Mountains with their southern extension.

The coast of Palestine is embarrassingly regular. The only bay of any size in its entire length is the Bay of Acre, and it is but slightly sheltered from the sea. South of Carmel the line of the coast is practically straight, offering no place for a natural harbor. But north of Carmel are a number of small projections of land, which in ancient times provided harbors sufficient for the small boats then used, and thus furnished the natural equipment for the maritime activities of the Phœnicians.

The Lebanon and Antilebanon Mountains are divisions of a long range which branches off from the Caucasus Mountains. The ridge of the Lebanon extends clear down to the Sinaitic peninsula, with two breaks, one at the Plain of Esdraelon and the other at the Wilderness of Paran. The Antilebanons dip abruptly from Mt. Hermon to the Plain of Bashan, then rise to the tableland of Gilead and Moab, whence the ridge slopes gradually away to a few scattering hills in the southwestern corner of the Arabian desert.

Between the Lebanon and Antilebanon Mountains lies the great depression which forms the Jordan Valley. It begins where the great mountain ridge divides far north of Palestine, descends three thousand feet in a distance of one hundred thirty-five miles to the Dead Sea, thirteen hundred feet below sea level at the surface, beyond which it rises approximately sixteen hundred feet, to three hundred feet above sea level, and then descends gradually into the Gulf of Akabah.

These larger physical features are divided by other natural formations into smaller sections. The Lebanon ridge in its southern course departs increasingly from the sea, leaving the Maritime Plain. It is broken in the center of Palestine by the Plain of Esdraelon, which forms a natural feature in itself, as well as dividing the Lebanon ridge into the Northern and Central Highlands. The Jordan Valley forms a single feature, and beyond it lies the Eastern Plateau. Thus Physical Palestine is divided into six natural features.

1. *The Maritime Plain.* This is formed by the widening of the coast from the point where Mt. Carmel juts against the sea. The hills thrust themselves seaward again just south of Joppa, and divide this plain into two parts. The northern part is the famous Plain of Sharon, and the southern part the Philistian Plain. Sharon is an average of ten miles in width and about fourty-four miles long. The average width of the Philistian Plain is twelve and a half miles, and it is nearly one hundred miles in length. Upon this fertile Plain lived the Philistine tribes, the age-long enemies of Israel.

2. *The Central Highlands.* At their northernmost point the Central Highlands rise to the summit of Mt. Carmel, which is seventeen hundred forty-two feet above sea level at its highest point. Mt. Carmel is not a peak, but a long, narrow ridge, which lifts itself abruptly from the coast on the west, and on the east gradually slopes away to the Plain of Dothan. At the northeastern projection of the Central Highlands stands Mt. Gilboa,

a tall peak rising to sixteen hundred ninety-eight feet above sea level. The Plain of Dothan is a huge basin, located in the northern end of the Central Highlands, at an elevation of nearly one thousand feet above sea level. On its northwest rises the lower slopes of Carmel, on the northeast those of Gilboa, and on the south those of Ebal.

The next interruption of the central range lies ten miles south of the Plain of Dothan. It is the Valley of Shechem, with Mt. Ebal towering three thousand seventy-six feet on one side, and Mt. Gerizim (site of the Samaritan temple) twenty-eight hundred fifty feet on the other. South of Gerizim the ridge is more regular, rising to fewer abrupt peaks. Its elevation reaches a great height at two points, the first at Jerusalem, where it is twenty-five hundred ninety-three feet, and the next at Hebron, where it is about thirty-three hundred fifty feet above sea level—the highest point in the Central Highlands. The southern portion of the Central Highlands shelves off to the west into a series of foothills, known as the Shephelah, and on the east falls away in rugged descent toward the Dead Sea.

3. *The Plain of Esdraelon.* The Lebanon range is interrupted in southern Galilee by a wide depression, the central and most important part of which is the Plain of Esdraelon, about nine miles in width. At its northwestern end the Plain of Esdraelon is closed in to a narrow valley by a projection of the Galilean hills. From this valley the Plain of Acre opens fan-like toward the sea, and extends an arm northward for about forty miles. This northward extension of Acre forms a narrow coastal plain, only a few miles in width, which is sometimes called the Phœnician Plain. On the eastern side Esdraelon is shut in by Mt. Gilboa on the south and Little Hermon on the north, with the narrow Valley of Jezreel between them, opening into the Jordan Valley. By some the entire depression, from the Plain of Acre to the Jordan, is called the Valley of Jezreel.

4. *The Northern Highlands.* This division is composed of the Lebanon and Antilebanon Mountains and the Mountains of Galilee. The Galilean mountains are really foothills of the Lebanon range. In the time of Jesus they were covered with luxuriant forest growth.[5] The highest point of the Lebanon ranges is far up in Syria, where they rise to more than ten thousand feet. The conspicuous feature of the Antilebanons is Mt. Hermon with its three peaks, the highest rising to nine thousand two hundred feet above sea level. Because of the great extremes in temperature between the altitude of Hermon and the low valleys about it, much moisture is condensed from the atmosphere, giving rise to the "dews of Hermon." The mountains in upper Galilee rise to a height of four thousand feet, but they shelve away in lower Galilee to an average of one thousand feet and less.

5. *The Jordan Valley.* This is the depression between the southern extension of the Lebanon and Antilebanon Mountains, through which courses the Jordan River. It is quite irregular in width, ranging from a narrow gorge between Lake Huleh and the Sea of Galilee to fourteen miles in width at Jericho.

The head-waters of the Jordan River consist of four large tributaries and a number of small ones, springing from fountains at the foot of Mt. Hermon. From near its source the stream flows through a dense swamp, filled with luxuriant vegetation. At the lower end of this swamp it widens into Lake Huleh (the ancient Waters of Merom), whence it dashes through a deep gorge, down a sharp descent, falling six hundred eighty feet in nine miles, then flows quietly into the Sea of Galilee.

The Sea of Galilee is approximately twelve miles long by six miles wide (eight at its widest point) and is six hundred eighty-two feet below sea level. On the north is a delta, formed by the deposits of the Jordan, and a little north of midway its western edge is a small coastal plain, the Plain of Gennesaret, some eight miles in length

[5]Hausrath, *op. cit.*, Vol. I, p. 5.

by four miles in width. At the southern end of the Sea of Galilee is the continuation of the Jordan Valley, which is four miles wide at this point. Elsewhere the lake is hedged in by the steep sides of overhanging hills. Especially are the shores precipitous on the eastern side.

From the Sea of Galilee the Jordan River moves swiftly on its course to the Dead Sea, falling six hundred ten feet in the seventy miles between the two seas. It ranges in width from ninety to a hundred feet, and is three to twelve feet deep. The current is zig-zag and rapid, and the waters muddy.

The Jordan empties into the Dead Sea, which is about one thousand three hundred feet below sea level at the surface, and about one thousand three hundred feet deep at its deepest part. It is forty-six miles long and ten miles wide. Its banks on the east, south, and west consist of the sides of the mountains which hedge it in. From the eastern side projects a boot-shaped promontory some fifty feet in height, and bordered by a sand-bar. Since it has no outlet, the waters of the Dead Sea are saturated with mineral.

6. *The Eastern Plateau.* The Antilebanon range does not descend into foothills and lower mountain ranges, as do the Lebanons, but slopes down into a rugged plateau, cut into three fairly distinct divisions by rivers which have plowed through its surface. The first is the Plain of Bashan, with the river Yarmuk at its southern border. Next comes Mt. Gilead, cut in twain by the Jabbok River. Mt. Gilead is about two thousand feet in elevation at the highest point, and is exceedingly fertile and fruitful. To the east of the Dead Sea are the plains of Moab, so prominent in Old Testament history.

Thus lies before us the natural features of that most renowned plot of land on all the earth. From the coastal plains of Philistia, Sharon, and Acre, it rises to the crest of a mountain ridge, cut through by Esdraelon and the Vale of Shechem, then dips to the deep rift of the Jordan Valley, rolls upward on the eastern side to the rugged table-lands of Bashan, Gilead, and Moab, and slopes away to the arid stretches of the Arabian desert.

Political Divisions

The political history of Palestine combined with its physical features to form certain divisions which influenced exceedingly its civil, social, and religious life. These divisions we designate by the territorial names Judea, Samaria, Galilee, Perea, and a group of little realms which we shall designate as Northeastern Palestine, and the Decapolis.

1. *Judea.* This was always the heart of the Israelite nation. It was the first territory conquered by Joshua, was the scene of the chief events of Hebrew history, contained the site of the Holy City, Jerusalem, and was the center of the Restoration. Thus it became preeminently the country of the Jews, and the center from which radiated the dominant Jewish influence. In New Testament times Jerusalem was the stronghold of Judaism. It was the chief source of standard tradition and the center of rabbinical authority. The name Judea is a corruption of Judah, and was applied because the tribe of that name was the chief possessor of that region.

2. *Samaria.* After the fall of the northern kingdom of Israel, in accordance with the fixed custom of the Assyrian conquerors, the vanquished peoples were deported, and in their place the country was colonized with Gentile tribes. The colonists mingled with the remnant of the Hebrews which the conquerors had left in the land, the number of whom was doubtless considerable, and the customs of the Hebrews were corrupted by heathen influence. The straggling and defeated Israelites had lost their religious leadership—what little they had—and their distinctive racial hopes and ideals seemed crushed beyond redemption; consequently they married among the heathen immigrants and produced a hybrid race. At the time of the Restoration, when these apostate Israelites of Samaria and their hybrid relatives wished

to join in the reconstruction of the holy nation of Jehovah, they were summarily rejected as unworthy. The resulting enmity persisted between the two races in the time of Christ and the Apostles.

The great majority of the Samaritans were descendants of Abraham, and had a religion quite similar to that of the Jews. Their claim was that they were the true descendants of the Hebrew patriarchs, for which reason the Samaritan woman in her conversation with Jesus referred to "our father Jacob" (John 4: 12). After being repulsed by the Jews at Jerusalem, they built their own temple to Jehovah on Mt. Gerizim, and there maintained worship until their sanctuary was destroyed by John Hyrcanus in 128 B.C. A remnant of the race survives at the present time.

3. *Galilee.* After Joshua's victorious campaign in the north, in the extreme northern part of Canaan he settled the tribe of Naphtali (Joshua 20: 7). But Naphtali failed to subdue and expel the native Gentiles (Judges 1: 33). Hence this region became known as "the district of the Gentiles." The Hebrew word for district is *galilah*, whence the name arose; first, *galilah haggoyim*, "Galilee of the Gentiles," then *haggoyim* was dropped, leaving just "Galilah" as a proper name, which became *Galilaia* in Greek and Galilee in English. At first the name applied only to the possessions of Naphtali, now upper Galilee, but was later extended to designate the possessions of Zebulun and Issachar as well, reaching to the southern border of Esdraelon.

This territory was ever disputed ground between the Israelites and their heathen enemies. During the Restoration there were but few Jews who settled in Galilee. It remained for one of the Asmonean princes, John Hyrcanus (135-105 B.C.), to really establish the control of the Jews in this section of their promised land. In the time of our Saviour it may properly be described as Jewish territory, but it was inhabited still by many more Gentiles than was Judea, and the Jewish people there were more liberal in their attitude. "Separated from the barren land of Levites and Rabbis by the intervening Samaritans, less leavened by the intense sectarianism which prevailed there, less hardened in Jewish orthodoxy, and in many ways influenced by their extensive foreign relations, the Galileans had not become of that narrowly exclusive character which was usually the product of Judaism."[6] It was for this reason that Jesus could pursue his ministry with more freedom in Galilee than in Judea. By standard Judaism of Judea Galilee was regarded as corrupted through Gentile occupation and unworthy of the highest privileges of Israel. This fact will help us in understanding the attitude of the Pharisees toward the Messianic claims of Jesus.

4. *Perea.* We now pass to the eastern side of Jordan. In New Testament times this meant more than simply crossing a little stream a few feet in width. It meant entering a different circle of life and history. Israel never had a firm hold, either religiously or politically, in the trans-Jordanic regions. This territory was always exposed to Gentile inroads, and was consequently never as thoroughly Jewish as Judea. It was brought under Jewish control by the Asmoneans, and had a predominantly Jewish population in the first century of our era. It thus afforded a passage over relatively Jewish territory which the Jews might use and avoid passing through despised Samaria.

5. *Northeast Palestine.* We do not have a name any more definite than this which we may apply to this region. It is that portion of Palestine which lies east of the Sea of Galilee and north of Perea. It includes several small districts of indeterminate limits. These are Gaulonitis, Iturea, Suranitis, Trachonitis, and Batanea.

There were only a few Jews scattered through this territory, and they lived chiefly in the western part, near the Sea of Galilee. The inhabitants were a wild,

[6]Hausrath, *op. cit.*, Vol. I, p. 11.

marauding set, who gave much trouble to their rulers. Herod had subdued them by force on several occasions, but found great difficulty in keeping them in subjection, even though he had the district carefully policed. In the time of Christ the region was governed by Philip, who was more successful than had been his father in controlling these wild Gentile tribes.

6. *Decapolis.* The region of Decapolis, the "ten cities," embraced a large portion of northeastern Palestine, but extended also into Perea and Galilee. Decapolis was a sort of municipal league, consisting originally of ten Greek cities (hence the name: *dekapolis,* ten cities), leagued together in a sort of confederacy, maintaining their pagan character and customs, and granted special protection by the Roman government. They were, of course, despised by the Jews as lawless intruders.

In the New Testament period there were more than ten of these cities, though they were still referred to as "Decapolis." The exact name and location of the original ten has never been ascertained, but a probably correct list gives Damascus, Philadelphia, Raphana, Scythopolis, Gadara, Hippos, Dion, Pella, Gerasa, Canatha.[7]

[7]This is an ancient list given by Pliny, the Latin writer, and is considered as best by Schuerer. Cf., *The Jewish People in the Time of Jesus Christ,* Div. II, Vol. I, p. 95. For a slightly different list, see Hurlbut, *Bible Atlas,* p. 102.

CHAPTER III

THE LITERATURE OF JUDAISM

We are dealing in this chapter with the literary activity of the Jewish people after the time of Ezra down to and including the first century of the Christian Era. The literary products of the Jews which belong to this period are commonly referred to under the broad, general designation of "Jewish Literature." But the use of this title logically includes the New Testament along with other Jewish writings. Hence to denote Jewish literature exclusive of the New Testament requires a more restricted designation. The title *Literature of Judaism* exactly serves the purpose, for two reasons: (1) This literature is the surviving expression of that type of life in the first and second centuries B.C. and A.D. universally accepted under the name "Judaism." (2) This term necessarily excludes the New Testament, for however intimate one may regard the connection to be between first century Christianity and Judaism, he certainly would not consider the New Testament as embraced in the term "Literature of Judaism."

We have before us here the chief documentary sources from which we shall derive the historical accounts that are to follow. It is therefore well that our attention should be turned at this point to the literature.

It is the popular impression that after the writing of Malachi no worthy literary effort was made by the chosen people of Jehovah until the Apostles of Jesus began to pen the books of the New Testament. This is far from the facts. Some of the finest products of Hebrew religious zeal belong to the period between the Testaments and contemporaneous with the New Testament. There were historical and intrinsic reasons for their not being included in the Old Testament, but their general character as religious literature is in some instances superlative.

Many of these books are embraced in the canon of the Roman Catholic Vulgate, and compose what is known as the *Apocrypha.* The origin of this title is not definitely known. The word is a transliteration of the neuter plural of the Greek adjective *apokruphos,* meaning "hidden, concealed." Its significance is quite certainly not Hebrew in origin. There was a late Hebrew phrase applied to the Old Testament which might be rendered "hidden books," but this term was used to denote the best of the canonical books and really meant stored away as a treasure, precious, extraordinarily sacred. The most likely explanation is that the term was of Christian origin. There were books used in some of the heretical sects of early Christianity, esoteric and ascetic in their practices, which books were kept secret. Hence they became known as *apokrupha,* hidden or secret books. These heretical works were severely condemned by orthodox Christianity, and hence the term *apokrupha* came to signify books excluded from the canon. The term, originally applied to Christian writings, came in course of time to denote books not recognized as embraced in the Old Testament canon. It seems to be used in this sense as far back as Origen.

In general terms we may say the Apocrypha are those books of the Latin Vulgate not contained in the Hebrew canon of the Old Testament. It is difficult to set definite limits, because a fixed standard of determination has not been agreed upon. The number of books in the Septuagint (the Greek Old Testament) differs from the canon of the present Roman church. But as generally known the Apocrypha consists of ten separate books, one addition to Esther, and three additions to Daniel—making fourteen in all.

The Christian world has never been agreed on the value and authority of the Apocrypha. In the first century the Christian Jews of Palestine likely did not accept them as on a par with the other Old Testament books. Outside of Palestine they were held in high favor by the Christians, especially after the beginning of the second century, but Christianity has never given quite unanimous recognition to the canonical standing of these books. The ecumenical council of Carthage in 397 gave them formal standing by declaring them canonical, but even this failed to gain universal consent. During the Reformation the question was revived, and the Protestant confessions of faith, though differing as to the value of the Apocrypha, were agreed in rejecting their inspiration. Some representatives of the Reformation attached value to the Apocrypha as means of edification, though they did not regard them as authoritative scripture and valid sources of doctrine.[1] Their edificatory value is indeed worthy of consideration, but the chief point of their value to us is the light which they throw upon the preparation of Judaism for the coming of Christ. Roman Catholicism still holds to them as canonical, and therefore inspired.

In addition to the Apocrypha, a large group of Jewish literary products are known as the *Pseudepigrapha.* This is a term of Greek derivation which signifies a writing under an assumed name. The day of bold and original prophecy had ceased with Malachi. No longer was there sufficient courage of religious leadership for one to raise his voice as being himself a spokesman for Jehovah. Consequently, they wrote under the names of the celebrated and influential leaders of the past, such as Enoch, Noah, Elijah, Baruch, Ezra, and so forth. These documents constitute the Pseudepigrapha.

Nothing better can be done for a student of the New Testament than to introduce him to this vast and important field of investigation. The brief sketch which

[1]The Thirty-nine Articles, the creedal statement of the Anglican Reformation, declares that the Apocryphal books may not be used "to establish any doctrine," but "may be read for example of life and instruction of manner" (Art. VI).

we give here is but a bare introduction.[2] We may best present the discussion under three heads: the *creative factors* in the experience of the Jewish people which inspired the production of this literature; the *geographical centers* about which the literary effort gathered; and a *general survey* of the literature under its different types.

Creative Factors

One is not able to appreciate the literature of this period without some understanding of the purposes in the minds of the writers. Some of the deepest impulses of the human heart are seeking to find expression in these writings. All the passion of religious fervor and pathos of martyrdom are voiced in this literature. To treat this matter exhaustively would of course necessitate an investigation into the history of each particular document, but it is possible in a brief way to make a general survey of the principal and common features.

1. *Intense Devotion to the Law and Worship of Jehovah.* The Captivity had taught the Jews a great lesson. It was the neglect of the prescribed worship of Jehovah which had brought about the great calamity, and in far away Babylon, absent from Jerusalem and the Temple, perpetuation of their worship became exceedingly difficult. The remnant of the race who remained loyal to their traditions hailed with joy the privilege granted them by Cyrus of returning to their own country. Thus it was a responsive group who yielded themselves to the leadership and influence of Zerubbabel, Nehemiah, and Ezra in the Restoration. This restored population of Palestine, made up largely from the tribe of Judah, were deeply devoted to the traditions and teachings of the fathers. To them the Law of Moses and the Levitical rites represented the highest interests of life.

The strict and loyal Jews believed that the only hope of the world resided in Jewish legalism. One of the distinguishing features about the expected Messianic pro-

[2]For comprehensive but more detailed treatment see Grant, *Between the Testaments*, pp. 109-146; for a full and thorough treatment see Schuerer, *Jewish People in the Time of Jesus Christ*, Div. II, Vol. III.

gram was that the Messiah would call the world to conformity with the Law, and to the Law as interpreted by the rabbinic schools of Judaism. That is, he was to be a sort of second Moses. This devotion to legalism colored practically all the literary effort of the period. Of course some writings were more intensely legalistic than others, but in all there was evident respect for the Law. This was not in itself a reprehensible motive. The mistake of the Jews was not in having a high regard for the Law, but in seeking an artificial and forced application of the Law.[3] The legalistic note in their literature is not always a defect; in fact, it frequently presents a virtue.

2. *Persecution by Heathen Nations.* The religious and racial exclusiveness of the Jews has subjected them to intense prejudice and hatred in all their history. At no period was this opposition more severe than in that now under consideration. While Palestine was under the control of the Ptolemies of Egypt the Jews enjoyed a large degree of religious liberty, but the Syrian kings sought to break down their stubborn loyalty to the traditions and practices of their race, and to compel their adoption of the culture and customs of their Greek conquerors. A large portion of the race refused to be Hellenized, and the unthinkable extremes of persecution came as a consequence. In the midst of its terrors some of the best of the literature of Judaism originated. It echoes the heartaches of a despised and baffled people. Some of the richest strains of religious pathos ever produced by the Jews are to be found in the Psalms composed in these hours of national crisis.

3. *Efforts at Compromise Made by the Liberal Jews.* Here lay the cause of the most intense antagonism which Jewish life ever experienced. Loyalty to traditional Judaism was never quite unanimous, even among the

[3]Professor E. F. Scott correctly observes: "Too often we think only of the protest which Christianity offered to the Law, but we ought also to remember that Christianity grew up in the soil of the Law, and derived from it some of the most precious elements." (*First Age of Christianity*, p. 89.)

Jews of the Restoration. Especially after the Alexandrian campaigns, and the aggressive propaganda of the Syrian rulers, a strong Hellenistic drift set in among the Jews, and the ardent supporters of the national religion arose in mighty protest against the threatened apostasy.

With the Jews patriotism and religion were one. The nation was an object of divine favor, and their national history composed a large element in their scriptures. Their traditions were in a peculiar sense the account of God's revelation of himself to them. To defend Israel against the inroads of heathen influence was to serve Jehovah directly, for Israel was the specially favored handiwork of Jehovah. The Holy City was the capital of the nation, and the Temple in which they worshiped was the national headquarters. So above every other concern of life the loyal Jew felt it his obligation to preserve intact the customs and traditions of his nation.

Those remaining true to traditional Judaism were known as the "righteous," while those yielding to Hellenistic tendencies were called "sinners." Many traces of this conflict are to be found in the literature of the period. It is at once patriotic and religious, for patriotism and religion were one and the same to the Jew. Yet the literature of Judaism is by no means wholly exclusive, sectarian, and nationalistic. In much of it there is reflected a truly altruistic interest. While the conviction is everywhere evident that they wished to see all the nations of earth united under the influence of Judaism, at the same time it is clear that, in their view, this would be to the immeasurable benefit of the world. While this was by no means the view of all Judaism, for many were utterly indifferent to the fate of the Gentile world, it was the attitude of the better spirits of the nation.

The course of subsequent history has proved that, while wrong in their conception of its application, in the essence of this doctrine the Jews were right. The greatest single benefit the world has ever received it has derived from a religion which originated with a Jew and his Jewish followers.

God never ceased to work in the national consciousness of Israel in preparation for the coming of his Son, and the traces of his hand may be found in much of the literature of Judaism. It reflects high conceptions of the issues of human life, and a really unselfish interest in those issues.

GEOGRAPHICAL CENTERS

Though standard Judaism ever had its great stronghold at Jerusalem, there was much of Judaism which developed outside of Palestine. With that in the Mesopotamian valley we are not concerned here, for it only remotely affected the New Testament, and produced no literature of note. The two places which deserve treatment here are Jerusalem and Alexandria.

1. *Jerusalem.* In Palestine, and chiefly in Jerusalem, originated that literature which had most to do with shaping the world into which Jesus came. It did not represent the greater part of the literature of Judaism taken in bulk, for by far the most of it was written by Alexandrian Jews, but it was the most distinctly Jewish, and wielded the greatest influence in the development of Judaism as such. It was the least subject to the influence of Greek literature and thought, and hence best represents the potency of those interests which were discussed in the preceding section. It was likely all written in Hebrew (or Aramaic)[4] and was closest to the real heart of the Jewish people. It represents most accurately the real thought content of Judaism. In it the Jewish life and consciousness found its unhindered, unadulterated expression. Consequently, the most important literature of this period for the New Testament student is that written in Palestine.

2. *Alexandria.* While the Palestinian literature is of greater importance for New Testament study, yet the great body of literature produced in and around Alexan-

[4]Aramaic was one of the chief ancient Semitic languages, of which Hebrew was a literary offspring, and was the indigenous language of Palestine in the time of Christ.

dria is by no means unimportant, and is at the same time intensely interesting. This literature became less Jewish and more Greek until by the time we reach Philo we have Greek philosophy interpreted from a Jewish point of view. There are four representatives of the Alexandrian-Jewish literature which mark four stages of advancement toward the Hellenistic literary and philosophical type. The first is the pseudepigraphic letter of *Aristeas* written in Egypt about 100 B.C., and exhibiting the desire on the part of the Jews of Alexandria to gain recognition and respect from their heathen neighbors and rulers. *The Wisdom of Solomon*, written in Egypt about 50 B.C., is a piece of Jewish wisdom literature deeply colored by Greek speculation, and marking a further advance in Hellenistic character. *IV Maccabees*, written between 25 B.C. and 25 A.D., represents the third step in the approach to Greek culture. The climax came in *Philo*, who died probably not far from A.D. 50. Philo was more a Greek philosopher than he was a Jewish religionist. All this Alexandrian-Jewish literature presents much of interest to the New Testament student.

It was Alexandrian Judaism which gave to the world the first great Bible translation in the form of a version of the Old Testament books of Law in Greek. It was called the *Septuagint*, by reason of the tradition that seventy-two Jewish scribes did the translating.[5]

Up to about the third century B.C. there had never arisen an occasion for the translation of the Old Testament. When the Jews were carried as captives to Assyria and Babylonia they carried their language and, to some extent, their customs with them. But when Alexander established a colony of Jews in Egypt the situation was different. The Greek language rapidly became the prevalent tongue of the eastern Mediterranean world, and was of course the language of Alexandria. The colony of Jews at Alexandria were given full citizenship, assigned a large section of the city for their exclusive occupation,

[5]The Latin for seventy is *septuaginta*.

and accorded the full liberty of worship in their own way. Naturally this kind of treatment made them feel favorable toward the existing government, and hence disposed to adapt themselves to their new environment and be contented therein. The Ptolemies continued the liberal measures of Alexander, and in consequence the Alexandrian Jews soon became thoroughly naturalized. Within a few generations the great majority were unable to speak or understand the Hebrew language.

Their distinctive Jewish form of worship was carried on with perfect freedom. Several synagogues arose,[6] in which the Alexandrian Jews studied the sacred Law of their people. This created a demand to have the services conducted and the Scriptures read in the language which all the people could understand—the *Koiné* Greek.

The exact facts about the origin of the Septuagint are not known. The letter of Aristeas gives a very miraculous and highly fanciful account of how the translation was accomplished. By sifting out the fiction from this account we arrive at the following as the probable facts. During the reign of Philadelphus (285-247 B.C.) there was recognized a demand for the Jewish Scriptures in Greek. This demand likely came chiefly from the Jews themselves, from reasons intimated above, though it is quite possible that the Egyptian king was glad to lend his patronage to a movement which would add to the unity of his kingdom as well as increase the Library which he was interested in promoting. A group of Alexandrian-Jewish scribes[7] was got together—possibly the

[6]About 170-160 B.C., the Egyptian Jews, under the leadership of Onias the son of the high priest, built a temple near the town of Leontopolis in which worship was conducted similar to that in the Holy Temple. For a full discussion of this Egyptian temple see Ewald: *History of Israel*, Vol. V, pp. 354ff.

[7]The representation in the letter of Aristeas that the scribes were secured from Judea is hardly to be accepted, for the very obvious reason that Palestinian scribes would not be adept in both languages, as Alexandrian scribes would of necessity be. The Greek of the Septuagint presents occasionally good classical idiom, which is unthinkable for Palestinian scribes. Those who did the translating were familiar with the Greek of their time, but also well versed in Hebrew. This characterization exactly fits what we would expect of a Jewish scribe in Alexandria.

traditional number of seventy-two, and the work of translating the books of the Law was accomplished by them.

It is likely that the first translation contained only the Pentateuch, but other books were translated in rapid succession as fast as rolls and translators could be secured. This Greek Old Testament was gladly received and widely used by the Jews of Egypt and of the entire Hellenistic world until after the time of Christ. It was, of course, very little used in Palestine, as the Jews there would prefer the Hebrew, which was closer to their native tongue (Aramaic) and made sacred by national traditions. After the beginning of the Christian movement the Septuagint became so widely used by the Christians and so freely appealed to in their controversies with the Jews that the orthodox Jews grew skeptical of the translation and had other translations made. But the Septuagint remained the Bible of the Christians down to the Middle Ages. It was frequently quoted by the New Testament writers, especially the author of Hebrews. It was used frequently by Paul, who showed also ability to use the Hebrew text. There is but slight trace of the Septuagint in the Synoptics, but considerable in John's Gospel. The early church fathers used it almost exclusively. It was for a hundred years after the birth of Christ the only Bible of the Christian world.

General Survey

In this classification it is not possible to draw rigid lines of distinction. No piece of literature belongs exclusively to any one type. But however many elements it may contain, we find some one element which is preeminent, and which enables us to classify the document with a particular type. By the use of this method we may divide the literature of Judasim into five types.

1. *Historical.* There is no Jewish literature which is wholly historical. As has already been observed, to the Jew the history of his people was an important re-

ligious asset, and a sacred matter. They were therefore not primarily interested in history for history's sake, but as an important element in religion. This attitude affected more or less all their historical productions.

(1) Doubtless the nearest approach to purely historical literature is to be found in *I Maccabees.* While there is a clear religious interest, and an evident sense of God's relation to his chosen people, yet the author is admirably faithful to his historical purpose. There is a striking lack of the usual Hebrew emphasis upon special divine intervention, such as we find in the Old Testament, and much other historical literature from Jewish writers. It is of inestimable value as a source document for Jewish history. The author has sought to draw up an accurate account of the heroic and eventful struggle of the Jews for national independence under the leadership of the Maccabean brothers. The book derives its title from the history which it records.

(2) Quite different in quality from this book is that known as *II Maccabees.* It is not thus named because it is second in the sense of sequence, but because it contains an additional account of the Maccabean revolt. But while it covers very much the same period as I Maccabees, its historical value is not to be compared with that book. Yet by no means is it to be regarded as historically worthless. There is certainly a basis of fact supporting its account of the Maccabean struggle.

(3) Somewhere between the two extremes of historical merit represented in I and II Maccabees we may place the works of *Josephus.* He is of special interest to the New Testament student both because of his close relation to Jewish history of the first century and the value of his writings as historical sources.

Josephus was born at Jerusalem about A.D. 37 or 38. While Paul was in Jerusalem for the purpose of becoming acquainted with Peter (Gal. 1: 18), Josephus was an infant in a Jerusalem home. He was of priestly lineage, and trained for the priesthood. His original Jewish name was Joseph, which he Latinized by adding the ending *-us* and taking the surname Flavius.

From the beginning of his career Josephus attained to prominence in Jewish affairs. According to his own account, he visited Rome at the age of twenty-six in an effort to obtain liberty for some of his fellow countrymen. When he was a little above thirty years of age there broke out in Palestine the Jewish revolt of A.D. 66-70. Josephus took an active part in this uprising, but with no very zealous spirit, because he was without confidence in the outcome, and perhaps sympathetic toward Rome from the first. He was placed in charge of the forces in Galilee, but recognizing his inability to offer successful resistance he capitulated at the first approach of the Romans. He was taken captive and became a prisoner of war, but was treated with unusual favor, possibly because of his manifest sympathy with the Roman cause.

After the fall of Jerusalem, Josephus became a resident and citizen of Rome, and devoted the remainder of his life to literary activity. His work was of a general historical character, but Josephus was essentially an apologist rather than a historian. His writings were in Greek, in which he naturally developed great proficiency after he took up residence in Rome. His first work was on the Jewish struggle for independence from Rome A.D. 66-70, and bore the simple title, *The War*. It was likely written about A.D. 80. The most important literary product of Josephus was his *Antiquities*, written at Rome about 90-93. It is an account of Jewish history from the beginning down to his own time. The historical reliability of this work is frequently open to question, due to the untrustworthiness of some of his sources and his own disposition to exaggerate, but it is nevertheless an important source of historical data. Two other works of Josephus need but bare mention. *Against Apion* is a defense of Judaism against the unjust and often untrue attack of a blind anti-Semitism which existed in the world of his day. *Life* is a not altogether modest account of his own career.

He died at Rome about 95-98 A.D., having attained to over sixty years of age.

2. *Historico-Romantic.* This type has been quite appropriately called "Didactic Romance." Schuerer describes it as "Hortatory Narrative."[8] Either designation is fitting. The character of the literature is quite clearly distinct. It was fiction employed as a means of impressing ethical, patriotic, or religious lessons. It is hortatory romance, purporting to be based upon historical events. The modern historical novel is a suggestive parallel, though quite different in purpose.

(1) The most of this type of literature seems to have been produced in Egypt. Only one of any importance was produced in Palestine. This was the book of *Judith,* a Hebrew document, written about 200 B.C. The title of the book is the name of the heroine of the story, and means "Jewess." The story was designed to portray dramatically proper Jewish patriotism and devotion. It is a fictitious narrative of how a brave young Jewish widow, through her beauty, patriotism and wit, saved her people from foreign invasion. The book represents ardent national Judaism, and probably came from among the Hasidim, forerunners of the Pharisees.

(2) The other three books included in this class were written in Egypt. Their original language was the Koiné Greek. The earliest was the book of *Tobit,* written about 225 B.C., if not earlier. It is probably the oldest extant piece of Jewish literature produced in Egypt. It represents a high type of Jewish religion and ethics. The title of the book is the name of the hero of the story. It is written in the form of an autobiography. It is the story of the marvelous experiences of a Jew in Babylonia, who goes on a journey with the archangel Raphael as a traveling companion, in consequence of which he is blessed by miraculous escapes and achievements. It is

[8] *Jewish People in the Time of Jesus Christ,* Div. II, Vol. III, p. 32.

one of the most fascinating pieces of Jewish literature, a story which was exceedingly popular in the early centuries among both Jews and Christians, and was included in the Alexandrian canon of scripture.

(3) Another book in this group which is intensely Jewish, though written outside Palestine, is that known as *III Maccabees*. The title has been superficially attached. It is entirely a misnomer, there being no connection between the book and the Maccabean struggle. It quite probably arose from the association of this book with the other Maccabean books in a common manuscript or scroll. Its grouping with these books probably resulted from the fact that they are all concerned with problems of persecution and deliverance. This book is a Jewish apology in the form of historical romance. It is the story of how Ptolemy IV of Egypt, in an effort to defile the Temple, was miraculously repulsed and returned to Alexandria in a rage. His effort to wreak his vengeance upon the Egyptian Jews was frustrated by a direct interposition of divine providence. The story probably has some historical basis, but must be treated with critical caution.

(4) The nearest approach to the Greek point of view to be found in this type is the so-called *Letter of Aristeas*, written in Egypt about 100 B.C., purporting to give an account of the origin of the Septuagint. The document is not, strictly speaking, historical. The Septuagint is only the historical norm for a highly fanciful piece of fiction produced in an effort to present to the Greek mind a fusion of the religious and moral teachings of Judaism with the life and philosophy of Hellenism. It has some value as throwing light on the history of the Septuagint, though its representations must be critically sifted to get at the small residue of authentic fact.

3. *Poetical.* This period was not especially characterized by psalm writing, but nevertheless some of the best products of Hebrew poetry arose out of the struggle and heartache of these turbulent years.

(1) A few Psalms contained in the canonical Psalter were quite probably written during the Maccabean revolt, and are called *Maccabean Psalms.* Old Testament scholarship is not agreed on this matter, but there is no longer much question whether there are Maccabean Psalms, but how many there are and which. There is fairly general consensus of opinion on four: 44, 74, 79, and 83. One cannot be dogmatic, for it is difficult to date a Psalm. There may be many more belonging to the Maccabean period than has been commonly supposed.[9]

(2) There is no doubt about one group of the Psalms belonging to this period. These are the pseudonymous *Psalms of Solomon.*[10] There are eighteen of these psalms in all. The seventeenth is the one of greatest interest to the New Testament student because of its pronounced Messianic element. The standpoint of these psalms is strict Pharisaic Judaism. They are intensely nationalistic, but pervaded by an earnest moral tone and sincere piety. Their purpose was to condemn and correct liberal and political Judaism, and to check the growing tendency toward Hellenism.

4. *Apocalyptic.* We approach here the most distinctive literature produced by Judaism. Judaism was characterized by an intense Messianism, and it was thought that the Messianic age would usher in the end of the present world order; hence the abundance of Apocalyptic writings. The term "apocalyptic" is a transliteration of a Greek word made up from two other words, one meaning "from" and the other meaning "to cover"; hence to take the cover from, to disclose, to reveal. The Jews had no such word in their language. For this sort of literature they used the word prophecy. Apocalyptic

[9]The fact that the psalm was so peculiarly adapted to the synagogue services, and undoubtedly extensively used in that way, has been regarded by some as a strong reason for inferring that many of them originated as products of the synagogue. Cf. Fairweather, *The Background of the Gospels,* pp. 36f.

[10]A group of psalms denominated "Odes of Solomon," which came to light in 1909, and are dated by Rendel Harris A.D. 75-100, are by a Christian hand, and cannot be placed in a class with the products of Judaism.

represents the predictive element in prophecy. This predictive work of the Jews was occasioned by a desire to know the future. They wished to know the future because the present seemed to them wholly unsatisfactory, even sometimes unbearable, and they believed it was God's purpose in some way to remedy conditions. In this apocalyptic literature the highest idealism and hope of Judaism is expressed. It represents a noble effort and deserves our deepest appreciation.

This period was particularly adapted to apocalyptic, because apocalyptic was a literature of persecution. When political powers oppressed, and those within Judaism apostatized, when the dearest object in the possession of the devout Jew—his religion—was critically jeopardized, then he instinctively turned to God and to the future for hope. The superb faith of Judaism, when borne down by tyranny and persecution, renounced the present order, and escaped its fetters of bondage by soaring high on the wings of hope into another world order, wherein God and righteousness would reign supreme.

Apocalyptic literature was thoroughly futuristic in its point of view; hence the peculiar style was that of vision. But it must always be borne in mind that the futuristic bearing was general rather than specific, and that the vision was a figure of certain great issues and ideas related to the situation which was real and present to the apocalyptist. The prediction was generally of the consummation of God's plan for Israel, and the ultimate triumph of righteousness and the Law.

The pathetic heart-throb of Jewish hope in the midst of trial and persecution found its most satisfying expression in the form of apocalyptic writings. This Jewish apocalypticism formed its earliest models in Ezekiel and Daniel, and its noblest and most enduring product in the New Testament Book of Revelation.

(1) The literature of Judaism contained several of these apocalyptic documents, but four are of particular interest. The greatest one, both in its length and in the

breadth of its prophetic horizon, is the book now generally known as *I Enoch*. The work is likely composite, produced by piecing together five smaller apocalypses, and has but little unity. The dates of these five documents range from 200 to 64 B.C. The work clearly took its title from the Old Testament patriarch of that name. There was a considerable amount of such Enoch literature. We have here five such documents, and in the composite work known as II Enoch there is another collection. Because of the description of Enoch in Genesis 5: 24, he was supposed to have had the privilege of special knowledge of the heavenly categories. It was this idea of the patriarch having been conversant with the secrets of God that led to the production of the abundance of Enoch literature. I Enoch was composed in Palestine, and its original language was Hebrew or Aramaic, or possibly both, as in the case of Daniel.

(2) The only apocalyptic production of importance outside of Palestine was *II Enoch*, also known as "Slavonic Enoch," because of the language in which we find the only extant copy, and the "Book of the Secrets of Enoch." This document is a comparatively recent discovery, having been first brought to public notice in 1892. The honor belongs to R. H. Charles, the greatest scholar in this field which the nineteenth and twentieth centuries have produced, of first investigating and giving to the public the real nature and value of this apocalypse. The last half is of gnomic or wisdom type, and probably originated in Palestine. The apocalyptic portion, forming the first half of the book, was apparently not written under the stress of persecution, as was usually the case with apocalyptic writings, but is a calm exposition of current Jewish apocalyptic ideals. It was likely composed by an Alexandrian Jew about A.D. 50, for the purpose of acquainting his kinsmen in Egypt with the apocalyptic ideas of standard Judaism.

(3) The third apocalypse deserving of notice here was written (or compiled) in Palestine by an ardent Pharisee.

It is known as *II Baruch,* and is represented to be a writing of Baruch the friend of Jeremiah, relating what he did before and after the destruction of Jerusalem. The contents of the book consist of three divisions, an introduction, a central portion, and a conclusion. The introduction (Chaps. 1-12) appears to be historical in aim, recounting Baruch's connection with the destruction of Jerusalem. The central portion (Chaps. 13-76) is the apocalyptic part, consisting almost entirely of visions and revelations. The conclusion (Chaps. 77-87) records admonitions and epistles of Baruch to the people of Israel. The religious standpoint is standard Judaism of the first century A.D. The work was written contemporaneously with the rise of the Christian movement.

(4) The apocalypse known as *IV Ezra* was written in Palestine about A.D. 90. The book bears this title because purported to have been written by the ancient Hebrew scribe of that name. There is, however, no great emphasis upon this pseudepigraphic character of the book, as the name occurs only three times. The book is made up of seven visions, all of them devoted to an effort to explain the fall of Jerusalem. It is concerned with the same general theme which occupies II Baruch, but approaches the problem in a far different attitude. In II Baruch we find the viewpoint of satisfied, standard Judaism; but this book is in a sense a criticism of standard Judaism, especially as to the doctrine that only a few are saved, and that God is entirely pleased that there should be only a few. This last was the standard Jewish view, but to the author of this book it is not satisfactory. He earnestly seeks for a different and better view, finally falling back upon the standard Jewish eschatology of his day for an explanation. He takes the view that the trials of Israel are disciplinary and preparatory in their purpose. He also resorts to the argument that the ways of God are beyond human understanding.

5. *Gnomic.* This type is also called "wisdom literature." It is of that general type represented by the

canonical Book of Proverbs. While apocalyptic dealt with the theoretical and eschatological, wisdom dealt with the practical and ethical. This gnomic literature represents Jewish moral philosophy at its best. It was written for the guidance of the people in their everyday lives. It consists of conclusions which have been reached by reflection upon the experiences of human life. This wisdom activity was not only literary, but was also carried on in personal instruction. What we have, preserved in writing, is the best ideas produced by that phase of Jewish activity. It was one of the most important phases of Jewish life, and produced the most extensive literature. It may be regarded as extending back as far as the time of Solomon, and is represented in the teaching of Jesus and the Epistle of James in the New Testament.[11] Five representatives of this type may be considered here.

(1) The oldest book in the group is known as *Sira* (Greek, *Sirach*). What its original title was we cannot be certain, for it is extant in Hebrew only in fragments, all of which are defective in the opening verses. In the Greek manuscripts it is called "The Wisdom of Jesus the Son of Sirach." The title "Ecclesiasticus" has been in use in the Latin Church since the middle of the third century. This title is ill-chosen. It means church book, and this book is not such in any peculiar sense. Nevertheless, it is the title which the book carried in the Vulgate, and has survived to modern times. The simple name Sira seems to be the preferable title. As is true of all books in this class, the contents are miscellaneous, and lack systematic arrangement. This absence of logical sequence in these books is not to be regarded as disorder, but was the wisdom method. The typical Jewish mind was not analytical and logical, but practical and concrete. Such is the character of this book. It offers a manual of conduct, by which the author designed to promote higher living. He studied human experience and sought to point the way to a better life. The book

[11]Cf. Fairweather: *op. cit.*, p. 79.

was written about 190-170 B.C., in Hebrew, probably at Jerusalem. Its teachings are in line with orthodox Judaism.

(2) In this group belongs the book known as the *Testaments of the Twelve Patriarchs.* The title is derived from the historical setting of the story. The book purports to be the testaments of the twelve sons of Jacob, given to their sons at their deathbeds. There are twelve sections, one devoted to each of the twelve patriarchs. The pseudepigraphic character of the book was probably not intended as a deception, but as a matter of literary form. The story is not told from historical motives, but as a medium of teaching. It belongs to that literary form known among the Jews as *Haggadha.* The original language was Hebrew. It was probably written during the years of John Hyrcanus, about 109 to 106 B.C. The author was a loyal Pharisee and an ardent admirer of the Maccabean family. Each testament presents three distinct parts. (1) The patriarch gives a sketch of his own life history, confessing the wrongs he has done and calling attention to his virtues. (2) He then offers his sons an earnest word of exhortation. (3) Each testament closes with a sort of apocalyptic message setting forth the redemption of Israel as mediated through the tribes of Levi and Judah. Because of this apocalyptic element the book is sometimes classified with the apocalypses, but considerably the major portion of it is of the wisdom type. The chief interest of the book is in its ethical teachings and their similarity to the moral tone of the New Testament.

(3) This wisdom activity also extended to Egypt. The earliest work of the gnomic type in this region was the *Wisdom of Solomon,* also known as the "Book of Wisdom," or just "Wisdom." It is unquestionably pseudepigraphic, though many Catholic scholars have tried to defend its Solomonic authorship. It was written in Alexandria between 100 and 50 B.C. The original language

was, of course, Greek. Its theology shows clearly the traces of Greek philosophy.

(4) A second Alexandrian product of this type is *IV Maccabees.* The book bears this title because it is built upon the story of the Maccabean martyrs. It is wisdom teaching presented in the form of highly rhetorical public address, after the manner of Greek philosophical speech-making. It is a synagogue sermon or anniversary address of some sort. The language is good idiomatic Greek of a literary style. It was written in Alexandria A.D. 1-25 by an unknown author.

(5) To this class of literature belongs the work of *Philo,* the greatest individual produced by Judaism as such. He was the most energetic and voluminous writer in all the history of the Jews. He represents the acme of Hellenized Judaism. His style, terminology, and mode of thought are Greek. He was nevertheless loyal to Moses and to the traditions of Israel. His supreme effort was to interpret standard Judaism in the terms and thought forms of Greek philosophy current in his day. More will be said about his life and work in a later connection.

There are four other documents in the literature of Judaism which deserve brief mention. With the apocalyptic type belongs the Book of Jubilees, a voluminous work written by a Pharisee about the last quarter of the second century B.C. for the purpose of restraining the Hellenizing tendencies in Judaism and of exalting the Law. It is cast in the form of a *midhrashic* treatment of the Old Testament. Another representative of the apocalyptic class appears in the *Sibylline Oracles,* which are fragmentary remains of ancient records of supposedly divine sayings, dating in composition over a period from 300 B.C to A.D. 150. The *Assumption of Moses* is a composite work of apocalyptic character produced in the first quarter of the first century A.D. for the purpose of safeguarding the interests of strict Pharisaism. Of the wisdom type we have, in addition to the works treated above, *I Baruch,* a composite document which came into existence in its present form about A.D. 70-80, having been written to bewail the tragic fate of Jerusalem. There are a number of other fragments or portions of documents, but not of importance sufficient to justify treatment here. The literature of Judaism in its distinctive character and chief contents has been presented to the student in the above sketch.

The vast amount of rabbinic literature, now found in theological libraries in numbers of printed volumes, was not in written form until several centuries after New Testament times. It existed during this period in the form of oral tradition, committed to memory *verbatim* in the rabbinical schools. The oral law, or elaboration of the *Torah*, was organized into a systematic arrangement by Rabbi Juda about A.D. 200, but none of it was reduced to writing until later.

CHAPTER IV

THE ORIGIN AND DEVELOPMENT OF JUDAISM

When one takes his stand in the midst of the New Testament world and contemplates his surroundings, the first and most prominent object to meet his attention is the Jew. The most imperative requisite to New Testament interpretation is to become thoroughly acquainted with this Jew. The investigation of his character and environment soon reveals that he is the product of more than a single generation. He presents a combination of elements contributed by many centuries of the past. In fact, all the history of Israel is represented in him. But especially is he affected by the five centuries immediately preceding the age in which he lives. The initial task in the study of the New Testament world is to investigate this period of history and to gain a knowledge of the origin and nature of the Jew.

We are to recognize first that the Jew is strictly a distinctive character. The Israelite of the Old Testament may not correctly be referred to as a Jew. The Jew was an Israelite, but the pre-exilic Israelite was not a Jew. The Jew is properly a creation of the Exile, and appears in history at the time of the Restoration. Josephus says of the term Jew: "This is the name they are called by from the day they came up from Babylon" (Antq. 11: 5). He occupied his ancient promised land, but "Judaism grew up as a new thing on the ancient soil."[1] The name Jew is a modification of the ancient tribal name "Judah," transliterated through the Greek into the English. It was applied to those coming up from Babylon in the Restoration because in the main they were of the tribe of Judah.

[1]Fairweather, *The Background of the Gospels*, p. 61.

But the terms Jew and Judaism have more than a tribal significance. They denote a distinctive type of life. The Hebrews of the tribe of Judah who were carried into captivity had suffered a real change. They saw in their privations in the Exile the chastening hand of Jehovah laid upon them because of their disobedience to the Law, and they heartily repented. And besides, it was only the more devout who returned under the benevolent patronage of Cyrus, and undertook the re-establishment of the holy nation. So the descendants of Israel who came up from Babylon had a new devotion to the Law and to the traditions of the fathers. They were possessed of a keen distaste for idolatry, and all things Gentile, and were therefore far more intense and exclusive in their racial loyalty than had been their fathers before the Exile. It was this renovated people who became known to history as the Jews, and their tenets and type of life constituted Judaism. We will now seek to trace the development of the agencies and processes which produced this most important feature of the New Testament background.

The Formative Factors

We are not studying here history for history's sake. It is not chronological periods but operative forces in which we are interested. Our aim is to find the relation of the five preceding centuries to the Jew we meet the moment we open the New Testament. Interpretative investigation of this history discloses one fundamental concern in Jewish life, manifesting itself along three essential lines of expression. The one fundamental concern was the relationship between Jehovah and his people, and this relationship was regarded as national, legal, and ritual. That is, the basal conception of Judaism was the *covenant,* which embraced three essential elements, the Nation, the Law, and the Priesthood. The Nation was the object of the divine favor and the chief end contemplated by the covenant; the Law was the condition required for the fulfilment of the covenant; and the ritual administered by the Priesthood was the ceremonial manifestation of the covenant. We see, then, that there were three normative factors in the development of Judaism, the Nation, the Law, and the Priesthood. These three interests may be unmistakably detected as they establish themselves in the beginnings of Jewish history.

I. The Nation

It was this fundamental interest which generated the rekindling of hope and the revival of patriotic devotion and enthusiasm in the exiles in far-away Babylon. Only through the re-establishment of the Nation could the operation of the Law be renewed and the worship of Jehovah resumed in the sacred courts of the Temple. Without the assembling of Israel as a nation there was no hope that the covenant relation could be restored.

1. Consequently, the first step in the re-establishment of the covenant must be the *restoration of national integrity*. By virtue of the generous patronage of Cyrus, at least fifty thousand people returned from Babylonia between 537 and 444 B.C., and resumed residence in Judea. They returned in three groups. The first came under Zerubbabel, a prince of the house of David, in 537 B.C. Their number, according to the most reliable sources, was 42,360.[2] A second group came with Ezra in 458 B.C., and probably a third when Nehemiah returned in 444. Besides these we might well suppose that others migrated thither from time to time, but not in connection with any event which caused them to receive mention in the chronicles of the time. The great majority of those who returned were of the tribes of Judah and Levi, but there were also representatives from the other tribes.[3]

The returning exiles purposed the rehabilitation of the ancient national life. They regarded the people of Israel as a holy nation and their native territory as a holy land.

[2]Josephus, *Antq.*, 11: 1, places the number at 42,462.

[3]For a dependable and enlightening discussion of the fate of the Ten Tribes, see Ewald, *op. cit.*, Vol. V, pp. 90ff.

To reclaim these holy possessions for Jehovah and the Law was the noble and earnest aim of the returning pilgrims.

As compared with the number who went into Exile, only a few returned in the Restoration. These consisted of the most devout and patriotic spirits to be found among the exiles, those who could find no satisfaction in life outside the service of God and the observance of the Law. The Captivity had taught the people a new regard for the Law, and those national and religious ideals so nobly advocated by the prophets. In the sufferings and religious privations through which they had been forced to pass while in exile in the midst of heathenism, much of the dross had been purged out of the race. Ewald describes this fact in vivid and striking language. "The ruinous errors and perversities of earlier centuries were over now; and all the storm was past of that wild passion into which even the essentially noble efforts of Israel had so often degenerated in the time of the nation's independent life. Only the immortal and eternal in Israel could maintain itself, and the sole method by which it was enabled to hold out against the trials of the time was by severing itself more sternly than ever from all that was foreign to it, and returning more quietly and firmly upon itself." He describes the transformation as a "twofold movement, leading on the one hand decidedly away from every form of heathenism, and, on the other hand, approaching with such earnestness and determination to the ancient God of Israel."[4]

All external support and protection had been lost; the faith of Israel must maintain itself by its own intrinsic forces. The Captivity destroyed all the forms and material symbols of Israel's religion. It was Nebuchadnezzar's policy to utterly crush the conquered. Out of this ordeal there came that faithful remnant foreseen in prophetic vision, possessed of a deathless loyalty to the traditions and hopes of Israel. It was a purgated and

[4]*Op. cit.*, Vol. V, pp. 19, 25.

patriotic people who took up again the broken threads of their nation's history, and, under the name Jew, resumed the holy enterprise of restoring the covenant relations of Israel in the Holy Land of the covenant.

The selfish and indifferent members of the race remained where they were. Josephus tells us: "Yet did many of them stay at Babylon, as not willing to leave their possessions."[5] However, there were many Jews who remained in Babylon who were still loyal to the Law and cherished the covenant, as is instanced in the cases of Daniel and Esther. Many of the wealthy Hebrews contributed liberally of their means to the program of rehabilitation. Nevertheless, we may conclude that the cream of Jewish patriotism and piety repeopled the land of Judea.

In its bearing upon New Testament interpretation this was by far the most significant development of the period. The Judaism thus established made possible, historically speaking, the career of Jesus. It found its extreme development in the Pharisees, where it was characterized by extreme legalism and national exclusiveness. The nobler and less rigid development of the race was represented in the multitudes who turned with such favorable attention to Jesus and became his disciples.

2. It was the determination of the Jewish people to preserve their national integrity which furnished the grounds for the *breach with the Samaritans.* A familiar fact in New Testament history is the intense animosity existing between the Jew and the Samaritan. This important development originated largely during the Persian period (537-332 B.C.). It is a fact well known by the Bible student that the Samaritans were repulsed when they offered to participate in the building of the Temple.

The Samaritans thus appearing in late Old Testament history are not the Gentile races immigrated into Samaria after the conquest of the northern kingdom of

[5] *Antq.*, 11: 1.

Israel, but chiefly the descendants of the Israelites themselves who were left when the mass of the nation was carried into Assyrian bondage. Though they were in the main of pure Hebrew lineage, they had been in close contact with the Gentile immigrants who had settled in Canaan after the Captivity, and had amalgamated with them to a considerable extent. Moreover, they had neglected the Temple and ignored the desolation of Jerusalem, disregarded the Law, and forgotten the covenant, through all the years that Judah was exiled in Babylon. Then, doubtless, it was not forgotten that they were descendants of the Ten Tribes who, under Jeroboam, had rebelled against the royal house of David. These combined reasons convinced the Jews that the Samaritans were not qualified for participation in the restoration of the nation.

Matters reached a climax when Manasseh, a close relative of the high priest, married the daughter of Sanballat, the Samaritan chief. When he declined to repudiate and abandon this unlawful union he was banished from the land of Judah. With several others who associated themselves with him because of being in the same plight, he repaired to Samaria, and applied to Sanballat for the privilege of erecting a distinctive Samaritan temple. This rival temple was built on Mt. Gerizim, where it stood until destroyed by John Hyrcanus. It was to this sacred spot that the Samaritan woman had reference when she said to our Lord, "Our fathers worshipped in this mountain" (John 4: 20).

The hostility generated by this development has persisted to this day, and accounts for the animosity of the Samaritans toward the Jews, especially when the latter were journeying in the direction of Jerusalem.

II. The Law

A distinct and vitally important line of development originated with the influence of Ezra. This mighty scribe, and founder of the standard Judaism which we meet in the New Testament, brought to Jewish life its excessive emphasis upon the Law. It was he who inspired the resumption of the morning and evening sacrifices upon the long neglected altar of the Temple (Ezra 3: 1-3). He led in the campaign conducted among the returned exiles to expunge from the life of the nation the bane of mixed marriages (Ezra 9: 1ff.). He inaugurated the first systematic study of the Law, by the people at large, known in Jewish history (Neh. 8: 1ff.). He was an ardent protagonist of the Law and of the racial exclusiveness of Judaism. Though his influence undoubtedly produced far more extreme results than he himself ever designed, yet we cannot fail to recognize him as the first and greatest promoter of legal bondage in Judaism. Through Ezra the Law was enthroned anew in the conscience of the people. As a result of the impetus thus given the Law there came two other developments.

1. Ezra's great stress upon the observance of the Law called for the greatest possible knowledge of it on the part of the people. For their instruction, and the study and promotion of the Law in general, there arose a class in Judaism known as *scribes* or rabbis. These scribes were not "clergymen," in the ordinary sense of that term, but were laymen who gave themselves to the study and teaching of the Law. As logical corollaries of this chief function they gave themselves to defending and preserving the traditions of Israel, and deducing from the Law more detailed regulations for the direction of personal conduct. These traditions and regulations were transmitted in oral form, and were regarded as an authoritative interpretation of the Law, styled by subsequent generations as the "hedge about the Law." This oral tradition extended to the most trivial matters, and became absurdly and unbearably rigid. It was to this that Jesus referred when he rebuked the Pharisees as those who "bind heavy burdens and grievous to be borne, and lay them on men's shoulders" (Matt. 23: 4). The regu-

lar minister of religion among the Jews was theoretically the priest, but actually the scribe was the molding factor in religious life. Through the scribe the synagogue soon advanced to a place of power and influence, and from it the Law exercised its supreme authority in Jewish life.

2. The advent of scribism brought the *cessation of prophecy*. This was inevitable. Prophecy is essentially original—a creative process; scribism was deliberately hostile to originality. Its very existence depended upon a design to repress innovation; to "build a hedge about the Law." Such a policy created an atmosphere which was obviously unfavorable to the exercise of the prophetic function, and in consequence the voice of prophecy was hushed in Israel from Malachi to John the Baptist. The exigencies of the Restoration called forth the burning messages of Haggai and Zechariah, and the corrupt practices of the high priest and his associates, accompanied by a decline of respect for the Law and neglect of the Temple worship, evoked the prophetic ministry of Malachi, the last of that long line of Old Testament prophets who, as the special spokesman of Jehovah, courageously denounced the backslidings of Israel and enunciated the great principles of that redemption which they dimly glimpsed as the fruition of the Messianic hope of their nation. With Malachi the curtain of prophecy falls.

III. The Priesthood

The covenant with Jehovah involved a ritual element, because it was a covenant of worship as well as of obedience. Jehovah was to be present with Israel as his God through all the ages. The Temple was the visible symbol of this aspect of the covenant, and the priest was the functionary. Consequently an essential part of the Restoration was to reinstate the priesthood and renew the ritual.

1. Naturally the first step in restoring the worship of Jehovah was the *rebuilding of the Temple*. It was on the occasion of the Feast of the Tabernacles that the return-

ing exiles finally arrived in Jerusalem, to build again the altar of Jehovah and offer sacrifices as required by Law. Later the foundations of the Temple were laid amid mingled tears and rejoicing, but due to serious opposition and difficulty the building was not completed for several years. As soon as the program of reconstruction was inaugurated the Samaritans proposed to join the enterprise and become members of the restored nation. Being rejected and repulsed by the Jews they were filled with hatred and jealousy, and offered hurtful and embarrassing opposition. It is probable that the Egyptian campaign of Cambyses also served to seriously retard the work of reconstruction.[6] But in spite of the difficulties, the work was finally finished, the Temple dedicated amid great rejoicing, and the sacred feasts resumed.

2. The history of Judaism presents a new regime for the priesthood, for it early witnessed the *elevation of the high priest.* In the Old Testament period the supreme functionary of the Temple ritual had been generally designated simply as chief priest, but after the Restoration he appears in a new light as high priest, and with greatly increased prerogatives.

The government of the restored nation was first placed in the hands of Zerubbabel, the last prince of Judah. He was not permitted by his Persian overlord to establish an independent monarchy, but only to govern Judea as a province of the Persian empire. Due to friction and criticism, Zerubbabel was forced to retire before the close of his life, and the high priest became the head of the government. This seemed to the Persian sovereign the natural and rightful policy to pursue, for the benighted heathen ruler could know nothing of the genius or safeguards of true religion. How long the high priest remained in power is not certain. When Nehemiah came to Jerusalem in 444 B.C. he secured appointment from Artaxerxes as governor,[7] and obtained full control of af-

[6]Cf. Ewald, *op. cit.*, Vol. V, pp. 105f.

[7]It appears possible that, prior to this, Ezra had exercised the prerogatives of governor. Cf. Ewald, *op. cit.*, Vol. V, p. 139.

fairs seemingly without opposition from the high priest. But after he retired the high priest again secured control. Judea was made a part of the satrapy of Coelesyria, and subject to its ruler. The local administration of affairs was consigned to the high priest, who was responsible to the Persian satrap.

Thus the government of the nation, its political administration and destiny, fell into the hands of the priesthood. This is a fact of noteworthy significance in the development of Judaism. It meant that the Temple, which was designed as the place for the worship of Jehovah and the purification of his chosen people, should instead become the center of political scheming and promotion of selfish ambition. The priesthood, ordained for the spiritual guidance of the people, was to lapse into a mere partisan clique, to be wielded as the instrument of unholy political aspirations. The position of high priest was debased from its exalted place of custodian of the religious life of the Hebrew people, and became the prize of carnal yearning and the object of the most disgraceful trickery and conflict.

Scarcely had the pontifical office obtained the government of the nation when it was stained with blood and sacrilege. Jonathan, son of Joiada, secured the office of high priest by legal succession to his father. Thereupon his brother Joshua became incensed with jealous fury, and emboldened by the partiality of Bagoses the Persian general, he sought to displace his brother. He was unsuccessful in his attempt, and was slain by his brother in the Temple courts. This disgraceful contest was an omen of the subsequent history of the priesthood.

The Invasion of Hellenism

It has been observed that under the influence of Ezra the Law became the supreme factor in Jewish life. But the reign of the Law was not without its vicissitudes and fluctuations. It experienced periods of great advancement, but also met serious reverses, which at times seemed to threaten its total extinction.

From the very beginning the yoke of heathen bondage lay upon the Jews. They returned from captivity under the sovereignty of the Persians, and under Persian dominion they remained for two hundred years, 537 to 332 B.C.[8] The Persian rule, however, did not militate seriously against the supremacy of the Law, for the Persians were generally kind and considerate in their dealings with the Jews, and allowed them the free exercise of their religious privileges and practical national autonomy.

I. Macedonian Conquest

In 332 B.C. a dark cloud appeared upon the horizon of Jewish history. Its ominous nature was not at first realized, but when Jewish history is viewed in full perspective the menacing aspect of this development becomes vividly apparent. Alexander the Great, the Macedonian conqueror, subdued the East and brought Palestine under his control. It was this turn of events which brought upon Judaism the blighting impact of Hellenism, the most serious hazard ever experienced by the Law.

II. Egyptian Rule

After the death of Alexander his vast empire was divided among his several lieutenants, and after considerable conflict between rival claimants Judea fell into the hands of the Egyptian rulers, known in history as the Ptolemies. As an Egyptian province the Jews continued to be treated with great leniency, and enjoyed material prosperity, but at the same time it was an era of religious decadence. The favor shown the people by their Greek conquerors made them very susceptible to the influence of Greek culture and manners, and brought on a

[8]Scholars are not in exact agreement on these dates. For instance Ewald (*Hist. of Israel*, Vol. V) places the limits of the period at 536 to 333, Graetz (*Hist. of the Jews*, Vol. I) divides at 537 and 300, Stanley (*Hist. of the Jewish Church*, Vol. III) gives 538 to 333, and Doubnow (*Outline of Jewish History*, Vol. I, p. 287) employs the limits used here, 537 to 332.

serious influx of Gentile manners and ideas, and a corresponding laxness in their attitude toward the Law. Many Jews openly repudiated their religious standards and ceremonial rites, and adopted the Greek mode of living.

Two instances from the period are illustrative of its general character:

1. In general, the Egyptian rulers were markedly considerate and tolerant in their treatment of the Jews, but, as naturally would be expected, differences in individual character of the rulers made differences in policy. Oriental monarchy was at heart tyrannical, and occasionally its essential nature would show itself. The most extreme case on the record of the dealings of the Ptolemies with the Jews was an attempt at a wholesale massacre of the Jews of Alexandria by Ptolemy Philopator, successor to Euergetes. In a conflict with the Syrian king Antiochus ("the Great") he won a brilliant victory at Raphia, and marched on exulting to Jerusalem, where he offered gifts and sacrifices in the Temple. In a fit of morbid curiosity he sought to enter the Holy of Holies, but was in some way summarily ejected, probably by a panic of his own superstitious fear. Deeply chagrined, he returned to Egypt in a rage and wreaked his vengeance on the Jews of that country by depriving them of many political liberties and attempting to slaughter a great number of them, but his effort was unsuccessful.[9]

2. The Hellenizing propaganda found its ardent advocates even among the Jewish leaders. Of such character was Joseph the son of Tobias. He was a crafty and ambitious profligate, who by shrewd diplomacy secured the favor of the Egyptian court and was made custodian of tribute, which gave him virtual control of Judea. He brought peace and prosperity to the land,

[9]In placing this incident in the reign of Philopator we are following III Maccabees, which we believe to be based upon a substratum of real history, though undoubtedly containing a considerable admixture of fiction. Others, rejecting III Maccabees entirely, place this persecution in the reign of Physcon, nearly a hundred years later. Cf. Graetz, *History of the Jews*, Vol. I, p. 519.

but with them their all too frequent concomitants, luxury and vice. The corrupt indulgences into which he led the nation ill prepared it for the distress which was to follow. At one time the high priest Onias II came near provoking trouble by refusing to send the tribute money to the Egyptian court, but the crisis was averted and the nation saved by the wit and affability of Joseph. This ingratiated him all the more deeply with rulers and people, and strengthened the cause of the Hellenists.

At the religious heart of the nation, however, there yet remained a faithful remnant who abjured all things Gentile, and continued to demand the absolute supremacy of the Mosaic code and labored ardently to perpetuate the race of Israel. This party of loyal patriots were called *Hasidim;* that is, the "righteous ones." They were destined to exercise a vast influence over the subsequent history of the Jews. They developed into that religious caste known to the New Testament as Pharisees. At the opposite extreme from them were the Hellenists, those who were aggressively active in promoting the Greek propaganda, the historical predecessors of the Sadducees.

The Nationalist Reaction

The age-long conflict in Judaism between the Hellenistic tendency and loyalty to the Law was inaugurated by the policies of Alexander, who sought not only to conquer but to Hellenize the world. Throughout the reign of the Ptolemies it continued to be but a controversy over rival policies, and brought on no open combat of any considerable significance. In fact, had the Egyptian mode of government continued, open hostilities might have been kept indefinitely in abeyance. And this would likely have been to the untold detriment of distinctive Judaism, for it would have meant the gradual Hellenizing of the whole nation. But in 198 B.C. Judea was wrested from the Ptolemies by the Græco-Syrian kingdom of the Seleucids, and there was soon set on foot a governmental effort at compulsory Hellenization. This soon led to open rebellion, and eventually resulted in the independence of the Jewish nation.

I. The Causes of Rebellion

During the three decades of Syrian domination the Jews suffered more than they had in all the hundred and twenty-two years in which they were under the control of the Ptolemies. Antiochus the Great respected their customs and courted their sympathy, but his successors treated them with shameless cruelty. This period represents the midnight of interbiblical history. Insult and persecution were inflicted upon the Jews in every conceivable way. Seleucus IV, the son and successor of Antiochus the Great, sought through one of his generals to rob the Temple of certain treasures which had been deposited there for safe-keeping, and the sanctuary of Jehovah escaped only by a special interposition of protective providence. But the apex of tyranny and persecution was reached by the next incumbent of the Syrian throne, Antiochus Epiphanes.[10] Three causes contributed to this period of distress:

1. The nation had been reduced to tragic impotency by the *disintegrating effects of Hellenistic influence.* The Jews had now been under Greek dominion for nearly two and a half centuries. This long continued contact with Grecian life and customs could not fail to have its effect. Thousands of Jews had gone from Palestine into Alexandria, which was rapidly becoming the world-center of Greek life and thought—the station which it held in New Testament times. These Alexandrian Jews often revisited the homeland, and their influence inevitably reacted upon the life in Judea. Then there were Jews from other parts of the Greek world returning to the homeland, and bringing their Greek culture with them.[11] The use of the

[10]*Epiphanes* meant in Greek "the illustrious," but Antiochus deserved far more the nickname attached to him by his subjects, *Epimanes,* "the madman."

[11]Cf. Gilbert, *Greek Thought in the New Testament,* pp. 35ff.

Greek language became widespread in Palestine as a result of the immigration of so many Greek-speaking peoples. Several almost exclusively Greek cities were established on Palestinian soil.

The fact of the presence of these Greek cities is one of the most pronounced evidences of the extent and strength of Greek influence. Some of the chief Palestinian cities which disclosed their Greek character by their names were Gerasa, Philoteria, Pella, Dion, Gadara, Scythopolis, and Ptolemais. Other cities lost their ancient names and came to be known by new Hellenic names. The ancient Dan was called Paneas, Rabbath-Ammon was rebuilt as Philadelphia, and Ar-Moab as Areopolis.

The attractiveness of Greek culture and practices, in their contrast with the far more sober and restricted life under the Law, won many Jews away from their allegiance to the traditions of Israel. Many Jewish children were given Greek or Greek-sounding names. A Greek amphitheatre was erected at Jerusalem, and an academy established for instruction in Greek literature and philosophy. Judean youths were trained for participation in the Greek games, and Jewish leaders applied for admission as enrolled citizens of the Syrian kingdom. A royal edict was issued requiring the Jews to worship the Hellenic gods; the Temple was formally dedicated to Zeus, the supreme god of Olympus; and swine's flesh was sacrificed on the altars of the Temple. Such developments could not fail to arouse to violent resentment the conscience of Judaism.

2. The tenseness of the situation was accentuated by *internal disloyalty and strife*. There were many Jews who preferred the Syrian regime. They welcomed every opportunity to advance the interests of the Syrian King. Of such character was Joshua, or Jason (his Greek name), who secured by bribe the deposition of his brother Onias from the high priesthood and seized the office himself. He devoted himself with enthusiasm to the Hellenizing policy of Antiochus and to the promotion of Greek

culture and amusements. But he was not permitted to remain long in undisputed possession of his ill-got prize. Menelaus, a far more unscrupulous Hellenist, by bribing Antiochus, supplanted Jason. At a seemingly opportune moment the latter raised a force and sought to regain his place, but was prevented by the unexpected interference of Antiochus. Menelaus remained in possession of the pontifical robes, and by lying representations to the king increased the oppression of the Jews.

3. The inevitable climax was precipitated by the *extreme cruelty of Antiochus.* This capricious and heartless ruler imposed upon the Jews an unbearable burden of taxation, and drenched Jerusalem in blood. In punishing the revolt of Jason he slew forty thousand of the inhabitants of the city, and despoiled the Temple. Two years later, without even a substantial pretext, but in a fit of whimsical rage, he again attacked Jerusalem, slew the defenseless inhabitants by the thousands, made slaves of women and children, and left the city in a tragic state of grief and desolation. The final blow came when he published a decree commanding all the Jews to offer sacrifice to the gods of the Greeks.

II. The Progress of Rebellion

It seemed that the last hope of the Jews had sunk within the gloom of the tyrant's oppression, that the glory of Israel had forever waned, and the unending night of historical oblivion had settled over the hapless nation. But just at this dread crisis a constellation of morning stars appeared upon the national horizon, heralding the dawn of a better day. The Maccabean heroes entered the arena, and by a few deft and mighty strokes changed the whole face of Jewish history. The hand of patriotic defense had at last been raised in deadly protest against the oppression of heartless tyranny. Prostrate, bleeding Judaism took heart again, and loyal Jews on every hand raised the thrilling slogan, "To the hills, to the hills, for Jehovah and Judah!"

1. The first and most spectacular of the Maccabean heroes to unsheath the sword of rebellion was *Judas*. His aged father had begun the insurrection, but had succumbed to the inevitable privation and exposure. The cause of freedom he committed into the capable hands of his third and noblest son Judas.

No more impressive figure ever graced the stage of human action than Judas Maccabæus. Others might have been more spectacular, but none was ever inspired by nobler designs or controlled by more unselfish motives than he. From David to John the Baptist he was the greatest who challenged Israel to rally to his standard. Bravery, earnestness, patriotism, and piety combined to make a character worthy of the admiration of the best of men. Whatever may be one's religious interpretation of interbiblical history, he must surely admit that Judas Maccabæus was a gift of merciful providence. If ever a man fell upon a crisis hour for which he was exactly fitted, such was certainly the lot of this Judean hero. He was just the leader whom Judaism needed at this tragic turn in its history, and his people soon recognized in him the God-sent defender of the national faith and fortune.

As the Syrian king assayed to suppress this petty rebel foe, despotic contempt gave place to piqued rage, which in turn was succeeded by chagrined surprise, and finally yielded to an attitude of literal dread—real, though unconfessed. How Judas, with but a handful of poorly equipped followers, could hurl cringing terror into the proud court of the Seleucidian tyrant, can be understood best by one who believes in an omnipotent hand of providence. Well did his people nickname this hero "Maccabæus"—that is, "the hammerer"—for despotism never received the shock of heavier or more rapid blows than he gave the armies of Syria. To the end of time, independent of his religious significance, human history must accord a high place of recognition to the name and deeds of Judas Maccabæus.

The Hasidim saw in the Maccabean heroes the salvation of their cause. They rallied to Judas, and offered their lives willingly for the defense of the nation. By a series of brilliant military strokes of combined bravery and strategy, Judas was enabled to gain practical independence. His first act was to restore the worship of Jehovah as nearly as possible in accordance with the Law. Of course this greatly delighted the patriotic party, but they were doubtless not so well pleased when Judas turned the energies of the newly restored nation in the direction of territorial conquest. This showed clearly to the Hasidim that the Maccabean brothers were not indifferent to political aggrandizement. Doubtless this step on the part of Judas planted in the hearts of the ardent patriots the first seeds of distrust, which were eventually to fructify in an open breach between the Hasidim and the descendants of Mattathias. Judas, however, retained their loyal support until the time of his death, which he met on the field of battle fighting desperately to defend the freedom which against such odds he had won.

2. After the death of Judas the secret suspicion of the Hasidim began to express itself in open opposition, and the country for a time fell into a state of virtual chaos. The nation became divided into three factions—the Hellenists, the Hasidim, and the Maccabeans. Jealousy and prejudice grew rampant, and as the natural result came distrust and disorder. In these extremes the nation turned to *Jonathan*, the younger brother of Judas, for leadership.

It was sometime before the Hasidim became reconciled to the leadership of Jonathan. In fact, their acceptance of him was more a matter of acquiescing in a necessary policy than endorsing an administration; he appeared to be the only leader upon whom all factions could agree. But finally they rallied faithfully to Jonathan, and he succeeded in winning their sincere and hearty support, and with it the violent opposition of the Hellenists.

Jonathan was a diplomat, and his diplomacy was the chief means of his success. While Judas prevailed by the invincible force of his great courage and determination, Jonathan accomplished his desired ends by strategy. His opportunity presented itself in the form of internal strife in the Syrian kingdom. Conflicts perpetually raged between rival claimants for the Syrian throne, and the wary Maccabean kept them striving to outdo one another in the liberality of their promises. Thus we find "the fugitive of a few years ago, now one of the arbiters of the Syrian throne, courted alike by the man in possession and the man who wanted to be!"[12] By this policy Jonathan secured the control of all Judea and recognition as high priest, thus combining again the political and ecclesiastical leadership of the nation. As a result of this step, the confidence and loyalty of the Hasidim again became greatly strained.

While seeking to outwit and bring to favorable terms Tryphon, a usurper of the Syrian throne, Jonathan was captured, thrown into prison in chains, and later assassinated.

3. It was only natural that after the loss of Jonathan the people should turn to *Simon*, the last survivor of the five Maccabean brothers. Even by the Hasidim he was hailed with delight. He was a quiet and peace-loving ruler, more interested in the internal strengthening of the nation than in extending its boundaries. Peace and prosperity prevailed throughout the greater part of his reign. His administration is characterized by an ardent Jewish patriot thus: "The land had rest all the days of Simon, and he sought the good of his nation; and his authority and his glory were well-pleasing to them all his days. . . . And they tilled their land in peace, and the land gave her increase, and the trees of the plains their fruit. . . . He provided victuals for the cities, and furnished them with

[12]Grant, *Between the Testaments*, p. 49.

all manner of munition, until the name of his glory was named unto the end of the earth" (1 Mac. 14: 4ff.).

There still remained, however, the one objection of the combined offices of high priest and political ruler. The Hasidim believed strongly in the separation of church and state. But Simon greatly pleased them when he declined to be constituted as king of Judea, since none save the house of David could, according to the Law, sit on the throne of Israel. Simon chose to be known as nothing more than "prince of the realm." Throughout the reign of Simon the patriotic party was highly favored, and the Hellenists were at a great disadvantage.

Decline of the Law

The influence of the heathen, however, had not been entirely eradicated from the life of the nation. So deeply had the Greek influence penetrated, and so attractive had it proved to some, that there still remained a strong Hellenist party who favored greater liberality than was countenanced by the Hasidim, and were indifferent to the traditional application of the Law. This factor in the national life had only been suppressed for a season. The Hasidim had been the original supporters of the revolt against Syrian oppression, and were in general loyal friends of the Maccabees. But they were destined to fare ill for a long period at the hands of the dynasty which was established by Simon.

I. Breach with the Hasidim

John Hyrcanus, the son and successor of Simon, was just such a leader as would arouse the intense ill-will of the extreme legalists. Though nominally high priest, and formally fulfilling that sacred role, he was in fact an adventurous warrior and an ambitious monarch. He was adroit enough not to engender too great opposition by claiming the title of king, yet he freely exercised the prerogatives of a monarch. It was under his administration that the sectarian lines in Judaism became taut and clearly defined. A singular incident brought these developments to a climax. A representative of the patriotic party objected to Hyrcanus being high priest upon the grounds, false no doubt, that his mother had been a prisoner of war among the Syrians. According to Jewish law, one whose mother had been held captive could not occupy the office of high priest. Infuriated at this insult, Hyrcanus called upon the Hasidim to propose a penalty for the offense. The punishment suggested was very slight. Hyrcanus took this as a personal affront, and declared himself in sympathy with the Hellenist party.[13]

In connection with this incident, Josephus first speaks of these parties as Pharisees and Sadducees, so it is likely that these designations originated within the reign of John Hyrcanus.

II. The Ascendancy of the Hellenists

When Hyrcanus broke with the Pharisees and aligned himself with the Sadducees, the last vestige of real religious patriotism vanished from the Maccabean family. His successors were political potentates, interested only in extending their domains and filling their coffers with gold. Aristobulus, the son of Hyrcanus and his successor, was known as Phil-Hellen, which means, "Lover of Greek." His reign was marked by cruelty and selfishness, and must have been unbearably repulsive to the Pharisees. He seems to have been the first to openly lay claim to the title of king.[14] This was a flagrant vio-

[13]Josephus and the Talmud give similar accounts of the specific provocations of the break between John and the Pharisees. The story, however, is not accepted as authentic by some leading authorities. Cf. Schuerer, *Jewish People in the Time of Jesus Christ*, I, i, p. 289.

[14]The Harvard Excavations at Samaria, 1908-1910, unearthed a coin issued by Alexander Jannæus, bearing on one side the Greek words *Basileos Alexandrou* ("of King Alexander") and on the other in Hebrew "John the king," evidence which leaves it beyond dispute that this Asmonean ruler claimed the royal title. It is maintained by some that, before him, Aristobulus had claimed the title. Cf. Ewald, *op. cit.*, Vol. V, p. 385.

lation of the sacred traditions of Israel, which required that none save a descendant of David and Judah should sit upon the throne, and Aristobulus was a Levite.

After the death of Aristobulus, his brother Alexander Jannæus succeeded to the throne. The manifestly Greek character of his name was a token of the direction of his sympathies. He disdained the Pharisees, and so aroused their hatred that they attacked him upon a certain occasion as he was ministering in the Temple. In avenging this insult, Alexander had six thousand patriots slain in the streets of Jerusalem. But so difficult did this policy make the remainder of his reign that he counseled his widow and successor Alexandra to cast her lot with the Pharisees.[15]

The Pharisaic Revival

Queen Alexandra accepted the advice of her husband, and immediately raised the Pharisees to power. She made her brother Simon ben-Shetach the prime minister of the realm, and called in from Alexandria another able Jew named Judah ben-Tabbai. Both these leaders were ardent Pharisees. The supervision of the Sanhedrin was awarded to the Pharisees, and by them sweeping reforms were made. Under the regime of Alexandra they won a place of supremacy which they have not lost to this day. At the time of Jesus and Paul they were the party in power among the people. After the destruction of the Temple A.D. 70 the Sadducees lost their last stronghold, and the Pharisees thenceforth held undisputed sway. The orthodox Jewish synagogue of today is the historical progeny of the ancient Pharisee.

The fluctuating fortunes of the Law from the Restoration to the Time of Christ may be graphically represented as follows:

[15]According to Josephus, but his testimony on this point is held in question. Cf. Fairweather, *op. cit.*, p. 160.

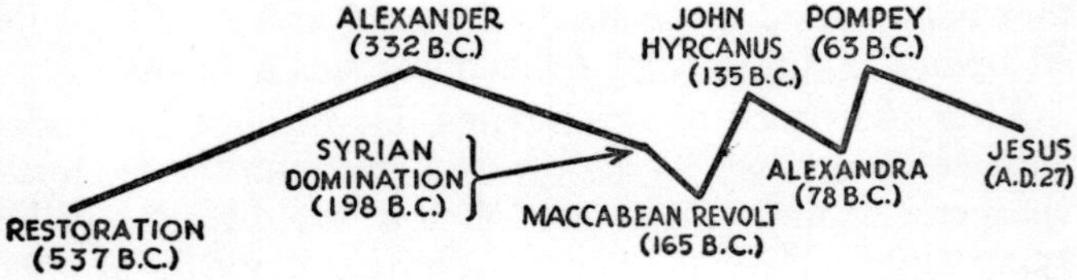

In this intermittent rise and decadence of the Law we have the chief determinative facts in Jewish history of interbiblical times.

CHAPTER V

JUDAISM UNDER ROMAN DOMINION

In understanding the Gospels and appreciating the environment of Jesus, there is nothing more important than a comprehension of the political situation. This political situation was determined by the reaction of Judaism to Roman rule and the policies of the Roman administration in meeting that reaction. Hence an important step in the preparation of the student for New Testament study is to review the progress of Roman domination in Palestine.[1]

Antecedent Developments

During the reign of Alexandra the high priesthood had been conferred upon her eldest son, Hyrcanus II, and at her death she designated him as her successor. As the firstborn, his was the rightful claim to the throne. But his younger brother, Aristobulus, an agressive, ambitious, shrewd, and unprincipled adventurer, began immediately to make plans for securing the throne for himself. He sought and obtained the support of the Sadducees, who were very much disgruntled because the royal favor had been transferred to the Pharisees, and with their aid he launched a rebellion against his brother. Hyrcanus, being an indolent weakling, had neither the disposition nor the ability to offer successful resistance. In a battle at Jericho he was defeated, and the greater part of his own following soon deserted to Aristobulus. Hyrcanus was forced to yield, and accept terms by which his brother should possess the throne and he be content with the office of high priest.[2]

[1]For a brief but highly enlightening discussion of this vital element in the background of the Gospels, one may refer to Simkhovitch, *Toward the Understanding of Jesus* (Macmillan).

[2]We follow here the interpretation of the agreement as given by Graetz, *op. cit.*, Vol. II, p. 58. Some authorities consider that Aristobulus secured both the throne and the priesthood, and that Hyrcanus agreed to become a private citizen. Such seems to be the meaning of the language of Josephus (Antq., 14: 2), but it has against it extreme improbability.

But the cause of Hyrcanus found championship from an unexpected source. Antipater, a crafty and capable Idumean, entered the contest and espoused the cause of the high priest. Without great difficulty Hyrcanus was persuaded to cancel the covenant with his brother, and lay claim again to the throne. They secured the aid of Aretas, the king of Arabia, who marched against Aristobulus with a large force, defeated him and drove him into the Temple fortress at Jerusalem.

Just at this crisis it became known that the Roman legions were in Syria, approaching Palestine on an expedition of conquest. This gave suddenly a new turn to the course of events. Both parties to the conflict knew that it was no longer a test of their respective military strength, but of which should first succeed in securing the favor of the approaching Roman. Aristobulus and Antipater had judgment enough to realize that to offer resistance to the Roman army would be utter folly. So both began at once to sue for favor, Aristobulus on his own account, and Antipater in the name of his weakling tool Hyrcanus. Aristobulus proved to be the successful contestant. The Roman general Scaurus ordered Aretas to raise the siege of Jerusalem and retire. Aristobulus fell upon the retreating army of the Arabian king and inflicted a great slaughter.

About this time news reached Judea that the incomparable Pompey was himself in Damascus. Once more both the brothers rushed to meet the Roman and treat for favor, and this time there went with them a delegation from the Jewish populace to entreat Pompey that he would oust the Asmoneans and restore the pure hierarchy of former days. The Roman conqueror was bent upon another expedition, and so notified them all that he would make no decision at that time, but would later visit Jerusalem in person and settle the dispute there. Aristobulus, impatient at the suspense of waiting, and doubtless fearing that the outcome would be disastrous to his ambitions, returned to his realms and prepared for a desperate resistance to the approach of Pompey.

Pompey immediately abandoned his contemplated campaign against another foe, and turned his attention to the defiant Judean. When attacked in his first position near Jericho, Aristobulus surrendered the fortress, but he himself escaped to Jerusalem. When Pompey laid siege to him there, he went forth in great trepidation to meet the Roman conqueror, and agreed to give over Jerusalem into the hands of Pompey, but a force of his followers took refuge in the Temple fortress and declined to yield. For three months they held out against the fearful impact of the Roman implements of siege, but the walls were finally penetrated by the Romans, and nearly all the besieged were slaughtered. Aristobulus was carried captive to Rome, and many of his fellow countrymen with him. These prisoners of war composed the nucleus of the Jewish colony in Rome which provided the original constituency of the Christian church at that place, to which Paul wrote his greatest Epistle. Hyrcanus was confirmed in the high priesthood, and Antipater was made governor of Judea.

Thus the Jews, who on frequent occasions before had parleyed for the friendship and protection of Rome,[3] now felt the invincible grip of her conquering hand, from which they were destined never to escape as an independent nation.

The Roman Policy in Judea

As was characteristic of the Roman Government in dealing with its provinces, the Jews were treated with

[3]Judas Maccabæus, toward the end of his career, sent an embassy to the Roman Senate making an appeal for aid against his Syrian oppressors. His ambassadors were favorably received and help promised, but the terms of the treaty were so indefinite that nothing of any value to the Jews ever resulted from it. Another effort in the same direction was made by Jonathan, but again without beneficial results. These nominal treaties were renewed by Simon, with the added provision that Judea be recognized by Rome as an independent nation, which was a real though not important advantage. An attempt of Hyrcanus during his reign to secure recognition and favor from Rome proved a failure. None of these efforts really secured any permanent advantage to the Judean kingdom. Rome was not in the business of strengthening independent kingdoms.

generous consideration so long as they were submissive to Roman rule. Their religion became one of the legally recognized religions of the Empire, which meant that it was protected by Roman authority. They were allowed to pursue their national and private affairs without interference as long as they maintained peace and remained loyal to Rome. They had their own judicial and legislative body, the Sanhedrin, which had jurisdiction in all civil and minor criminal affairs. The burden of tribute was not intolerable, though it was a matter of great chagrin to the strict Jews, who felt it was a national disgrace to be compelled to make any contribution, be it ever so small, to a Gentile ruler. The Jews really fared better under Roman rule than they had at any time since the Persian domination. But the fanaticism of an exaggerated religious bigotry and racial exclusiveness, agitated by a class of extremists called Zealots, kept the Jewish people in a perpetual foment, and added fuel to the fires of hatred until open rebellion broke out, which ultimately resulted in the annihilation of the nation. Had the Jews cultivated the favor of Rome their subsequent history might have been different.[4]

A short while after his arrival as a captive in Rome, Aristobulus escaped and aroused Judea to a rather ominous rebellion, but he was finally defeated, captured, and sent again as a prisoner to Rome. Later he was liberated by Julius Cæsar, and sent on an expedition against Syria. His son, Alexander, who eluded Pompey and escaped captivity, had already made unsuccessful efforts to regain the throne of Judea. If Aristobulus could subdue the soldiers of Pompey in Syria, there was hope that he and his sons might oust Hyrcanus and Antipater. But these hopeful prospects were all shattered by the murder of Aristobulus and the execution of Alexander. Only Antigonus, the other son of Aristobulus, was left as a rival to Hyrcanus, and he, too, was destined to meet a violent

[4]So intense was the hatred generated in the Jews against Rome that it has never entirely died out, and may be seen in the attitude of some modern Jewish historians.

death not many years later. The cause of national independence was forever lost to Judaism: the nation could but remain the unwilling subject of Rome.

THE IDUMEAN DYNASTY

As a matter of fact, Jerusalem had been all this time under the control of Antipater, who may justly be regarded as the first ruler of the Idumean dynasty. This royal line furnished the Herods,[5] who so frequently appear in New Testament history.

I. Antipater

The Idumeans were successors of the Edomites, the traditional descendants of Esau. In the campaigns of John Hyrcanus, Idumea was annexed to Judea and the people forced to submit to the rite of circumcision, thus becoming nominally Jews (cf. p. 71). Antipas, the father of Antipater, was appointed governor of Idumea by Alexander Jannæus. He was succeeded by Antipater, who proved to be a cunning, ambitious, and resourceful leader. Two features of his policy showed the shrewdness of the man. On the one hand he deliberately espoused the cause of the weaker side of the Asmonean family, because he knew that the self-willed and aggressive Aristobulus would never permit him to hold the reins of power; while on the other hand he courted and won the favor of each succeeding Roman conqueror, knowing that with their support he could overcome any kind of opposition. He succeeded in making himself "indispensable alike to the feeble Priest Hyrcanus and to the powerful chiefs of the Roman republic."[6] We have already seen how, using Hyrcanus as a tool, he gained possession of the government of Judea. Hyrcanus was high priest and nominal ruler; Antipater really administered affairs. Under Julius Cæsar he secured the

[5]For a list of the Herods in their lineal relations, see Appendix.

[6]Stanley: *History of the Jewish Church*, Vol. III, p. 361.

procuratorship of all Palestine. When he had made himself secure in the place of sovereignty, he proceeded to confer high honors upon his sons, Phasæl and Herod, by appointing the former military governor of Judea and the latter tetrarch of Galilee. But in the midst of his well-wrought plans for advancement he was poisoned by a fanatical Jew.

II. Herod

The mention of this name thrusts before our mental vision another Name which is above every name, JESUS CHRIST, the Saviour of the world; for it was while Herod was still on the throne that Jesus was born in Bethlehem of Judea. The bloody reign of this dramatic ruler may be divided into three periods: struggle for supremacy, progressive administration, and domestic chaos.

1. The beginning of his career was marked by a tense and sometimes very doubtful *struggle for supremacy.* The one fixed and unvarying policy of Herod to the end of his life was to remove every opponent, regardless of relationship or cost. Even those nearest and dearest to him were stricken down by his irrepressible ambition. Like his father, he succeeded in keeping himself on the side of the winning hand at Rome.

After the death of Antipater, Judea was left in the hands of Phasæl and Galilee under the control of Herod. But difficult days were before the two brothers. Julius Cæsar had been assassinated and the cause of the republic lost at Philippi. Thus the Idumeans were thrown on the vanquished side of the rivalry at Rome. By their subjects they were hated as foreign rulers and impostors. Antigonus, the son of Aristobulus II, called in the aid of the Parthians and captured Jerusalem. Phasæl was captured, and despairing of the cause, committed suicide. But Herod could not so easily be subdued. He evaded his enemies, and after much difficulty and privation reached Rome, where he requested Antony to place the young Aristobulus, son of Alexander, on the throne of Judea.[7] Just how sincere he was in this request we may not judge, but at any rate Antony declined to assign the kingdom of Judea to the youthful Asmonean, but conferred it upon Herod himself, granting him the title, "King of the Jews." He returned to Palestine with a small Roman army, gathered other forces who were in sympathy with his cause, and succeeded in capturing Jerusalem in 37 B.C.

Herod proceeded at once to rid himself of his opponents. Antigonus and most of the Sanhedrin were executed. Later the fair young Aristobulus, whom under pressure he had appointed to the position of high priest, he had some of his agents accidentally to drown. The aged Hyrcanus, so long the faithful tool of his father's ambition, was the next to fall under the unrestrained cruelty of the tyrant. After Octavian (Augustus Cæsar) had secured the supremacy of the world Empire by his victory at Actium, Herod won from him the promise of friendship and protection. He was now the absolute master of the entire situation, and prepared to reign in peace. But one more act of consummate barbarity must complete his bloody march to power. Mariamne, his beautiful and most beloved wife, was accused of unfaithfulness by his sister Salome and condemned to die. Her tragic fate was soon repeated in the execution of her proud and sagacious mother.

2. Herod's first career of bloodshed now gave place to a real effort at *progressive administration,* though even this era was not unmixed with cruelty. After he had disposed of all those who challenged his right to the throne, Herod turned his attention to the improvement of his domains. He became ostensibly (and perhaps really) an enthusiastic patron of culture and art, and

[7]According to a perhaps doubtful statement by Josephus, who says in *Antq.*, 14: 14, "For he did not come with an intention to ask the kingdom for himself, . . . but intended to desire it for his wife's brother."

induced several men of learning to take up residence in his realms. He provoked no unnecessary wars, thus giving the country opportunity for development.

Herod's program of reconstruction exhibited some real ability of statesmanship. He laid the foundation of new cities, the chief of which was Cæsarea, so named for his patron, Octavian. The city of Samaria was improved and enlarged, and a beautiful temple built there, after which the name of the city was changed to Sebaste (Greek for "Augustus") in honor of the Roman emperor. He built new forts for the defense of his domains, and built them so well that the ruins of some are standing today. He rebuilt the Temple at Jerusalem with even greater magnificence than that of Solomon, and erected a splendid palace for himself. Many other improvements were made in the city, such as building a large amphitheatre just outside the walls, and a theatre within. In these enterprises Herod exhibited evidence of real administrative ability and architectural taste. He showed that in a different situation and with a different temperament he might have been a truly great ruler.

3. Nevertheless, Herod was not to die in peace, but closed his despotic reign in a state of *domestic chaos.* He never recovered from the execution of Mariamne. Remorse preyed upon his conscience until he became almost insanely morose. It was only natural that such a state of mind should breed suspicion of all about him. His sons by Mariamne, Alexander and Aristobulus, he had designed as his successors. They were educated in Rome, and carefully prepared for regal positions; but upon their return to Herod's court, through the jealous machinations of Antipater his eldest son, and Salome, they fell under suspicion and were executed. A little later he learned that Antipater was devising a plot against his life, so he had him thrown into prison and later executed. One of the last acts of cruelty perpetrated by Herod was the slaughter of the innocents at

Bethlehem.[8] He died in excruciating agony about 4 B.C., having reigned thirty-four years.

In accordance with a will made by Herod shortly before his death, his three sons came into possession of his realms. Archælaus was made king[9] of Judea (including Samaria and Idumea), Herod Antipas became tetrarch of Galilee and Perea, and Herod Philip became tetrarch of Trachonitis and adjacent regions.

III. Archelaus

Archælaus was a signal failure as a ruler. Disturbances prevailed from the very beginning. Among his first official acts was the suppression of a riot in Jerusalem. While he was waiting for Augustus to confirm the will of Herod, rebellion broke out in Judea, and required the interference of the Syrian governor for settlement. Thus he began his administration in the

[8]By some historians, especially the Jewish and liberal Christian, the account in Matthew of the slaughter of the children at Bethlehem is rejected. There are two objections to it. (1) It finds no corroboration in Josephus or other accounts of Herod's reign; and (2) it is so intimately interwoven with the story of the Virgin Birth that the acceptance of it might appear to be a tacit endorsement of the supernatural. The first objection alone would offer little difficulty, for there is a considerable amount of Jewish history recorded in the New Testament which is accepted without extra-biblical corroboration, but it is eagerly seized as offering objective support to the second objection. No considerations of literary criticism appear against the record itself. It is a straightforward, simple narrative statement. "Then Herod, when he saw that he had been tricked by the Magi, was exceedingly angry, and sent and slew all the male children in Bethlehem and in all its environs who were two years old and under, according to the exact information which he had got from the Magi" (Matt. 2: 16). There is no trace of exaggeration or embellishment in this brief record. There can be no reasonable doubt that the author considered himself to be writing a simple statement of fact. And it accords precisely with the known habits and disposition of Herod. This is exactly the way in which Herod would naturally have acted under the given circumstances. It is hardly a historically sound policy to dismiss the whole matter by the single dogmatic statement, "But Herod, criminal as he was, was innocent of this crime" (Graetz: *op. cit.*, II, 116), and not even attempt the support of an argument for the repudiation of the simple New Testament narrative. In fact, one who has no difficulty with the supernatural finds no good reason for rejecting this account. It therefore is included in the main text of this historical review.

[9]While Archelaus was probably called "king" in the popular use of that term, his actual official title by appointment from Augustus was *ethnarch*. The coins of his reign which have been discovered indicate that he faithfully adhered to the use of this title. Cf. *Report of Harvard Excavations at Samaria*, p. 267.

face of difficulties with which only true statesmanship could cope, and Archelaus was wholly destitute of this qualification. His entire reign was a period of confusion and bloodshed. Opposition confronted him on every side. His right as a successor of Herod was challenged by his relations, especially by Antipas. His marriage to a divorced woman gave deep offense to the Jews, and augmented their hatred of him. The sole redeeming feature of his reign was that he engaged in considerable building operations. After ten years of tragically incompetent administration he was banished and his domains taken over by the Roman emperor.

IV. Herod Antipas

A longer and much more successful reign presents itself here. Herod Antipas was diplomatic and conservative, and was able to preserve relative peace. He carefully fortified his frontiers, and conducted extensive building enterprises. The darkest blots upon his record were his illegal marriage with Herodias, and the beheading of John the Baptist, whom, as we learn from Josephus, he had imprisoned at Machærus. It was he to whom Pilate sent Jesus for trial (Luke 23: 7-12). His greatest difficulties came from his unfortunate domestic relations, which in the end compassed his downfall. Herodias, in a fit of jealousy at her brother Agrippa, persuaded Antipas to go with her to Rome and entreat Caligula, who had recently attained to the throne (A.D. 37), to confer upon him the title of king. But instead of securing the object which he sought, he was deposed and banished.

V. Philip

Philip had but little connection with New Testament history, and hence may be dismissed with but brief notice. It was into his realms that Jesus retired when Pharisaic hatred became so intense as to imperil his life. His domains were kept in relative peace and order. He was by all odds the best of the Herods. Schuerer sums up his career by saying that "his reign was mild, just, and peaceful" (*op. cit.*, I, ii, p. 14).

The First Procurators

After the deposition of Archelaus the Judeans asked to be relieved of the rule of the Herods. They preferred a governor appointed directly by Rome; not, however, as a really desirable policy, but as the least of the necessary evils of heathen domination. So Judea was placed under the surveillance of the governor of Syria, and received a procurator.

The residence of the procurator was at Cæsarea,[10] though on special occasions, particularly during the great feasts, he took up temporary quarters in Jerusalem, probably because the large aggregation of people there at that time required his personal attention. At such times he resided in the palace of Herod, on the western side of the city.

The prerogatives of these procurators were three: to collect the taxes levied by the Roman Government; to command the military forces of the province; and to act as judge in the more important judicial cases. Because Judea was an imperial, and not a senatorial province, the taxes collected went directly to Cæsar (Cf. Matt. 22: 17ff.). In the collection of these taxes many Jews found employment. An individual would secure the right to collect the customs in a certain district, for which he would pay to the Roman Government a stipulated annual sum, and whatever revenues beyond that amount he could collect would be his own profit. A maximum was supposed to be determined by law, but it was so irregular that great opportunity was left for extortion. These collectors were called in Latin, the official language, *publicani*, the "publicans" of our New Testament, so much hated by

[10]This probably aggravated the prejudice against Roman rule on the part of the stricter Jews, since the origin and pagan associations of Cæsarea made it exceedingly hateful to them. Cf. Edersheim, *Jewish Social Life*, p. 72.

loyal Jews both as extortioners and as agents of a foreign power.

The procurator was a military commander. A force of provincial troops was placed in his command with which to preserve order and keep his realms in subjection. These troops were garrisoned at numerous points, so that a Roman soldier was a familiar object in Judea (Cf. Luke 3: 14).

The judicial function of the procurator was almost entirely confined to cases of capital offense, all minor cases being left to the jurisdiction of the local courts. Thus the Sanhedrin could try Jesus, and ostensibly determine his guilt, but the sanction of Pilate must be secured for his execution.

So the Jews were left entirely free in all matters of religion, and were allowed great liberty in civil affairs, and yet none of the procurators was able to give general satisfaction. As soon as Judea was made a Roman province, the Syrian governor Quirinius ordered a new levy of taxes, which precipitated a revolt. In fact, the attitude of most of the Palestinian Jews toward the Roman Government made it practically impossible for a representative of that government to give satisfaction, no matter how wisely and well he might seek to administer affairs. However, none of the procurators proved to be an able or tactful ruler.

The only one of the early procurators in whom we are especially interested is Pontius Pilate, who was in charge of affairs in Judea when Jesus was crucified. He held the office for ten years, not because of the justice or satisfactoriness of his administration, but due to the provincial policy of Tiberius, the ruling emperor. Extremely cruel treatment of his subjects finally brought his recall to Rome.

Herod Agrippa I

Agrippa was the grandson of Herod the Great. The story of his career reads like romance. He was educated in Rome and spent his early life there. Just as he was approaching middle age he was banished by Tiberius, and took refuge in an old tower in southern Palestine. While there he sought to bring his miserable life to an end by suicide. From this rash act he was prevented by his faithful wife. He continued to suffer ill-fortune until he made his way back to Rome, and found an entrance into the favor of Caligula. But by an ill-advised remark he again gave offense to the emperor Tiberius, who cast him into prison in chains. But this was the last dark hour before the dawn of his better day. When, within a short while, Caligula became emperor he appointed Agrippa king, bestowing upon him the tetrarchy of Philip, and a little later that of Antipas as well (A.D. 39). He did not, however, come into actual possession of his domains, but remained for a while longer a resident of Rome. He was a "king" for some time before he actually possessed a kingdom.

When Claudius came to the imperial throne, Agrippa again won the royal favor and secured, in addition to his former domains, Judea, Idumea, and Samaria. He then returned to Palestine, took up his residence in Jerusalem, and ruled with marked success for four years. He exhibited the tact and shrewdness of his famous grandfather, but without Herod's jealous and bloodthirsty spirit. He courted earnestly the favor of the Jews, especially of the Pharisees, as was demonstrated in the persecution recorded in Acts 12. But while manifesting ostensibly great deference to Judaism, Agrippa showed himself to be in reality thoroughly imbued with Hellenism. He provided his realms with many of the amusements common in the Greek world about him. Just as his prospects appeared to be brightest he was stricken suddenly by a loathsome disease, and died a horrible death (A.D. 44).

The Later Procurators

It was expected that Agrippa would be succeeded by his seventeen-year-old son, Agrippa II, but Claudius, upon the advice of his counselors, who regarded Agrippa as too young, decided otherwise. Palestine was placed under a procurator,[11] while Agrippa II was given the little principality of Chalchis, situated in the plain of Marsyas between Hermon and Lebanon, though later there was conferred upon him the former tetrarchy of Philip, embracing Trachonitis. He reigned with fair success, though with greatly restricted prerogatives, until his death, about A.D. 100.

Between A.D. 44 and 66 Palestine had seven procurators, Fadus, Alexander, Cumanus, Felix, Festus, Albinus, and Florus. This period was one of great stress and turmoil throughout the province. The Zealots, and later the Sicarii[12] adopted the most extreme measures of violence in opposing the Roman rule, even to the assassination of Roman officials and their sympathizers. The administrations of the first two were comparatively mild and peaceable, though even they were disturbed by occasional outbreaks, and the political stress was aggravated by the horrors of famine. But open rebellion came in the procuratorship of Cumanus (A.D. 48-52). In three clashes with the Jewish populace he subdued them with extreme cruelty and exacted a heavy toll of lives. The administration of Felix (A.D. 52-60) exceeded in cruelty and severity any of his predecessors. Conditions were considerably improved during the time of Festus, only to be thrown into a state of greater chaos during the term of his successor, Albinus, and reach a climax under Florus.

[11]During the period A.D. 6 to 41, only Judea was a Roman province, since the remainder of Palestine was under Antipas and Philip, but in A.D. 41 the former realms of Antipas were included with Judea, so that practically all Palestine was embraced in the Roman province.

[12]So called because they armed themselves with short daggers (*sicae*), and, mingling among the crowds at the great feasts, they covertly stabbed to death their enemies. They became a terror to the city of Jerusalem. Mathews regards those who plotted to kill Paul (Acts 23: 12ff.) as members of this party (*History of New Testament Times in Palestine*, p. 211). It is quite certain they are referred to in Acts 21: 38.

The racial hatred of the Jew, and the cruelty and avarice of the Roman, interacted to create a situation the horrors of which could scarcely be exaggerated.

Of the procurators of this period, Felix and Festus are of greatest interest to the New Testament student. It was by Felix that Paul was kept in prison at Cæsarea for two years, because of his hope "that money would be given him of Paul; . . . and desiring to gain favor with the Jews" (Acts 24: 26, 27). This brief descriptive notice in Acts is a remarkably accurate epitome of the man's character. It was before Festus that Paul appealed to Rome, and was later heard again by Festus in company with Agrippa II. The reflection of the character of both of these officials in the Acts account is in striking harmony with what we know of them from other sources.

During this entire period from A.D. 44 to 66 the Jews were in a perpetual state of rage and frenzy, getting ready for the bloody drama which would form the next period of their national history. It was when conditions were becoming most distressful that Paul was taking the collection among his churches for the destitute Jewish Christians in and about Jerusalem. Their destitution was likely due in part to the unsettled political affairs.

The Jewish Revolt

The Zealots had now been eagerly promoting their propaganda for nearly a century. The agitation had achieved its designed effects. It had created in the heart of patriotic Judaism an irrepressible hatred of Rome and all that in any way represented Rome. It was during this period of confusion that James the brother of Jesus met his martyrdom, about A.D. 62.[13] Many other faithful souls went down to death who really had no special sympathy with Rome, but who declined to take part in the mad protest of the Zealots.

[13]Schuerer is unable to accept this as the correct date, and presents evidence against it which does make it doubtful. Cf. *op. cit.*, I, ii, pp. 186ff.

The actual revolution broke out in the procuratorship of Florus (A.D. 66). This avaricious and unscrupulous official sought to plunder the Temple of some of its treasures. To avenge the insult thus perpetrated against Jerusalem and all Israel, Judea, after a brief interval of unsuccessful efforts at arbitration, arose in one mighty, bloody, desperate effort to throw off the Roman yoke. Carnage and devastation reigned on every hand. It was in vain that King Agrippa sought to allay the rage of the infuriated masses. Cestius Gallus, the governor of Syria, undertook to quell the rebellion, but was unsuccessful. He was driven back with great slaughter, and arrived at Antioch with only a remnant of the army with which he had set out.

On the tidal wave of this victory the revolutionists swept everything with them. The advocates of peace were forced to yield, and take part in the rebellion. The Jewish leaders now began—though doubtless with little hope of success[14]—to organize the nation for war. Josephus was placed in charge of Galilee, and went through with elaborate preparations, though as a matter of fact he had no hope of success in the war. In the other districts of Palestine military leaders were placed to set the land in order for war. The Sanhedrin remained in charge of affairs in Judea and Jerusalem.

Vespasian, one of the greatest of the Roman generals, and afterward emperor, was sent to put down the rebellion. In rapid succession he captured the strongholds which had been prepared for defense. In Galilee, Josephus capitulated as soon as the Romans attacked him. By the close of the first year of the war Vespasian was before Jerusalem. Just at this juncture an event occurred which was calculated to give the revolutionists an advantage. The death of Nero brought confusion in

[14]It was the opinion of Ewald that the entire Jewish nation, intoxicated by the victory over Cestius, had been deluded into the belief that they might successfully revolt against Rome (Cf. *op. cit.*, VII, pp. 511ff.). However, it seems highly improbable that the more judicious and farsighted leaders would have allowed a tide of mere enthusiasm to bear them into so great a deception, which had not in its favor even a vestige of substantial reason.

the imperial city, which caused a cessation of hostilities for a season. This gave the Jews a chance to reorganize their forces, but instead of taking advantage of the opportunity they spent the time in petty civil warfare. The forces within the city were rent into several contending factions, who sought one another's blood as ferociously as they had battled with the advancing Romans. The Zealots were re-enforced by an army of Idumeans, whom they brought into the city under cover of night, but these very soon departed, presumably in disgust at the civil strife among the Jews. Numbers of the forces of defense were slain, and valuable supplies were destroyed, hence when Titus, son of Vespasian and his successor in command,[15] renewed the siege with a force of four legions of regulars and many auxiliary troops, the defenders of the city were unprepared to successfully resist. After five months of horrible suffering, Jerusalem fell, and was destroyed by the Roman conqueror. Numbers of the inhabitants were put to the sword, while many were taken as prisoners to be used in gladiatorial combats or to grace the triumphal procession of the conqueror, which was later staged in Rome.

Thus ended a revolution which from its beginning was inevitably doomed to failure. With this calamity the national identity of Judaism was completely and forever lost. The last two institutions of their distinctly national life, the Sanhedrin and the sacrifice, were abolished, never to reappear. From this time the rabbis, representing the Pharisees, dominated the race, for with the destruction of the Temple and the abolition of the Sanhedrin the Sadducees passed into history. The center of rabbinic influence was located at Jamnia, in western Judea, where the leading rabbis of the Jews had taken refuge before Jerusalem fell.

Two other vain efforts were made by the Jews to assert themselves and gain larger liberties. The first was made

[15] Vespasian had meanwhile been placed upon the imperial throne by the Roman legions of the East.

by the Jews in Cyrene, Egypt, Cyprus, and Mesopotamia, A.D. 115 to 117. It was suppressed by Trajan with great slaughter, and resulted in more rigid restrictions upon the race. The second, which was also the last, was confined to Palestine. It took place during the reign of Hadrian, in A.D. 132 to 135. A fanatical leader known as Barchochba adopted the role of Messiah, and led in a terrific insurrection, probably occasioned by the reported designs of Hadrian to build a pagan shrine on the site of the Temple. In quelling the rebellion, the Romans practically annihilated the scattered remnants of the nation, and imposed severe persecution upon the Jews in other parts of the Empire. Palestine was thenceforth the undisputed property of the pagan, and Palestinian Judaism was at an end.

CHAPTER VI

THE RELIGION OF JUDAISM

The title of this chapter in its fullest sense comprehends all of Judaism, for to the Jew every detail of his experience and every element of his environment had a religious significance. His history, his country, his people, were all a part of his religion. It is our purpose here, however, to treat of those elements of Palestinian Jewish life which were distinctively connected with that which we would regard as essentially and purely religious. There were certain institutions involved in the religious life and worship of the Jews, the progress of their religious history had produced distinct sects, religion as they knew it was essentially expressed through the Law, and the religious heart of Judaism regarded the future as containing the full realization of their national hopes and ideals. To these distinctively religious matters we devote the present chapter.

The Institutions of Judaism

There were four institutional factors in the religious life of first century Palestine, the synagogue, the Temple, the annual feasts, and the Sanhedrin.

I. The Synagogue

When the curtain falls upon Old Testament history we have heard of no place of worship other than the Temple, save as apostate leaders sought to debase the religion of Israel by establishing "high places" in imitation of heathen ritual. When we open the New Testament we are confronted immediately by a new institution, very prominent in Jewish religion, known as the synagogue. The word is of Greek derivation, and means "gathered together"; that is, an assembly.

1. As to the *origin* of the synagogue, we are unable to be certain. There was a tradition among the Jews that it was established by Moses, but of course this was incorrect. The theory on which biblical scholarship is now practically agreed is that it originated in Babylon during the Exile, and gained a permanent and definite place in the life of the nation after the Restoration. After the tribes had been carried into captivity, since they were hopelessly separated from the Temple with its worship, the more devout met together in some convenient place to read and discuss passages from the Law. This custom of assembling became more regular and widespread, until stated places and occasions of meeting were adopted. Under the reform instituted by Ezra, which placed great emphasis upon the study of the Law, great impetus was given to the systematic study of the Law.

2. The primary *function* of the synagogue was to provide a place for the study of the Law. The Temple was the place of worship, while the synagogue was the place of instruction: the educational institution of Judaism. "Our houses of prayer in the several towns are none other than institutions for teaching prudence and bravery, temperance and justice, piety and holiness," says Philo.[1] The teaching was done by scribes, or rabbis, who were specially trained for this purpose, and set apart to this service by special ceremonies of ordination.

3. It is probable that the *services* in the synagogue were at first held only on the sabbath, but long before New Testament times it became the custom to conduct synagogue services on the great feast days for the benefit of those not able to go up to Jerusalem. In the time of our Lord the custom prevailed of having synagogue services on Monday and Thursday, in addition to the sabbath services, for the convenience of the country people,

[1]Cf. Hausrath, *op. cit.*, Div. I, Vol. I, p. 85.

who, as Hausrath says, "brought their fruits to the market and their disputes to the judges"[2] on those days.

The synagogue services were according to a more or less set form. After the preliminary exercises, consisting of opening "benedictions" and the reciting of a ritual of confession known as the "Shema," and prayer, a prescribed section was read from the Law, then usually one from the Prophets, after which some one was called upon, or volunteered, to add expository or hortatory comments. A concluding benediction, pronounced by a priest, concluded the service.

4. There was connected with the synagogue a group of *officers.* The most important were the elders, who were elected by the congregation to have general supervision of the community life.[3] Within Palestine, in the cities dominated by the Jewish population, the elders had control of both civil and religious affairs, but in the Dispersion their prerogatives, of course, were exclusively religious. The regular synagogue services were in charge of an officer known as the "ruler." This officer saw to the upkeep of the building, took care of the scrolls of scripture which the synagogue possessed, and conducted or appointed some one to conduct the synagogue services. Other officers known as "receivers" were responsible for collecting and distributing alms. A subordinate official known as the "minister" (Greek, *diaconos*) acted as an assistant to the ruler of the synagogue, and another, who was an official "reciter of prayers," served as secretary of the synagogue in its transactions with the outside world.

In the days of Jesus and Paul there was not in Judaism an institution more influential than the synagogue.

II. The Temple

To the Jew the Temple was the only place in which Jehovah could be worshiped in a real and adequate way.

[2] *Op. cit.*, p. 36.

[3] Cf. Edersheim, *Life and Times of Jesus the Messiah*, Vol. I, p. 438.

It is true, there were prayer and praise in home and synagogue, and no doubt many devout souls of mystical temperament held communion with God in secret devotions, but worship in the strict sense, as the Jew conceived it, was confined to the Temple. Hence the Temple occupied an exceedingly vital place in the religion of Judaism.

1. The Temple in the courts of which our Saviour walked and taught was a most beautiful *building,* one of the most imposing structures ever produced by human skill. The Roman Empire had no greater building, outside the imperial city. It had been begun by Herod in 20 B.C., and was still under process of construction during the ministry of Jesus. Work was continued on it for forty-six years, then improvements and finishing touches added here and there until its final completion—A.D. 64, just six years before it was destroyed by Titus, never to be rebuilt.

Herod's Temple was in the shape of an irregular oblong, broader on the north side than on the south. It was located on Mt. Moriah, an eminence in the lower or eastern side of the city of Jerusalem. The entire area[4] was enclosed by a battlemented wall, penetrated by several gates, the exact number of which we do not know. There were at least five, four on the west side and one on the south, with possibly three others, an additional one on the south, one on the north, and one on the east.[5] The chief and most elaborately constructed entrance was the south gate on the west side. Through this gate one entered first the Court of the Gentiles, so named because Gentiles were allowed there. It was richly adorned with huge porches and colonnades, the Royal Porch being on the south side and Solomon's Porch on the east. Similar porches bordered the northern and western side, all massively colonnaded. On an elevation slightly above the

[4]Sources vary as to the shape and size of the Temple enclosure. It was probably about 750 feet wide by 1,000 feet long. For a sketch of the Temple plan see any Bible dictionary.

[5]For particulars, see Edersheim, *The Temple,* pp. 36, 37.

Gentile's Court, and surrounded by a marble partition four or five feet high, was the Sanctuary. Within its sacred precincts a Gentile dared not pass,[6] though Gentiles might present through the Temple ministrants their gifts and offerings to Jehovah. This inner court was penetrated by nine gates, four on the south, four on the north, and on the east the Beautiful Gate (Acts 3: 2), the most magnificent entrance to the Temple and the one through which the majority of worshipers entered.

The length of the Sanctuary lay east and west. Beginning at the Beautiful Gate on the east and moving westward one found first the Court of the Women, so called because Jewish women were allowed to enter it, but could go no further. Next came the Court of Israel, into which any male Israelite might go, provided he had attained proper age and conformed to the elaborate rules of purification. It was separated by a low balustrade, about eighteen inches high, from the Court of the Priests, which was before and about the Temple proper. In the foreground of the Priests' Court was the altar of burnt-offering, at which the priests ministered daily. The Temple proper was elevated above all its surroundings, built of white marble, elaborately ornamented, and furnished with sacred implements of worship. In the Holy Place were the altar of incense, a table for the shew-bread, and the seven-branched golden candlestick. Before the Holy of holies hung the richly embroidered curtain, called in the New Testament the "veil of the Temple" (Matt. 27: 51). There was no furniture whatever in it, save a large stone upon which the high priest set the golden censer when he entered once a year, on the Day of Atonement. No other human foot could ever press its sacred floor.

[6]In 1871 Clermont-Ganneau discovered a stone tablet which had been used as one of the posters placed at the entrance to this court of the sanctuary. It bore in Greek the words: "No stranger is to enter within the balustrade round the Temple and enclosure. Whoever is caught will be responsible to himself for his death, which will ensue." Cf. Cobern, *New Archeological Discoveries*, p. 355.

2. The *worship* in the Temple of the Jews was carried on every day in the year. In this daily worship the most prominent feature, and doubtless the most important, was the burnt-offering made for the people as a whole. It was made every morning and evening, and consisted of a male lamb a year old and free from blemish of any kind, and accompanied by a "meat-offering" and a "drink-offering," the burning of incense, vocal and instrumental music by the priests and Levites, and the prayers of the people. Throughout the day the priests were busily engaged, officiating in the vast number of sacrifices for individuals who were seeking to comply with the various requirements of the Law.

3. The services in the Temple were under the exclusive direction of the *priests*. They were universally regarded in Israel as a distinct order, serving under divine appointment in the solemn capacity of offering sacrifices to Jehovah. The limits of the order were determined by lineage, only the sons of Aaron being allowed to function in the priesthood. The priestly genealogies were guarded with the utmost care; seemingly, in the time of Christ, having become a matter of public record.[7] The lineal order of the priesthood was regarded as so exceedingly sacred that strict regulations were imposed upon them in marriage, and the person of the individual priest was so sacred that special laws of ceremonial purity were applied to him. He was installed in office by a special ceremony of consecration. They were divided into twenty-four groups or "courses," serving in rotation, and the individual priest for a particular function was chosen by lot.

4. As a subordinate class of Temple officials we find the *Levites*. A frequent error of the casual student is to suppose that priests and Levites were one and the same class, "priest" designating the office and "Levite" the tribe. Only the lineal descendants of Aaron, or "sons of Zadok" as they were sometimes called, were allowed

[7]Cf. Josephus, *Life*, I.

to actually officiate in the Temple sacrifices. The Levites served as attendants upon the priests, performing the more menial services of the sacrifice, caring for the Temple equipment, and so forth. Theoretically, only descendants of Levi could fill this office, but it is likely that members of other tribes had been admitted in former times to more lowly Temple duties, and their descendants came eventually to be numbered among the Levites.

5. The *support* of the Temple was provided for by an elaborate system of contribution and revenue. The chief source was the tithe, which was paid to the Levites, who in turn tithed to the priests. Then there were the ransom for the first-born male children, the first-born from flocks and herds, the first-fruits from fields and vineyards, the free-will offerings, Temple tax, and various other sources of income. The Temple of Jesus' day was a vastly wealthy institution.

III. The Feasts

Jesus, in fulfilment of his human relationships, was a loyal Jew, and conscientiously observed the religious customs of Judaism. In line with this well-attested policy of his life, he was regular in his attendance upon the feasts at Jerusalem. The Gospel of John is distinguished for its attention to this phase of our Lord's ministry. The principal sacred occasions were six in number. The three primary or Mosaic feasts were Passover, Pentecost, and Tabernacles. All male Israelites, after they attained thirteen years of age, were required to attend these three feasts, and parents were expected to bring them along even two years prior to that age, that they might become familiar with the routine of ceremonies. The post-Mosaic feasts were Purim and Dedication. The Day of Atonement was a fast rather than a feast. Purim and the Day of Atonement are not mentioned in the New Testament.

1. *Purim* was the first feast of the year according to our calendar. The Jews calculated time by the lunar month, and counted the beginning of the civil year at

about the first of our October, while the ecclesiastical year began about the first of April. Purim was observed near the first of March. It commemorated the deliverance of the Jews from the treachery of Haman, as narrated in the Book of Esther. Merrymaking and exchange of gifts characterized this festal occasion. It was observed in the typical holiday spirit, much as we celebrate Christmas. The chief feature of the ceremony was the reading of the Book of Esther.

2. *Passover* occurred on the fourteenth of the Jewish month Nisan, or about the first of our April. It was the most ancient of the Jewish feasts, and was held in high esteem. It was observed to celebrate the preservation of the Israelites from the effects of the tenth plague, and their escape from bondage. Its importance was even recognized by the Roman Government of Judea, a prisoner being released on that day subject to the choice of the people. Associated with Passover, and commonly regarded as a continuation of it, was the Feast of Unleavened Bread, which began on the fifteenth of Nisan, the day following Passover, and continued for seven days. On the second day of this festival (sixteenth of Nisan) there was observed the ceremony of waving the sheaf of new grain before the Lord in the Temple, indicating that the feast was one of thanksgiving for the early harvest as well as a celebration of the deliverance from Egypt.

3. *Pentecost* came fifty days after Passover, which usually placed it within the last two weeks of May. It was observed in celebration of the grain harvest, which at this time was about complete. The special ceremony of celebration was the presentation in the Temple of the two "wave-loaves," made of flour from new wheat; that is, wheat harvested that season. Pentecost was also looked upon as a celebration of the giving of the Law to Moses, since that great event occurred at about the time of year when Pentecost was observed. This feast was made

famous in Christian history by the advent of the Holy Spirit (Acts 2: 1ff.).

4. The *Day of Atonement* was observed the last of September. As indicated above, it was a fast rather than a feast. On this day the high priest entered the Holy of Holies to offer incense and sprinkle the blood of the sacrifices, after which he sent the "scape-goat" off to the wilderness, bearing away the guilt of the nation, and had the carcasses of the sacrificial animals burned outside the city. This was an intensely solemn occasion for the Jews, and they devoted the entire day to fasting and prayer.

5. The feast of *Tabernacles* occurred five days after the Day of Atonement, usually around the first of October. It was in commemoration of the divine protection of Israel during the wilderness wanderings, and an occasion of thanksgiving for the blessings of the year. While this feast was in progress those participating lived in improvised booths, which were constructed on the flat roofs of the houses, in the courtyards and open squares, and even along the streets and highways, though never farther away from Jerusalem than a Sabbath day's journey. The two chief ceremonies were the pouring out of a libation of water, brought by a priest in a golden pitcher from the Pool of Siloam, and the "illumination of the Temple," made by four huge lamps placed for the purpose in the Womens' Court. It was an occasion of joyous festivities, elaborate rites, and abundant offerings.

6. The feast of *Dedication* was observed about the middle of December. It commemorated the restoration and rededication of the Temple by Judas Maccabæus. At this feast I and II Maccabees were read publicly.

IV. The Sanhedrin

This was a group of seventy-one Jewish elders, presided over by the high priest (making seventy-two in all). In this body was vested both legislative and judicial authority. When all Palestine was included in one province, the Sanhedrin had jurisdiction over the entire region, but during the time of Christ it had control only of Judea. Nevertheless, its opinions were at all times respected by the Jews of all Palestine, and even those of the Dispersion. In fact, it appears that the Roman Government recognized its jurisdiction in matters of religion throughout all Judaism. In Palestinian Judaism its authority was civil and religious while in Hellenistic Judaism it was religious only. Hence Paul could go to Damascus under authority from the Sanhedrin to apprehend Christian Jews on a charge of heresy. The civil functions of the Sanhedrin were principally judiciary. All civil cases within its jurisdiction could be disposed of by the Sanhedrin, and criminal cases not including capital punishment. The one exception in the matter of capital cases was that they might put to death any one who desecrated the Temple.[8]

The name was of Greek derivation (*sunedrion*), and meant "seated together." It is first mentioned in connection with events which occurred about 55 B.C. Its prerogatives, as exercised in the New Testament period, were received from the Roman Government sometime shortly after 63 B.C. The period in which it flourished was from the establishment of Roman domination to the destruction of Jerusalem, A.D. 70. However, there seems not to have been permitted to it any large freedom of operations during the reign of Herod. After Jerusalem was destroyed the Sanhedrin was abolished. Thus the distinctive history of the Sanhedrin covered but little more than a hundred years. But during this brief period it wielded a mighty influence over Jewish affairs.[9]

The Jewish Sects

It has been observed above that there were three fundamental elements in the life of Judaism, the Nation,

[8]Schuerer believes that even in these cases ratification of the death sentence by the Roman governor was necessary. Cf. *op. cit.*, II, i, p. 188.
[9]For a discussion of its origin and history, see Graetz, *op. cit.*, Vol. I, pp. 394ff.; Ewald, *op. cit.*, Vol. V, pp. 167ff.

the Law, and the Priesthood. Devotion to the Nation had brought the Restoration. As the Nation progressed the life of Judaism naturally gathered about the other two basal elements, the Law and the Priesthood, and developed two distinct currents of religious interest. The one attached to the Priesthood had to do with the perpetuation of the ritual, performed through the ceremonies of the Temple worship. In this realm the high priest dominated, and gathered about himself the political interests of the nation. This was especially true after the Maccabean period, when high priest and king were so often combined in one person. The other line of interest arose from the teaching of the Law, a work carried on by the scribes and centering in the synagogue.

At the beginning of Jewish history the two lines of interest were practically indistinguishable, but a cleavage soon appeared, and the further their history proceeded the wider became the breach. Eventually the priestly group became absorbed in political affairs; the scribal group, impatient of politics, devoted themselves with utter abandon to the individual application of the Law. As the varied and conflicting currents of racial strife surged back and forth through Palestine, that "bridge of the ancient world," the priests as political leaders were perpetually striving to keep Judaism so adapted and conformed to the ruling powers as to secure a profitable and satisfactory national existence. To the ardent devotees of the Law such adaptation appeared to be unpardonable compromise, and was therefore abhorrent to them. It was but that age-long opposition of the conservative and liberal elements which appears in all the history of human progress. The scribes were chiefly on the conservative side while the priests were mainly liberal.

Thus the Law and the Temple, normally supposed to be mutual sharers in a common holy task, became pitted against each other in perpetual schism. It is not to be understood, however, that all priests were concerned in political interests alone, nor that all scribes were indifferent to politics. Many priests were devout students of the Law, and many scribes were intensely interested in political developments. That is, if we may anticipate distinctions which are explained later in our discussion, there were Pharisees among the priests and scribes among the Sadducees. But in the main the priestly element of the nation turned its interests in one direction while the scribal element took a different course. Out of these two divergent currents of Jewish life, with their interaction, came the Jewish sects of the New Testament period.

I. The Pharisees

The Pharisees appear in the New Testament as by far the most prominent sect of the Jews, and the prominence accorded them there is but commensurate with their undoubted place in first century Judaism. All our sources give evidence that no other sect was nearly so influential or numerous. It probably would be more accurate to describe them as a fraternal order than as a sect, for they had a definitely qualified membership and certain prescribed obligations. Their chief emphasis was upon *tithing* and *ceremonial purity*. They were the unrivaled teachers and exemplars of the people, because recognized by them as the true and loyal standard-bearers of traditional Israel.

The name Pharisee meant "Separatist." They were so called on account of their loyalty to the traditional exclusiveness of Judaism, which they went to the extreme of applying even to members of their own race who were not consistent with their interpretation of the Law: hence their intense prejudice against "publicans and sinners" (Cf. Luke 15: 1, 2).

By a comparison of Josephus with the New Testament we can discern quite distinctly the chief characteristics of the Pharisees.

1. The fundamental feature of the sect was their extreme *legalism.* The Pharisees exhibited the acme of the

development of that legalistic tendency which originated with the Restoration, and became the most potent force in the religion of Judaism. They may therefore be thought of as the inner core of Jewish life. That is, Pharisaic Judaism and standard Judaism are identical conceptions.

2. They put great emphasis upon special divine *providence,* though they also recognized man's free will. They did not deny moral responsibility. Josephus asserts that the Pharisees ascribed everything to "fate" (*War,* 2: 8), but likely we meet here a Jewish idea in Greek garb. What they really believed in was special providence as affecting every item of human life.

3. The Pharisees accepted the reality of the *spiritual realm.* They believed in a future life and the resurrection of the righteous of Israel. The literal existence of angels and spirits was accepted by them.

4. They *lived simply* and despised delicacies.

5. Antiquity and *tradition* were held in high esteem by them. Josephus explains that "the Pharisees have delivered to the people a great many observances by succession from their fathers, which are not written in the laws of Moses" (*Antq.* 13: 10: 6). They were the chief conservators and exemplars of the oral tradition, "the hedge about the Law."

6. They were characterized by strong group *fellowship* and loyalty, and kindness to one another.

7. They took *little interest in politics* as long as the existing government interfered in no way with their religious pursuits. It was this trait which so frequently won for them the hearty dislike of the ruling class. However, the exigencies of historical developments eventually forced them to take a stock in political affairs.

It is not just to conclude that all Pharisees were ostentatious extremists. There were certainly some of them, and in all probability a considerable number, who were diligently and sincerely seeking to promote piety, and who took an honest delight in their effort to keep in favor and fellowship with Jehovah. It was the ostentation and casuistry of the Pharisees which Jesus condemned, and not the Pharisees as a sect. There appear in the Gospels evidences of a better and really pious type of Pharisee. Such a type is surely represented in Saul of Tarsus. The extreme type of Pharisaism entered early Christianity in the form of the Judaizing controversy.[10]

II. The Sadducees

This was the second in prominence of the Jewish sects, both as to the attention which they receive in the Four Gospels and as to their historical position in Judaism.

As to the name Sadducee, according to its form in rabbinic literature, it appears to have been derived from the name Zadok. Consequently, a popular explanation of its origin is that it arose by reason of the fact that the priestly order, the majority of whom were Sadducees, claimed to be descended from an ancient high priest named Zadok. The priests were "sons of Zadok," and the sect which they fostered were the "Zadokites," corrupted into "Sadducees." The fact that a sect by just this name appeared just before the dawn of the Christian Era (see below) throws doubt upon this explanation, for it is not probable that two different sects would have begun with the same name—though not impossible. It is more probable that the name came from *zaddikim*, a Hebrew word meaning "the righteous," assumed by them because of their boasted faithfulness to the letter of the Old Testament Law in contradistinction to the oral tradition of rabbinism, so ardently supported by the Pharisees.[11] The problem must remain an open question unless further documentary evidence can be brought to light.

[10]For a full and able discussion of the Pharisees, as to both character and history, see Edersheim, *In the Days of Christ*, pp. 227-238.

[11]Cf. Edersheim, *op. cit.*, p. 243, and *per contra* Ewald, *op. cit.*, Vol. V, pp. 275ff.

Our sources indicate several clearly defined characteristics of the Sadducees.

1. They were the *aristocratic* party. Schuerer says that, "the characteristic feature of the Pharisees arises from their *legal tendency*, that of the Sadducees from their *social position*."[12] That is, their aristocratic standing was their fundamental characteristic. As such the sect embraced the politicians and office-holders of the nation. Politics was a matter of great concern to them, by virtue of their position in the nation's life. As mentioned above, the sect contained the great majority of the priests. Thus the Sadducees found their chief stronghold in the Temple, while the Pharisees operated principally in the synagogues.

2. The Sadducees had a very *low view of God* and religion, and denied that God had any very minute concern in human events and activities.

3. They *rejected the doctrine of immortality* and the resurrection, and denied the existence of angels and spirits.

4. They accepted as authoritative only the *written Old Testament*, and opposed the rabbinic tradition held in such high regard by the Pharisees. But while theoretically repudiating tradition, in actual practice the Sadducees were compelled to conform to many of its ritual provisions, for so great was the influence of the Scribes and Pharisees that many of their interpretations of the Law had become established as standards which even the Sadducees dared not ignore.

5. They were a *suspicious group*: not only being wary of others, but without confidence in one another, and having no group loyalty.

6. Their belief in the rigidly literal application of the Law, without interpretation or modification, resulted in extreme *judicial severity* in their dealings with the people, which fact augmented their unpopularity.

[12] *Op. cit.*, II, ii, p. 10.

One finds nothing about the Sadducees to admire, and no very positive fault to condemn. They were chiefly negative in their point of view, and appear to have been largely inoffensive in their mode of life.

III. The Essenes

This was the development on the extreme right of Pharisaism. The Pharisees emphasized meticulous observance of the Law. The Essenes were so rabidly bent upon exact compliance with every requirement of the Law that they separated themselves into isolated communities, and devoted themselves to a rigidly ascetic form of life. They were especially partial to the desert region about the Dead Sea, where they seem to have established several colonies.

When we contemplate the Essenes we find ourselves on a plane of sectarian life entirely different from the other Jewish sects. We have in them, not really a sect within Jewish society, but a distinct social order separate from Jewish society, quite like the monastic orders of Christian history. They composed an ascetic community, arising from a survival of the strictest Hasidim of Maccabean days, perpetuating a wing of that original sect more extreme than the Pharisees, and modified by influences from Greek philosophy, Judeo-Persian eschatology, and Oriental mysticism.[13]

This sect is not definitely mentioned in the New Testament, though there are a few possible reflections of their teachings and customs. We may be sure that they affected profoundly many currents of life which flowed about Jesus and his disciples.

IV. The Zealots

This sect represented the development on the extreme left of the Pharisees. The Pharisees were interested in politics only as it affected the freedom of the nation

[13]Cf. Edersheim, *op. cit.*, pp. 244ff.; Fairweather, *op. cit.*, pp. 203ff.; Graetz, *op. cit.*, Vol. II, pp. 24ff.; Schuerer, *op. cit.*, II, ii, pp. 190ff.

to worship Jehovah and to observe the Law. The Zealots were interested in the independence and autonomy of the nation to the neglect of every other concern. According to Josephus (*Antq.* 18: 1), their founder was Judas of Gamala, who incited the Jews to revolt on the occasion of the taxation census of A.D. 6. That is, most of the interpreters of Josephus so take his language in the passage cited, though some do not regard this conclusion as correct.[14] If it is not, then we cannot regard the Zealots as having existed at the time of Christ. Nevertheless, one turns from the chapter under question in Josephus with the distinct impression that the Jewish historian meant to trace the Zealot movement of the sixties back to Judas of Gamala, and that the movement at least finds its forerunner in the leader of the census rebellion. From his time forward the Zealots increased in numbers and influence, and also in ferocious hostility toward Rome, until they precipitated the civil war of A.D. 66. Their one aim was to throw off the Roman yoke and usher in a Messianic kingdom of a temporal and political character, and to achieve this end they resorted to the rankest extremes of fanaticism. Their most extreme development was represented in the *sicarii.*

V. The Zadokites

As the Essenes were on the extreme right of the Pharisees, so the Sadducees had their development on the extreme right. More than a century before the Christian Era there began in the circles of the Jewish priesthood a reform movement looking toward a religious revival and the correction of irregularities in the Temple worship. These reformers were pleased to characterize themselves as the "sons of Zadok"—unless it be true that the name was a taunt of ridicule cast at them by their resentful colleagues. Failing in their effort at reform, these reactionaries abandoned the Temple and the Holy Land and retired to Damascus,

[14]Cf. Grant, *Economic Background of the Gospels,* p. 128.

where they established a community under a new set of regulations; or, as they termed it, a "New Covenant." Later they returned as missionaries to their homeland, where they met with bitter opposition from both Pharisees and Sadducees.

They were ardent Messianists, looking for the early arrival of a "Teacher of Righteousness" who would call Israel back to his national ideals, and usher in the advent of Messiah. They accepted all the written Word—Law, Prophets, and Hagiographa (Aramaic, *kethubin*)—but rejected in the main the oral tradition of the rabbis. In their private life they were rigidly self-denying and loyal to the regulations of Levitical purity. On such matters as the future life, spiritual beings, and divine providence, they agreed with the Pharisees. Great stress was laid on the necessity for repentance.

It is clear that the adherents of this party would be especially susceptible to the appeal of Christianity, and it is therefore not unlikely that many were won to the Christian movement. They constituted a factor, how extensive in effects we do not know, in preparing Jewish society for the acceptance of the message of Jesus. The "great company of priests who were obedient to the faith" (Acts 6: 7) during the early years of the church in Jerusalem might have come from Zadokite influence.

Of the details of their history not a great deal is known, and their ultimate fate is lost in obscurity.[15]

VI. The Herodians

On the extreme left of the Sadducees developed a party who were almost purely political. Only because

[15]The documentary source for information relative to this Jewish party is the fragmentary "Book of Zadok," given by Charles in his *Apocrypha and Pseudepigrapha.* Its historical reflections are remarkably clear and full, so that a fairly complete historical sketch has been derived from it, but later than the date of this document (18 to 8 B.C.) nothing definite can be learned of their history, until other evidence comes to light. For a thorough discussion of this party and the document which furnishes the information concerning them, see Charles, *Apocrypha and Pseudepigrapha,* Vol. II, pp. 789-834. They are treated as a distinct party in Judaism by Eakin, *Getting Acquainted with the New Testament,* p. 191, and Purdy-Macgregor, *Jew and Greek: Tutors Unto Christ,* pp. 109-113.

they are a sect of first century Jewish society can they be included under a discussion of the religion of Judaism, for religion to them was quite a secondary interest.

After the deposition of Archelaus A.D. 6, Augustus, in compliance with a petition from influential leaders in Judea, appointed a governor for that section of Palestine. To this action some of the Jews objected, and favored a perpetuation of the Herodian dynasty.[16] When the ministry of Jesus was accumulating popularity among the masses these Herodians feared that he might precipitate a nationalistic movement which would thwart their designs for their favorites, and hence they joined the Pharisees in opposition to him. (Cf. Matt. 26: 16; Mark 3: 6; 12: 13.)

Thus we see that the Pharisees developed one extreme in the Essenes and the opposite in the Zealots, while the Sadduces produced on one side the Zadokites and on the other the Herodians. These developments grew out of the Law on the one hand, and the Temple on the other.

The Law

It has already been seen quite clearly in our sketch of the history of Judaism that Jewish life as a distinct development in the Restoration was established upon a high regard for and strict observance of the Law. As seen in its historical perspective, Law observance was practically a synonym of Judaism. A serious retrograde movement was in progress during the Greek period, particularly under late Egyptian and Syrian supremacy, but the Law was re-instated in its high place of influence by the Maccabean revolt. The successors of the Maccabeans, however, showed what was to the devout among the people a shocking indifference to the observance of the Law. But the last of the Asmoneans, Queen Alexandra, restored the Law to its pristine power and gave

[16]The view is quite plausible that the Herodians looked upon the Idumean dynasty as fulfilling the Messianic hope, and were to that extent religious in their interest. Cf. Fairweather, *op. cit.*, p. 185.

its ardent protagonists, the Pharisees, the supreme positions of civil and religious authority under her rule. Under her patronage the dominance of the Law became so fully established that its rigid hold upon Jewish life and conscience, particularly in Palestine, was not released until rudely and summarily broken by the mailed fist of Roman oppression. And even then its sway persisted in the Dispersion. An adequate comprehension of New Testament life is entirely conditioned upon a proper understanding of this supreme position of the Law.

I. Legal Bondage

The conditions of Jewish life relative to the Law are vividly portrayed in the language of our Saviour: "they bind heavy burdens and grievous to be borne, and lay them on men's shoulders" (Matt. 23: 4). Such the rabbinic interpretation of the Law had become for the moral and religious life of the people.

There was a legal regulation at every turn, so that the most minute details of life might not be undertaken without dread of forgetting or violating some precept of the Law. The picture of Jewish legalism which is drawn in the Gospels is unquestionably accurate. The minute legal regulations of the Pharisees "were made the substitute for real piety and morality by the majority; and to tender consciences they were an intolerable burden, for it was scarcely possible to move a step or lift a finger without the danger of sinning against one or the other of them."[17] Yet these regulations may be classified under five phases of application—namely, Sabbath observance, food laws, laws pertaining to tithes and offerings, laws regulating obligations and relations between the sexes, and laws relative to cleanness and uncleanness. This fact has led some scholars to question whether in reality legal regulations were the intolerable burden upon the devout Jew that it has been supposed they were,

[17]Stalker, *Life of Christ*, p. 95.

but when we consider the vast number of details in which these five groups of regulations were applied, and the fact that they embrace practically all the ordinary routine of life, the conclusion remains inescapable that the Jew in the New Testament period found a legal restraint confronting him in nearly every activity of life.[18]

For the earnest and devout soul, who desired to live well-pleasing to Jehovah, life under the Law must have presented an unbearable strain. Indeed, when the Law came, with the labyrinth of Pharisaic interpretation, one died: for life could no longer hold much attraction or inspiration (Cf. Romans 7: 9). The observance of legal regulations looked only to the hope of personal or national reward; the violation of the minutest restriction was believed to entail a divine penalty. Righteousness as a vital principle and a means of happiness and progress in life was unknown. Retribution was the sole sanction of the Law. Under such conditions it is not strange that the masses of the people despaired of measuring up to Pharisaic punctiliousness. The Pharisees in turn scorned these masses, disdainfully designating them as *am-ha-aretz,* "the country people."

II. Rabbinic Domination

The tyranny of the letter of the Law and its traditional interpretation gave a supreme place of regard to the rabbis, the official teachers of the Law. The veneration in which this class were held found no rival in all the life of Israel. No accomodation was denied them, no request was allowed to pass unheeded. In the highest sense, the rabbi was regarded as the chosen representative of Jehovah and his will. The priest in the Temple at Jerusalem was looked upon with respect, but this attached to his office more than to his person; and besides, the priests but rarely came into religious communication with the people. "The near and living

[18]Cf. Montefiore, Peake's *Commentary on the Bible,* p. 621.

institution was not the Temple, but the Synagogue, at once a house of prayer and of study; the near and important officials were not the priests but the scribes, the rabbis, the teachers of the Law."[19] The rabbi was present at all times, a guide in the most minute details of life, the source of enlightenment in every problem, the last appeal in every mooted question. Therefore his hold upon the interest and reverence of the people was unequaled.

Even in the Temple, where the priests were formally in control, the interpretation placed by the scribes upon the laws pertaining to the Temple worship determined the methods of ritual observance. This state of affairs was, of course, not at all pleasant or satisfactory to the priests, but the high place in popular esteem held by the Pharisaic scribes as the competent and authoritative interpreters of the Law made it expedient for the Temple officials to conform with their views of proper Temple routine.[20]

This legalistic bondage is not to be thought of as wholly evil in results. The motive was generally selfish and the performance mechanical, yet it did result in a state of moral rectitude which elevated Jewish life far above the average level of the Gentile life contemporaneous with it. And these conditions prevailed chiefly in Palestine. It is improbable that Hellenistic Judaism was so casuistic and mechanical in observing the Law, at least to any considerable extent.

The Messianic Hope

We have reviewed the Temple and the Law in first century Judaism; now we turn to the Nation. The nationalistic ideal of Judaism was essentially theocratic. That is, they believed Jehovah should directly rule the Land which he had given them. When they returned from the Captivity it was with this hope in their hearts.

[19]Montefiore, *op. cit.*, p. 620.

[20]Hausrath, *op. cit.*, Vol. I, p. 80.

Their part in the Covenant which was the basis of their religious and national life was so to enforce the Law and promote the Ritual that Jehovah would be completely supreme in the Nation. Time after time progress toward this ideal was frustrated and hope of its realization through ordinary means was progressively fading. As the earthly accomplishment of this hope became less evident, the anticipation increased that Jehovah would intervene in a great crisis of deliverance, and a direct divine regime usher in the Messianic age.

The Jews knew themselves to be God's chosen race, the special object of his care and favor: and yet their history gave grim and undeniable evidence that the ideals of this relation had never been realized. As a result, the eyes of Israel were trained ever more and more toward the future. This extension of faith into the future finds its earliest manifestation in the Old Testament prophets, but its most definite expression is given through the literature of Judaism, wherein we may clearly trace this ever-brightening hope.

I. Development of the Messianic Hope

Jesus of Nazareth was the culmination and highest expression of a noble hope which was all but universal in the ancient religious mind. The Messianic hope was by no means peculiar to Judaism. The history of religion discloses that in varying forms it appears in the majority of the ancient religions. Sometimes it is the expectation of a Golden Age of peace and plenty, sometimes it is the hope of a divine deliverer, sometimes it is the eagerness to follow a great prophet or religious teacher, but ever it looks toward the revelation of God's better plan for humanity. We construe this as the providential provision of an inherent susceptibility of the religious mind to the divine provision of redemption. There can be no question that Jesus offers what is beyond comparison the highest and fullest answer to this natural quest of the soul.

That which is distinctively denominated as the Messianic hope of Judaism was originally and essentially the expectation of a future Golden Age for Israel, rather than the definite conception of an individual deliverer who was to come. The earliest records we have of Hebrew religious consciousness reveal a conviction that the people of Israel were ordained to a grand destiny which would bring all nations under their sway and make them the pre-eminent power of all the earth. This view is to be clearly seen as early as Gen. 12: 1-3, and recurs at frequent intervals throughout the oldest literature. In the development of the prophetic view this came to include the sovereignty of Jehovah over all nations and the salvation of the righteous among the Gentiles. At a very early period in the life of Israel this national hope becomes personified, if not a person, in a great individual representative of Jehovah, who is to appear as the leader and teacher of Israel. In some of the later prophets and Psalms this personal conception becomes distinct and unquestionable.[21] A personal Messiah, however, is rarely ever found, some even of the latest prophets presenting the Messianic age and its glories without any definite conception of the mediatorial personality who is to be its central figure.

That this hope persisted in and after the Restoration, we may certainly with safety conclude, and it is entirely possible that many still thought of the Messianic era as the achievement of a personal Messiah. Such an expectation is amply clear in the first eight chapters of Zechariah.[22] "But from the little . . . evidence that remains to us it would seem that in the period between the Captivity and the rise of the Maccabees the Mes-

[21]The conviction that the Messianic hope found its fulfilment in the person of Christ makes the personal force of the Old Testament prophecies very clear to the Christian, but we must beware of assuming for prophetic consciousness as it peered into the distant future the definite clearness of view which we have in historical retrospect. However, there is certainly personal significance in such passages as Gen. 49: 10; Num. 24: 17-19; Deut. 18: 15. Cf. Huffman, *The Progressive Unfolding of the Messianic Hope*, pp. 26-37.

[22]Zech. 3: 8; 6: 12, 13; 8: 23. Cf. Adeney, *The Hebrew Utopia*, p. 303.

sianic hope resolved itself into vague anticipations of a glorious and happy future, in which the presence of God would be more manifest, but of which a Messiah would form no essential feature."[23]

Again in later Judaism there reappears, more clearly and definitely conceived than ever before, the idea of a personal Messiah as a great, divinely appointed leader who should become the national champion against Israel's foes. But even their views differed widely as to the nature and policies of this national champion, and in the minds of some Israel's deliverance and triumph continued to be looked upon as the direct accomplishment of Jehovah himself.

But on one essential point interbiblical Judaism agreed. *God would eventually deliver his people from heathen bondage and elevate them to the supreme place of power and influence among the nations.* The method by which this triumph was to be accomplished was the point at which opinion varied.

II. Forms of the Messianic Hope

In Israel the idea of religious leadership gathered about four cardinal conceptions. All authority was ultimately based in the will of Jehovah, but the will of Jehovah might be mediated through certain personal instrumentalities approved by him. This personal representative might be a prophet, who spoke directly from Jehovah; a priest, who approached Jehovah on behalf of the people; an angel, sent on some special mission of warning, promise, or instruction; as a king, who was selected under Jehovah's direction to guide the affairs of Israel. The personal aspect of the Messianic hope took form in all four of these conceptions.

[23]Drummond, *The Jewish Messiah,* p. 199. Cf. also pp. 185-195. It should also be noted that Drummond (pp. 195f.) denies the Messianic significance of the passages cited in Zechariah, but we agree with Adeney (*op. cit.,* p. 303), *et. al.,* that the Messianic hope is in the background of these statements. Drummond's great caution, however, is not an unwise policy in this field of investigation, for it is easy here to picture a prophet as seeing things in the light of subsequent developments.

1. The prediction of Malachi that Elijah the *Prophet* should be sent to prepare the way for the Messiah (Mal. 3: 1; 4: 5) was taken by some to refer, not to the forerunner, but to the Messiah himself. It is probable that the idea of a prophetic Messiah was also encouraged by Deut. 18: 15, "Jehovah thy God will raise up unto thee a prophet from the midst of thee, of thy brethren, like unto me."[24] This led to the expectation that God would bring in the Golden Age for Israel in the person of a great prophet who would fulfil the Messianic role. Such an expectation unquestionably appears in 1 Maccabees (4: 46; 5: 16), and survived into New Testament times, as is evident from the current opinions concerning Jesus described in Matt. 16: 14 and in the questions which the delegation from Jerusalem asked John the Baptist (John 1: 21). In fact, it is obvious that the ministry of the Baptist appealed with peculiar force to such an expectation. It is now generally accepted as an historical fact that many of the disciples of John the Baptist refused to abandon their belief in him as the true Messiah, and perpetuated into the second century a sect in which John's Messiahship was preached in opposition to that of Jesus. This conception must have been based upon the expectation of a Messianic prophet, for John could hardly have been assigned to any other category.

This aspect of the Messianic hope was quite probably sustained and perpetuated by the yearning in the hearts of the more spiritual for a return of the spirit of prophecy. This prophetic hope, however, was not very prevalent in Judaism. The Samaritans were expecting a prophetic Messiah, but the Jews had in the main other expectations.

2. In later interbiblical history there appears the idea of a Messianic *priest*. The revival of hope in the heart of Israel engendered by the Maccabean heroes directed the expectations of the people toward the tribe of Levi. When the offices of prince and high priest were combined

[24] Williams, *Evolution of New Testament Christology*, p. 87.

in Simon, an exceptional impetus was given to the development of such a hope. *The Testaments of the Twelve Patriarchs*, in the earlier portions, which were composed within the Maccabean period, look for a priestly Messiah from the tribe of Levi, but later additions reflect the more general view that the Messiah will be from Judah. Probable traces of such a view are found in other literature of pre-Christian origin, but beyond the Maccabean period it seems to have found very limited acceptance.[25]

3. Many in Judaism looked for a *supernatural* Messiah. As earthly powers continued to oppress, and the dissatisfaction of Judaism with the present world order increased its intensity, it was inevitable that the conception of the Messiah should become more and more transcendent. Israel had never found any abiding relief from human sources, but on the contrary perpetually recurring disappointments in human leaders as they arose and shone forth in resplendent promise for a season, but to degenerate and decline, and leave the nation in a worse plight than before. Hence many of the better minds despaired of human deliverance, even under divine appointment and leadership. Intervention must surely come from heaven, and not from earth. Hence the Messiah was conceived of as an angelic being, pre-existent and supramundane in character, who would be sent from heaven by Jehovah to deliver his people from their oppression.[26]

4. By far the most popular view of the Messiah was as a warrior *king*, who should appear as a political champion and military hero to rally to his standard the Jews from every nation and lead them in a victorious

[25]Cf. Jones, *The New Testament in the Twentieth Century*, pp. 96ff.

[26]Drummond's denial of the idea of a supernatural Messiah in pre-Christian Judaism is not supported by valid arguments. He decides upon an unreasonably late date for the "Similitudes of Enoch," and then undertakes to prove that it is *possible* for the references in other literature to be interpreted as signifying something other than a supernatural Messiah, assuming that because the language *may* mean something else it does not mean what its plain significance seems to be. His opinion has found little support among the other scholars in this field. Cf. *op. cit.*, pp. 290-295.

onslaught against their enemies. Heathen oppressors would be annihilated and God's elect race would become the world's conquerors. In this view the Messiah was expected to be the descendant of David. "That the future ruler should be thought of as the descendant of David was only natural. David had been the great hero-king of the united tribes, and his line had proved so much more stable than that of Jeroboam."[27]

This conception of a royal Davidic Messiah gained ascendency in the popular mind of Judaism especially in times when heathen domination became most obnoxious and tyrannical, as in the period of Syrian persecution and during the two centuries of Roman rule. During such times the hope of the nation quite naturally turned to a warrior champion. It appears from the New Testament records (Matt. 21: 9, 15; 22: 42; Mark 13: 35; Luke 20: 41, et al) that this was the standard view in the time of Christ, and there are numerous evidences from other sources which corroborate the view in the Gospels. It had its genesis in the Old Testament prophets, where the restoration of the Davidic line is explicitly predicted (Cf. Isa. 9: 7; 11: 1; Jer. 23: 5, 6). It appears in 1 Maccabees (2: 57), and is quite specifically set forth in the Psalms of Solomon (Cf. especially 17: 5, 23). Undoubted traces of the conception appear elsewhere in the literature of Judaism (Cf. e.g., IV Ezra 12: 32). The rabbinic Targums on Isa. 11: 1; 14: 29, et al, bear witness to this idea.

It is certain that the current view at the time of Christ was that the Messiah would be a regal figure and of the lineage of David. After the time of Christ the expectation of a warrior prince continued for several generations as the predominating Messianic conception of Judaism, and occasioned the final destruction of its national life.

Thus the view of Israel's deliverer varied from the anticipation of a purely political potentate, who, by military force, would secure national independence and

[27]Rose, *Antecedents of Christianity*, p. 61.

subdue the enemies of Israel, to a great apocalyptic being who would make his advent from heaven, accompanied by supernatural manifestations and destroying his enemies by supernatural means. The latter view was held by only the more mystical minds, but is for that very reason the one most widely expressed in the literature of Judaism. The former was the popular conception, the favorite view of the masses. However, even the popular view seems to have expected the origin of the Messiah to be shrouded in mystery (Cf. John 7: 21ff.) and his mission to be attested by supernatural demonstrations (Cf. Matt. 12: 38; John 7: 31).[28]

III. Basal Characteristics of the Messianic Hope

Notwithstanding the variety and confusion in the form of the conception, there were at least three basal elements which belonged to the essential character of the Messianic idea, and were therefore the common possession of practically all of Judaism. It is here that we discover the heart of the matter, and in these essentials of the doctrine the student can secure an intelligent and comprehensive grasp of the fundamental character of the Messianic hope.

1. The Messianic hope contemplated a *special interposition of divine power.* This hope of the Jews found its ultimate basis in their faith that Jehovah had set them apart as a peculiar and choice possession, and had made with them his covenant that he would never repudiate his special relations with them. Hence they believed that in his own time God would interpose, and manifest himself in some spectacular fashion as the deliverer of Israel. The standard view was that this divine interposition would be accomplished through an intermediate

[28]The best documentary source from which to secure evidence for the popular Messianic notions of the Jewish people in Jesus' day is to be found in the Four Gospels. The reaction of the masses to the ministry of Jesus unquestionably reflected the conceptions of the Messianic era. An able discussion of the Messianic hope based largely on evidence from the Gospels may be found in Muirhead, *The Times of Christ*, pp. 112-150.

agency, the Messiah whom Jehovah had chosen. But another view, especially characteristic of the Sibylline Oracles, the Book of Jubilees, and the Assumption of Moses, was that God himself, without any intermediate agency, would bring about the triumph of Israel. Under this view the glorified kingdom of Israel would not be a Messianic monarchy but a theocracy. This was the ideal of the Zealot movement.[29]

2. An essential element of the Messianic hope, common to all Judaism, was an expectation of the *supreme elevation of the nation of Israel.* The divine choice of Israel was to the end that Jehovah might have a people who would establish his name in all the earth and make his Law supreme. Therefore the national interests of Israel were one with the cause of Jehovah. To oppose or oppress the chosen people meant to defy Jehovah and to disdain his righteous demands. This status of the Hebrew race constituted them the rightful object of special respect by the surrounding nations. They were God's specially chosen representatives among the nations, and considered that they should be treated as such. But, on the contrary, they were despised by the Gentiles, ruthlessly seized and consigned to bondage by one despotic conqueror after another, to be buffeted and maltreated in the most humiliating fashion. To the devout Jewish religionist this could only mean that Jehovah was keenly incensed at the heathen nations and regarded them as his own defiant enemies. The coming of the Messianic age must in the very nature of the case bring the consummate destruction of the incorrigible and the humble submission of those who yielded and repented. Even those who had never known Israel, and consequently could not be guilty of conscious defiance of Jehovah, must nevertheless become subject to the chosen nation

[29]Cf. I Enoch 5: 56; 6: 6; 51: 3; 61: 8; Psalms of Solomon 17: 3; Sibyl. Orac., 5: 114 cf. 3: 702-709; Assum. Mos., 10: 3, 7. The Sibylline Oracles do not present a consistent view throughout, which is to be expected, for they are composed of a compilation of fragments of varying dates. All the references given here are based upon the text of these writings as contained in Charles, *Apocrypha and Pseudepigrapha of the Old Testament.*

(Cf. 2 Baruch 72: 5). The hostile powers were expected to make a final desperate and concerted effort to resist the power of Jehovah and his elect, only to be overthrown and destroyed. Israel was to become victorious over all his enemies, with all other heathen powers, the Diaspora was to return, and the re-united and renovated nation would reign in triumph and blessedness.[30]

In its earlier stages the Messianic hope seems to have been purely national, with little interest in the ultimate fate of the Gentile world. The destiny of Israel was regarded as Jehovah's only concern. But as the conception of God enlarged, and the unity of the human race was more clearly perceived, and Israel's relations to the nations of earth were multiplied, the view became more and more universalized.[31]

The doctrine took on also in its later developments an individual application. Many of those who belonged by race to Israel had proved themselves traitors to the sacred interests of the nation. These could not be expected to share in the glories of the Messianic Age. Hence there must be an elect remnant who would participate in the ultimate triumph of Jehovah and the righteous. On the basis of germinal teachings in the Old Testament, influenced by contacts which have been observed above, there arose with this individualistic conception the ideas of resurrection and judgment. Around these views there was woven an elaborate eschatology, the fundamentals of which were standard Jewish doctrine in New Testament times and furnished a basis for the doctrines and hopes of the Christian religion.

But notwithstanding this development of the universal and individual application of the Messianic hope, Israel as a nation reigned supreme in the anticipations of the future. The nations of earth were to be but subordinate

[30]Even Philo shares with his fellow-countrymen in this view. Some scholars are skeptical about Philo's acceptance of the Messianic hope, but it cannot be reasonably denied in the face of such evidences from his own writings as we find cited by Hausrath, *op. cit.*, Vol. II, pp. 196f.

[31]Cf. Schuerer, *op. cit.*, II, ii, pp. 130f.

recipients in the blessings of the new age. The influence of this view is reflected even in the writings of Paul (for example, Romans 11: 1ff.). The basal conception of the Messiah was that he should be Jehovah's representative to, and in the interest of, his chosen people.[32]

3. Another basal conception upon which Judaism as a whole was agreed was that the Messianic Age would bring the *subjection of the world to the rule of Jehovah and his Anointed.* This hope for the supremacy of Israel should not be regarded as purely selfish. The devout Jew believed that it would be infinitely the best for the peoples of earth to be subject to the absolute dominion of Israel, for such would mean the complete sovereignty of Israel's God. Of course the penalty of utter destruction, or eternal punishment in Gehenna, would be inflicted upon a great host of the impenitent, but for those who were preserved the change of conditions would be a gracious blessing. The Messiah would reign in glory and beneficence, and peace and plenty would prevail in all the earth. The Jews believed, and rightly, that the unhindered sovereignty of God's will would bring the highest possible state of human happiness. This was to be the chief accomplishment of the Messianic Age. The common cravings of human nature marred this ideal to some extent, but it is nothing short of remarkable how little the animal cravings of human nature influenced the Jewish anticipations of their Golden Age. It was expected to be an era of transcendent righteousness, when the will and Law of Jehovah would hold unchallenged sway, and the Messiah would promote and enforce the highest principles of right living.[33]

At the dawn of the Christian Era no other element held a larger place in Jewish life at large than this Messianic expectation. It is certain that at this period "no

[32]I Enoch 48: 8, 9; II Baruch 72: 2-5; Sibyl. Orac. 3: 657, 658; 5: 120-133; Assum. of Mos. 10: 8-10; Tobit 13: 12-18; 17: 7; II Mac. 2: 18; Psalms of Solomon 11. Cf. especially I Enoch 56: 5; 57: 3.

[33]Cf. Tobit 13: 11; 16: 6, 7; Judith 16: 17; I Enoch 38: 2; 48: 4, 5; 52: 4; 62: 6-16; Psalms of Solomon 17: 3, 23-26; Rev. 11: 15.

important movement could take place upon the soil of the history of the Jewish people and religion without either being introduced by the Messianic idea or becoming involved with it at a later stage."[34] Whatever of hope the future contained was associated with it. It was the vital center of Jewish religion, and was productive of a far more spiritual type of religious experience than could have been otherwise possible in the midst of Pharisaic formalism. It was the preserving salt of Jewish religious life, and did more than any other historical cause in preparing an audience for Jesus. Yet it is also true that the life of first century Judaism contained no more violent stimulus to the inflammable passions of racial hatred and religious prejudice than this very Messianic expectation. It became the cause of a series of disturbances, and was ever ready to break out into violence. One of the grand spectacles of history was the way Jesus utilized the better elements in this factor of Jewish life, and yet restrained its more extreme demonstrations. Unsympathetic critics have emphasized this excitable phase of the Messianic hope, to the neglect of its valuable features, and thus made it to appear as a reprehensible passion and unreasoning illusion. But while frankly admitting the fanatical rage of self-deluded pseudo-Messiahs and conniving Zealots, yet there are two other products of the Messianic hope which far more than atone for its extreme demonstrations. These are, first, the rich and noble religious experience which was constantly associated with it and dependent upon it in the lives of the sanely devout; and, second, and infinitely superior, the ministry and achievement of that One who was the real fulfilment of the Messianic hope, if it be admitted that such fulfilment has ever been or is ever to be.[35]

[34]Baur, *Church History in the First Three Centuries*, p. 39.

[35]A clear, comprehensive discussion of the Messianic hope, considered from the Jewish point of view, may be found in the *Jewish Encyclopedia*, Vol. VIII, pp. 505ff.

CHAPTER VII

THE STATE OF JEWISH SOCIETY

It is obviously impossible to distinguish sharply this subject from the matters already discussed, for the sects and institutions of Judaism were elements and factors in its society. But for convenience we select this as a title for separate treatment, and present under it those matters which have to do with the common conduct, customs, and intercourse of the people as a whole. That is, we have been considering in the previous chapter Judaism in its distinctive religious phases; we now turn our attention to the Jews as a social group, living in Palestine in the first century.

Hellenistic Influence

In spite of the persistent efforts of the Pharisees and their sympathizers, the leaven of Hellenism had done its work in Palestine, and had introduced many elements of Græco-Roman life and culture. From the time of Alexander, Greek influence had been encroaching on Judaism, though meeting considerable restraint in the developments of the Maccabean period. Especially were severe restrictions created by the reign of Alexandra. But Roman domination again opened the door for the inroads of Hellenism, so that its effects pervaded Palestine in the first century. Herod was especially aggressive in the promotion of Greek culture and practice. The Greek language was used to a varying extent by the majority of the people, though the native tongue was still Aramaic. Latin was used by the officials connected with Roman government,[1] and the primitive Hebrew was used in the rabbinical schools and in parts of the synagogue services. Roman roads traversed the country in many

[1]In the rabbinic literature of this period are found, transliterated into Hebrew, a number of Latin terms pertaining to civil and military affairs.

directions, and the people were taxed or paid tolls to keep them in good condition. Much Hellenistic culture prevailed among the higher classes. Herod had manifestly sought to surround himself with Greek culture.[2] Greek names were used even by the loyal Jews, as may be seen in the names Philip and Andrew among the apostles of Christ. The devout Jews knew these only as familiar names, and gave them to their children ignorant of their Greek origin; but this all the more manifests the penetration of Hellenistic influence into Jewish life—it was so familiar that they were not conscious of its presence in many instances. Greek amusements and conveniences were freely used. The architectural work of the Herods bore an unmistakably Hellenistic stamp. Economic affairs had been considerably affected by Græco-Roman custom. The coinage used was prevailingly Græco-Roman. In fact, there was no phase of Palestinian life in the first century which had escaped the effects of Hellenistic influence. Its results were traceable in everything from intellectual culture to such incidents of life as food and clothing.

Many Gentiles lived in Palestine in the New Testament period, especially in the Greek cities of Decapolis and the cities along the Mediterranean coast. Judaism penetrated to the sea at only two points, Joppa and Jamnia, and even in these cities there was a large Gentile population. As a whole, the Maritime Plain was dominated by Hellenism, and largely devoted to the worship of Greek and Oriental deities.[3] In Galilee and Perea the Gentile residents were numerous, and even Judea itself was not free of them. Where Gentile life dominated a community, Greek influence held supreme sway. At the site of Gerasa, one of the cities of the Decapolis, there have been discovered the remains of a triumphal arch, of magnificent baths and temples, of a vast theatre with a seating capacity of six thousand, and of an arti-

[2]Cf. Schuerer, *op. cit.*, I, i, pp. 442ff.

[3]Schuerer, *op. cit.*, II, i, pp. 11ff.

ficial harbor for mock naval battles, all of which are distinctly Græco-Roman features.[4]

Central Judea was almost entirely Jewish, and was the influential center of Jewish life. Galilee and Perea had in the main a Jewish population, though in both there were Græco-Roman communities and Hellenistic influence was strong. The Jews of these two sections of Palestine, because of the large Greek constituency and their distance from the center of Jewish life and influence, were not nearly so rigid in their legalistic restrictions and national exclusiveness. In view of this fact it may be more readily understood why Jesus could do more effective work in Galilee and Perea than in Judea. The domains of Herod Philip in Northeastern Palestine were inhabited by both Jews and Gentiles, the latter predominating. Its chief city, Cæsarea-Philippi, had been a center of Hellenistic culture for many generations, as is signified by its former name, Panias, derived from the name of the Greek god Pan.

Hellenism was thus a potent factor in the world in which Jesus and his disciples moved. Yet Palestine presented some outstanding differences from the Gentile world about it. In spite of the inroads of Hellenism, at its vital religious and social heart Judaism still possessed its distinctive character. The Pharisees still maintained their rigid adherence to the Law and their traditions, while the faith and hope of historic Israel were still alive in the heart of the great majority of the Jewish masses. Women were treated with far more consideration than in the Roman world, and the sanctity of the home—a thing almost unknown among their pagan contemporaries—was held in high regard among the Jews. Illegal unions and polygamy were exceedingly rare, though divorce was all too common. Altogether, Palestinian Judaism had been remarkably successful in resisting the demoralizing tendencies of the pagan life of its day.

[4] Cf. Cobern, *New Archeological Discoveries*, p. 372.

Civil Organization

The conditions and changes in civil affairs have already appeared in our investigation of the history of Judaism. In the first century the government was in the hands of a procurator or vassal king, who ruled as the representative of Rome, and was expected to utilize as far as possible the existing forms of civil administration. It is these existing modes of government which we are now to consider.

1. *Palestinian Government in General.* From far back in Old Testament times the government of Palestine was essentially municipal. That is, the civil administration of the country was committed to the larger towns and cities. The largest municipality in a district had a council of elders who administered all branches of civil government, whether legislative, judicial, or executive. This mode of supervision was in general continued during the Roman period. Of course the entire system was under the general control of Roman law and Roman officials, but Rome gave to the local administration very large liberty in the direction of civil affairs. Under the supervision of the council of elders, and doubtless selected from their number, were "judges," who presided in trials, and "officers," who looked after the executive side of civil affairs. Frequent reflections of these features of government appear in the New Testament.

2. *The Government of Judea.* The civil organization of Judea followed the same general lines found in other parts of Palestine, but some particular features were sufficiently different to warrant separate treatment. Jerusalem was the dominant municipality, or provincial capital, functioning as the general center of control, issuing laws, trying cases, and collecting taxes. But for greater convenience and efficiency in administration, the province of Judea was divided into ten districts, or toparchies.[5] In a prominent municipality of each to-

[5]The sources differ here, some giving eleven toparchies, but this number includes Jerusalem which should properly be viewed as the general center or "capital" of the province.

parchy there was a council or local sanhedrin which served as a center of control, representing and acting in subordination to the Sanhedrin at Jerusalem.

3. *Independent Municipalities.* Distributed throughout Palestine there were a considerable number of towns which were denominated "free cities," such as Ascalon, Cæsarea, Ptolemais, Samaria (Sebaste), Scythopolis. These cities, with the country districts immediately surrounding them, formed independent municipal communities. The majority of them had secured their most extensive prerogatives of self-government during the declining years of Syrian rule. It appears that all of those on the coast except Ascalon and Ptolemais had been forced to submit to Judean rule by Alexander Janneaus, but were liberated again by Pompey in 63 B.C. In dealing with these free cities the Romans had followed their wise policy of adapting their own government to that already in existence, or which the conquered peoples preferred. The form of government in these independent municipalities and the extent of their liberties varied considerably, but in general it may be said that they were largely, though not entirely, exempted from imperial taxation, had their own administration carried on by representatives from the free citizens of the municipal community, and possessed special privileges and distinctions granted by Rome. However, they were expected to recognize the general supervision of the provincial governor, and in some instances the head of the provincial government appointed a representative to reside in the free city and have final oversight of affairs. The word "free" as applied to these cities must be taken with considerable qualification. They were nevertheless independent of the prevailing system of Palestinian government.

Economic Life

However intense and pervasive may be the religious interest of a people, the material necessities and relationships of life cannot be disregarded. This inevitable aspect of existence had its significant and distinctive place in Palestinian society of the first century. Nothing is more important in a proper understanding of the Gospels than to comprehend the economic background.[6]

I. Economic Destitution

The economic status of Palestine in the first century was far from ideal. The people as a whole were in a deplorable state of material privation.

1. We will review first the *causes* of this economic destitution.

(1) As one of its chief embarrassments, the country was crowded with an excessive population. Even the permanent Jewish inhabitants were more than the land could adequately support, and when we add to these the Gentile immigrants, the Roman officials and military forces, and the thousands of pilgrims gathering at Jerusalem for the feasts three times each year, if not more often, it is obvious that there existed a serious economic problem in sustaining the proper balance between production and consumption.

(2) Accentuating this difficulty of over-population was the Jewish aversion to engaging in any sort of trade relations with the outside heathen world, or to barter and exchange under any conditions. Every Israelite had his individual heritage in the form of a portion of "the Land," and upon this he was supposed to subsist, in humble gratitude and loyalty to Jehovah who gave it. To look to any other source of support was to dishonor his divine heritage. Such a conception of necessity presented a serious deterrent to economic progress. The land, on an average, was of only ordinary fertility, and droughts were of frequent occurrence.

(3) The vast building enterprises of Herod had left a huge financial burden upon the civil government,

[6]An excellent discussion of this very important feature of Gospel environment may be found in Grant, *The Economic Background of the Gospels* (Oxford).

which of necessity brought on exorbitant taxation. This economic problem presented an immediate handicap to the reign of Archælaus, and augmented the opposition to him. After Archælaus was deposed the people hoped that direct Roman rule would give them the much desired relief from taxation, but in this they were disappointed, for with the coming of a procurator they were required to pay revenues to Rome. And in addition to the regular tax there were various other imposts, customs, tariffs, and so forth, which were exacted of them. So much for their civil taxation; yet there was over and above all this the demands for religious revenues, the enormous contributions required by the Law for the administration of the Temple and the support of its elaborate services. And still there is left to be added the revenues necessary to support the local synagogue. This amazing accumulation of assessments made the burden of taxation intolerable, and an intensely acute question.

2. We observe next *the effects* of economic destitution in first century Palestine. In the light of such conditions we may easily visualize the state of economic distress. Poverty to the extent of privation and hunger prevailed throughout Palestine, and for multitudes life was but a problem of physical existence. In consequence dissatisfaction and unrest grew apace.

The fitful outbursts of robbery and insurrection which characterize this period were in a large measure the result of this stress in economic affairs. These conditions also account for the ease with which the crowds in Jerusalem could be aroused to ungovernable fury and mob violence, as when they would so readily seek to stone Jesus (John 8: 59; 10: 31), or thronged Pilate demanding the execution of Jesus (Matt. 27: 20), or pounced upon Paul when he was falsely accused of bringing a Gentile into the Temple sanctuary (Acts 21: 27ff). In fact, the general state of unrest and agitation which prevailed throughout Palestinian Judaism in the first century, and culminated in the revolt of A.D. 66, was probably due more largely to material destitution than has generally been recognized.

The difficulty of obtaining a livelihood drove many to desperation. Many a woman resorted to the Magdalene role because of sheer physical want. In view of this economic situation one does not wonder at our Lord's merciful attitude toward such unfortunates (Luke 7: 36ff; John 8: 1ff.). Men bartered the respect of their neighbors and defied the ban of rabbinic law in collecting taxes for the hated Romans; or, worse still, resorted to theft and pillage, so that even along the much frequented road from Jerusalem to Jericho one might fall among thieves (Luke 10: 20).

It is remarkable how Jesus prevented these tense economic conditions from affecting to any appreciable extent the determining issues of his ministry. He deliberately declined to yield to the popular Messianic demands, which were undoubtedly instigated to a considerable degree by those problems of support. It was definitely expected of the Messiah, when he should come, that he would "fill the hungry with good things" (Luke 1: 53). But Jesus addressed himself primarily to spiritual rather than to physical need. He fed hungry hearts rather than hungry stomachs. His gospel was by no means an economic gospel; nor can it be characterized in general as a social gospel; primarily and essentially the gospel which Jesus proclaimed was an ethical and religious gospel.[7] Yet it would be a serious mistake to assume that the economic conditions had no relation to the life and teachings of Jesus. He was in the midst of these conditions every day of his life, and the people to whom he ministered were the victims of this distressful state of affairs; consequently, much of what he said and did cannot be properly understood without full consideration being given to these economic facts.[8] In the light

[7]Abundant support for this position may be found in Scott, *The Ethical Teaching of Jesus.*

[8]An excellent treatment of this question may be found in G. A. Smith, *Jerusalem,* Vol. I, pp. 275-376.

of this situation we may feel more forcibly the tender strain of sympathy in that compassionate appeal: "Come unto me all ye that labor and are heavy laden, and I will give you rest" (Matt. 11: 28).

II. Economic Pursuits

Palestinians of the first century continued very largely in their old-time pursuits of farming, grape-raising, sheep-raising, and fishing. Fruit and grain were produced in abundance. This would seem to indicate that the majority of the population was rural. But authorities differ on this point. Josephus unquestionably represents the bulk of the population as urban, but many evidences are found which appear to prove him in error. It may be regarded as fairly certain that the great majority were rural in interests, but many of those who secured their living from the country had their homes in the villages or towns. This could conceivably have thrown the balance on the side of urban population, and in some measure have justified the situation as represented by Josephus. At any rate, most people earned their living from small tracts of land which they owned and cultivated themselves. There was little need of hired labor, though it could easily be secured, usually at the rate of a Roman *denarius* (about twenty cents) a day. Slave labor was also used, but generally by those who had large estates. Slaves were much better treated by the Jews than by the Romans. They were placed under the supervision of a "house-manager" (Gk. *oikonomos*), commonly called a steward. The products of their labor could be marketed very cheap, which caused unfavorable competition for the small farmer.

We have noted above that commercial progress in Palestine was seriously retarded by the traditional ban on barter and exchange and usury, which was still maintained by the more devout and loyal Jews. The rabbis had drafted laws regulating commerce which were extremely rigid and meticulous. But the growth of towns and cities made the growth of commercial enterprise inevitable. There were of necessity some commodities imported, but imports were limited largely to liberal aristocrats and foreigners, for the ideal of the Jew was to live strictly off the products of his own land. Imports were confined to wood and metal products, and articles of luxury for the well-to-do. For manufactured articles and luxuries, residents of Palestine were almost wholly dependent on imports, for but little of that sort of thing was produced by the Jews. In this class of imports there were a hundred eighteen articles, according to Edersheim. Export trade was more extensive, but consisted almost entirely of natural products. Fish was shipped to Antioch, Alexandria, and Rome. There was also export trade in oil, wool, wheat, balsam, honey, and figs.

Among the Jews professional life was limited. The one widely extensive profession was that of rabbi, if profession it may be called, for most rabbis followed some trade or secular pursuit for a livelihood, while devoting all the time possible to the study and teaching of the Law. The professions of law and medicine, which were widely practiced in the Græeco-Roman world, had little place in the life of Palestinian Jews. They held manual labor in very high esteem, and every Jewish boy was expected to learn some trade. Rabbinic tradition declared that "whoever does not teach his son a trade is as if he brought him up to be a robber."

Home and Education

I. Living Conditions

We have already seen that certainly much of the population of Palestine lived in towns and villages. The former were distinguished from the latter by the fact that they were walled in and, in most instances, had a synagogue.[9] Where the highway approached the town the

[9]By some scholars distinction is also made between villages and "townships," or hamlets. Cf. Edersheim: *op. cit.*, p. 87.

wall was penetrated by a gate, which could be closed and made fast with bars and bolts. Just within the gate there was usually a large open square, where the people congregated for trade and social intercourse. As Jesus went on his teaching tours through the towns and villages of Galilee, it is probable that he frequently addressed the assembled people in these open squares.

The houses of the masses were low and flat-roofed, built of material composed of mud and straw and baked in the sun, while the houses of the wealthy were taller, consisting frequently of two or three stories, and built of brick or stone. Windows were made of grating or lattice-work, and opened usually on the street or highway. The door-shutters hung on wooden hinges and were made secure by crude wooden bolts and keys. Often on the roof of a house a guest-chamber was constructed, called the "upper room." In urban communities, where the houses were close together, the roofs were generally connected. Frequently there were an outer and an inner court, the rooms opening into the inner court.

Sanitary and police provisions were of a remarkably high order. Sanitation was enforced by rigid rules. Anything that would vitiate or befoul the atmosphere was required to be removed hastily.

II. The Establishment of the Home

The customs relative to marriage among the Jews were distinctive and rigidly fixed. Betrothal was a matter far more sacred than the mere "engagement" with which we are familiar in modern times. It was effected by solemn ceremonies, and could be broken only by divorce. "From the moment of her betrothal a woman was treated as if she were actually married."[10] The husband chose the wife, but was expected to secure the woman's consent as well as that of her parents. It was expected that the bride would be provided with a dowry. Very elaborate preparations were made for the nuptial celebrations.

[10]Edersheim, *In the Days of Christ*, p. 148.

Presents were presented to the bride by the groom and friends. When time for the wedding arrived the groom went to the home of the bride and brought her to his own home for the ceremonies. If desired by the family of the bride, there might be pre-nuptial celebrations at her home. In Judea the groom would be accompanied by the groomsmen as he went for the bride; no groomsmen were required in Galilee. A brief ritual and benediction solemnized the union, after which there were the wedding festivities. The "marriage feast" seems to have been the important feature of the proceedings. Divorce was allowed, and was the one blight on Jewish domestic life of the first century.

III. The Family Circle

It is in their family life that the Jews shine out most brightly in contrast with the Gentile world about them. Most of the homes were characterized by systematic religious observance, such as the Sabbath, prayers, ceremonial ablutions, and the rite of circumcision. The offering of thanks at each meal is assumed as a universal custom. The relations between parents and children were excellent. The parents treated the children with great consideration, and the children reciprocated with honor and kindness. A prominent characteristic of Jewish life was deep reverence for old age, whether parents or strangers.

An important feature of Palestinian home life was the family meal. Here the fellowship of the household found its largest expression. The eating of a meal possessed for the Jew a large degree of religious sanctity, and included religious elements in the form of two blessings, one for the meat and another for the drinks. At formal meals they reclined, but at informal meals they sat at the table. The food consisted of such things as mutton, veal, fish, white bread, vegetables, and fruits. As a beverage diluted wine was used. The food restrictions provided in the Law were carefully observed.

The coming of children into a Jewish home was counted a great blessing. Especially was this true of male children. Much difference was made between the welcome accorded a boy baby and that demonstrated when a girl was born. When a male child was born there was great rejoicing. Neighbors assembled to congratulate the parents, and musicians were in waiting to celebrate the occurrence. But if the baby was a girl, the silence of disappointment and chagrin marked her arrival. We learn from the Talmud that, "the birth of a male child causes universal joy—but the birth of a female child causes universal sorrow" (Niddah 31*b*). The advent of the male child meant additional support and protection for the home and for the parents in their old age; added strength to the nation in its struggle for independence; and, above all, the possibility that the father and mother might have the peerless honor of being the parents of the Messiah! Of course the last mentioned hope depended upon the Messianic view which happened to prevail in the home. When the true Messiah was born there were no friends and neighbors to assemble and rejoice with the parents, but what men omitted angelic choirs and ministrants supplied.

On the eighth day the male child received circumcision as the sign of the covenant. This operation was performed with great solemnity, for it was regarded as "equal to all the commandments recorded in the Law" (Nedarim 32*a*). The boy was named at circumcision; the girl any time within the first month. The naming of the child was very important, for it was considered to fore-token, if not actually to influence, the character and accomplishments for which the child was destined.[11]

Families had no surnames, so when it became necessary to distinguish an individual from others bearing the same name, the father's name was used, with the Aramaic word "bar" (son of) prefixed. Thus Simon bar-Jonah meant Simon son of Jonah. Sometimes one's social or

[11]Cf. Keith, *Social Life of a Jew*, pp. 5ff.

religious affiliations furnished him a distinguishing name, as "Simon the Zealot"; or his occupation, as "Simon the tanner"; or his place of residence, as "Judas Iscariot," which meant Judas the man of Kerioth.

The law of the first-born in the Mosaic code required that the parents pay for the first-born male child a redemption fee of five shekels (about $3.75), which payment was made with simple but solemn ceremony, under the direction of a priest, and, if convenient, in the Temple. Forty days after the birth of a male child, or eighty days after the birth of a female child, the mother was expected to present herself in the Temple to make her offering of ceremonial purification, which consisted of a young pigeon or a turtle dove and a lamb of the first year. If her means were too meagre to provide the lamb, she could make the "poor's offering" instead, which was two doves or two pigeons. This was the offering made by the mother of our Lord (Luke 2: 22, 23).[12]

IV. Education

Great stress was laid upon the education of children. Josephus declares with pride, "We take the most pains of all with the instruction of children" (*Apion* 1: 12). Philo bears testimony to the same fact, saying that his people "were from their swaddling clothes, even before being taught either the sacred laws or the unwritten customs, trained by their parents, teachers, and instructors to recognize God as Father and as Maker of the world" (*Legat. ad Cajum,* sec. 16). The instruction, however, was devoted chiefly to boys, less attention being devoted to the education of girls. The teaching was begun in the home by parents, and continued in the synagogue by scribes. At the age of five[13] they began to teach the child the Hebrew Bible, beginning, not with Genesis, as

[12]Cf. Keith, *op. cit.,* pp. 16f.

[13]"Generally speaking, such early instruction was regarded as only safe in the case of very healthy and strong children; while those of average constitution were not to be set to regular work till six years old" (Edersheim: *op. cit.,* p. 105).

would normally be expected, but with Leviticus, because of the importance of Leviticus in the study of the Law. After completing Leviticus the child studied the rest of the Pentateuch, then at ten years he might be advanced into the Mishnah; and finally, if he desired still more advanced learning, he studied the Talmud. When it was desired to train a Jewish youth for a rabbi, he was sent to a rabbinic academy (*beth-ha-midrash*), several of which were scattered through Palestine. For final training as a rabbi, schools were provided in Jerusalem.

Thus we see that domestic life in Palestine was clean, energetic, cultured, and religious. This picture presents a decided contrast with that which we are later to contemplate in the Græco-Roman world. And these pleasant home conditions tended to offset the effects of the economic distress.

Social Distinctions

In first century Palestine social distinctions were very rigid. There were five rather clearly marked classes. (1) There was an aristocracy consisting of the priestly group, with the Sadducees and their sympathizers. This class also included royalty and high civil officials. (2) The Pharisees and their followers composed a religious caste, conspicuous for their arrogance and exclusiveness. (3) The chief component of Palestinian society consisted of a great middle class, the masses of Jewish peasantry, who respected the Pharisees and their views but were not eager to observe all their minute exactions. These honest, devout common people, though failing of Pharisaic punctiliousness, were intensely concerned in the religion of Jehovah and his sovereignty among his people, and especially in the coming of the Messiah. It was this great class of practical religionists which furnished the seed-bed of Christianity. They were represented in such characters as Simeon and Anna, the parents of Jesus, and the greater part of the multitudes who waited on the ministry of our Lord. The fourth and fifth classes constituted the nether strata of Jewish society. They were

(4) the "publicans"—hirelings of the Roman Government and "sinners"—those who, in the abject hopelessness of their poverty and oppression, cared little for the traditions of Israel and less for the restrictions of rabbinic lore; but little lower than the last-mentioned class were (5) the slaves.

Between the first two classes, embracing the Sadducees and the Pharisees, and the last three, including the common people, the publicans and "sinners," and the slaves, all of whom were called by the Pharisees "the people of the land" (*am-ha-aretz*), there was such a wide breach of difference that many scholars are led to divide Jewish society into only two classes. We believe it to be more accurate, however, to distinguish the five as given here. To summarize, then, Palestinian society was divided into an upper stratum composed of two classes, the Sadducaic aristocrats and the Pharisaic ecclesiastics with their following; and a lower stratum composed of three classes, the common people, the publicans and "sinners," and the slaves. There were other isolated groups, such as the Roman soldiers, Gentile traders and exploiters, Roman officials, and so forth, which could hardly be regarded as social classes, but were rather distinct circles of life outside Palestinian society.

Burial Rites

Death among the Jews was a matter of tragic import, and its consequent grief was relieved by but scant consolation, for views of life beyond the grave were vague and none too certain. No one brought to the bereaved any definite and positive message of comfort, such as the sustaining hope of Christian faith. There were formal acts of grief required by current proprieties, such as rending the outer garment, abstaining from food, and so forth. Hired mourners were employed, being generally women, though men also sometimes served in such capacity. Some one competent for the task was usually secured to deliver a funeral oration, which might take place at the home, on the way to the burial, or at the grave. The body, which had been carefully washed, anointed, and wrapped in burial clothes, was carried to the place of interment on an open bier, borne by friends who relieved one another from time to time as they proceeded. At the intervals when the change of pall-bearers took place there were great demonstrations of grief. In the procession the funeral orator walked in the lead, and, in Galilee, the bier was preceded by the hired mourners, while in Judea they followed. Behind the bier and mourners came the family and friends. The body was laid to rest in a cemetery, or, if means admitted, in a private tomb hewn out of rock.

PART TWO

HELLENISM

CHAPTER VIII

ROMAN GOVERNMENT

We have traced in the preceding chapters the development in Israel of that significant and strategic situation which furnished the background for the historical origin of human redemption. But Israel was not serving alone in this holy enterprise. In unwitting—not to say, unwelcome—co-operation with him, Greek and Roman were working toward the same grand attainment. "The flood of preparation for Christianity flows steadily down the ages in three main streams—the Greek, ever bearing on its sparkling surface the one burden, the humane character of man; the Jewish, gradually becoming clearer, till it mirrors the nature of the one true God, then losing itself amid the rocks of formalism, anon bursting its home banks and overflowing with fertilizing influence into many far-off lands; the Roman, swamping a world in its majestic current, then exhausting itself in the endless eddies caused by the junction of innumerable tributaries."[1]

Rome was bringing the world to a state of peace and order, and providing facilities of communication, which would make possible the unhindered advance of the message of redemption. Greece, having subdued and amalgamated the best elements of the Orient, was preparing a mind which could penetrate and interpret the profound truths of the Christian religion, a spirit which would furnish susceptible and fertile soil where there might be sown the seed of gospel propaganda, and a language which could express the message of redemption with a beauty and accuracy which has not been equaled anywhere else in human speech. It may readily be discerned that these historical developments are of vital interest

[1]Wenley, *Preparation for Christianity*, p. 160.

in the interpretation of the New Testament. Rome occupies the foreground as the ruling power of the time, and hence claims initial consideration.

The Rise of Rome

At the dawn of the fifth century B.C., while Greece was cringing in dread before the ever-encroaching menace of Persian aggression, and making every possible preparation for successful resistance, there had come into existence on the western shores of Italy a political power which was destined forever to deprive the proud Hellenic race of their peerless prestige as political rulers in the Mediterranean world. This new power was the infant Roman Republic. Wearied of the intolerable despotism of kings, probably of an alien dynasty,[2] she had cast off the yoke of monarchy, and committed herself to the uncertain fortunes of democracy. Or should we call it democracy? During the greater part of the period of the Republic the government was in reality an oligarchy. In the beginning the rule was aristocratic, being confined to the wealthy or *patrician* class, but after a succession of internal disturbances the common people or *plebeians* secured a part in the government of the Republic.

Having successfully repulsed barbarian invasions from the north, and subdued their neighbors in the Italian peninsula, at the beginning of the third century B.C. the Romans had made themselves a national power of the first magnitude. Such a position was certain to provoke its deadly rivals. The first to appear was the Carthaginian Empire, with extensive territorial possessions in North Africa and southwestern Europe, a large navy and a well-trained army. Especially unpleasant to Rome was the hold which Carthage had on Sicily. This, with the Carthaginian occupation of Spain, was the chief occasion of combat between the two powers.

Carthage found its champion and invincible leader in the person of Hannibal. Against this powerful foe

[2] Fowler, *Rome*, p. 23.

Rome threw all the weight of her renowned patriotism, valor, and military organization. After a series of conflicts, known as the First, Second, and Third Punic Wars, Carthage succumbed, and left the Roman Republic at 146 B.C. the dominant power of the West.

Thereafter, for more than half a century, little advance was made. The task of adjusting the administration to the widely-expanded territorial possessions brought inevitable difficulties and internal strife, and sharp contention between rival leaders; and invasions from without threatened the safety of the Republic. It was less than a century before the Christian Era that the next great forward movement came. Already, a hundred years before, the Romans had subdued Macedonia, and conducted successful campaigns against Syria. But no permanent foothold was gained in Asia until 63 B.C., when the indefatigable Pompey led the victorious legions of the Republic through Asia Minor, Syria, Palestine, and Egypt, thoroughly and unquestionably establishing Roman dominion in the East. Through the peerless military enterprise and courage of Julius Cæsar and the tact and organizing ability of Augustus Cæsar, the Roman Republic, in the last half century B.C., emerged into the Roman Empire.

As a result of these various conquests, the Roman Empire embraced practically the entire Mediterranean world. Its extreme eastern boundary was the Euphrates river, and on the west it extended to the Atlantic ocean. Its domains extended northward to the Danube and the southern borders of Scotland, and southward to the Sahara desert. Only the Atlantic ocean on the west and the arid stretches of the great desert on the south had succeeded in checking the victorious advance of the Roman legions. The Parthians on the east and Germanic tribes of the north were never subdued, but doubtless more because Roman life was surfeited with conquest than because of the invincible character of these border nations.

Thus the Mediterranean world was brought under the control of a single government. After a succession of bloody contests between rival factions and their leaders at Rome, this vast realm came under the scepter of a single man, Augustus Cæsar (Octavian), who achieved an efficiency of organization and an era of peace and safety which has been the marvel of all succeeding generations. In him the Roman Empire made its advent and attained its zenith.

Roman Administration

It would be difficult to exaggerate the importance of Roman rule in preparing the world for the spread of the Christian message. It accomplished in the east the culmination of a process which had been in progress for more than two centuries. This process was begun by Alexander the Great. After the Macedonian conqueror had subjugated and unified the scattered and jealous factions of the Greek states, he crossed into Asia Minor in 334 B.C., and began a campaign which accomplished one of the greatest historical developments of all time—the penetration of Greek culture into Oriental life. Henceforth Greek and Oriental marched forth hand in hand to conquer the world spiritually and intellectually. But at the very beginning of its advancement Græco-Oriental civilization met a serious check, which certainly would have proved fatal had not a parallel development in history saved it. The breaking up of Alexander's empire after his premature death, and the political chaos which followed, divided the new Græco-Oriental world into several warring factions, and resulted in a gradual disintegration of that colossal structure of Hellenistic dominion which the marvelous genius of Alexander had so widely established in so short a time. But we have seen how Rome advanced from the West, first into Macedonia, and then into the Asiatic realms, again combining the loose and deteriorating fragments of the Greek Empire into a coherent organization. Thus Rome saved the decaying Hellenism, and Hellenism reciprocated by turning upon Rome the enchanting powers of her superior cultural and religious influence. "Greece captive led enthralled her captor."[3] The Roman had soon adopted the education, philosophy, art, and religion of Greece. By spreading the stabilizing, organizing effects of her imperial administration over the Hellenistic world, the Empire rescued the waning results of Greek civilization and opened the way for its renewed advancement.

Thus Roman, Greek, and Oriental met in the world which was to furnish its unique opportunity for the spread of the Christian religion. A survey of their distinctive contributions was given in our introductory chapter, and the Greek and Oriental will appear for more detailed treatment later in the discussion. Here we are considering the contribution of the Roman: an organized world. The government which had effected this organized world was the most equitable and best adjusted which antiquity produced.

I. The Central Government

The form of the Roman Government in the first century was nominally republican, but in effect it was an absolute monarchy. The emperor was supposed to be but the highest public official, the *princeps*, or supreme magistrate, subject to the will of the people as voiced by the Senate.[4] But, as a matter of fact, his authority was practically absolute.

The governing powers were the Senate and the emperor. The Senate was composed of several hundred national leaders, who arose to their position, not by popular vote, but by virtue of a certain amount of wealth and influence, and because of having held some high office, to which they had been elected, either by a popular as-

[3]Myers, *History of Rome*, p. 85.

[4]The revival of this theory during the Renaissance led to the modern view that governments derive their just powers from the consent of the governed.

sembly or by the Senate itself.[5] Their prerogatives were supposed to constitute a check upon the powers of the emperor, but they were really subject to his pleasure. The chief office of the emperor was head of the army,[6] which he held absolutely within his power, and this gave him control of everything else connected with Rome or her realms. The emperor could also raise one to the "order" of qualification for a place in the Senate, and then secure for him a public office, the discharge of which obtained his entrance into the Senate. It was also in the power of the emperor to remove a senator, if in his opinion the senator was not properly performing his duties, or had forfeited or lost his qualifications. Hence the emperor had almost unlimited power over the membership of the Senate. Furthermore, the decrees of the Senate were subject to the emperor's veto. It is easy to understand how these facts made the Senate but little more than a figurehead, while the emperor was the real head of the nation. The offices of consul and tribune, which were the supreme positions of the state in the time of the Republic, were now little more than empty prizes of honor to be bestowed by the emperor upon his favorites. The Roman Government of the first century was an absolute monarchy in all but name.

II. The Provincial Government

Never were conquerors more cruel in their methods of conquest nor more rigid in their demands for submission, and yet seldom have they been more generous and wise in their mode of administration, than were the Romans. A conquered state was allowed to retain its own laws and customs, and even sometimes its own rulers, in so far as these were compatible with the rule of Rome. A few fundamental laws, necessay to the supervision of the

[5]The Senate originated as a council of elders functioning as an advisory cabinet to the King. Hence its history goes back to the days of the monarchy. Cf. Fowler, *op. cit.*, p. 69.

[6]His military title was *imperator*, whence the word "emperor."

Empire and the welfare of the conquered territory, were imposed upon all conquered peoples, but so far as the original machinery of government was in harmony with these it was retained.

The provinces had come into the possession of Rome in various ways. In the days of the Republic some had joined by voluntary alliance. Others had been peacefully annexed from time to time. But the great majority of the dependent states had been conquered by the invincible Roman legions, and annexed by military force.

A few of the provinces were ruled by vassal kings, who accepted the suzerainty of Rome and paid a stipulated tribute, as was the case with the Herods of the New Testament. In most instances the ruling official was a governor, appointed by Roman authority, either the Senate or the emperor, owing to the status of the province. The duty of the governor was to keep the province under subjection to Rome, collect taxes, and administer justice wherever Roman law was concerned. Violators of local laws were tried by local courts. In case the defendant was a Roman citizen he might appeal to the imperial court at Rome. It was under this law that Paul was able to appeal to Cæsar.

There were two kinds of provinces: The *senatorial* provinces were those whose governors were appointed by the Senate, subject to the approval of the emperor, such as Achaia, Macedonia, Asia, Cyprus, and Crete. Their governors were called "proconsuls." The *imperial* provinces were under the direct control of the emperor, and their governors were his representatives. In the larger or more important imperial provinces the governor was one who had been a member of the Senate, and was known as a "proprætor," while the smaller provinces were governed by "procurators" of equestrian rank. To the latter class belonged the province of Judea; hence Pilate was a procurator. In popular parlance the title "governor" was loosely applied to any provincial administrator. Among the imperial provinces of the first century were

Pamphylia, Galatia, Cilicia, and Syria. Judea was a procuratorial province under the supervision of the Syrian administration. The governor of a province had as an advisory cabinet a Council, composed of former magistrates of the domain and influential citizens.

Within the provinces there were often settlements of Roman citizens, frequently of veteran soldiers, known as "colonies." These were usually established at the site of some city already in existence. To such settlements belonged not only the city, but a small tract of the surrounding country. In government these colonies were practically duplicates of imperial Rome—they were "little Romes." Among the Roman colonies of the first century those familiar to the New Testament student were Caesarea, Lystra, Antioch of Pisidia, Troas, Philippi, and Corinth. There were also cities which were granted special privileges and the independent administration of their local government. This privilege was granted by Rome either in recognition of some distinguished service which they had rendered to the Empire, or because of their civil status when conquered. These were known as "free cities." Thessalonica was such a city. We have noted above several in Palestine.

III. Taxation

Beginning early in the reign of Augustus Cæsar, at intervals of fourteen years a census of the Roman Empire was taken for purposes of taxation. Such a census was the occasion of the visit of Joseph and Mary to Bethlehem at the time of the birth of Jesus, probably 8 B.C. The chief source of revenue was land tax, but there were many forms of personal and special revenues, even to the taxing of old bachelors!

The revenues may be divided into two classes: customs and taxes. The customs, which were duties charged on various commodities and facilities, were collected under the supervision of local governments. Through agents selected from among the people of the provinces these customs were gathered and remitted to the official representative of the Empire. Taxes on property and person were no longer farmed out, as formerly they had been, but were collected under the immediate supervision of Roman officials. Revenues were paid in either money or produce. The taxes of Egypt were chiefly paid in grain; those of Palestine in coinage.

The bulk of the revenues was spent in the administration of the local government and in public facilities and improvements. They were also used for repair and reconstruction in case of earthquake, fire, or other disaster. A considerable balance was sent to Rome. Revenues from the senatorial provinces went into the treasury of the Senate, and were used to defray the expenses of that body and for the administration of the province of Italy. The imperial provinces remitted to the emperor, and provided for the improvement and administration of the city of Rome, the support of the army, and the personal expenses of the emperor.

IV. The Army

There was no more familiar object in the first century world than the Roman soldier. Soldiering had become in practical reality a profession. After a twenty-year period of enlistment[7] the soldier might retire from active service, but he was still regarded by the Roman public as a soldier, and as such was quite an influential individual. We have seen how the military forces, with the emperor at their head, held the Empire in their power. Hence we may say that at the very foundation of Roman rule was the army. Thus military life was a prominent and impressive feature of the Græco-Roman world. This fact is recognized and utilized by Paul in his frequent

[7]One might secure a release from military service before his full term had expired if there were justifying circumstances, such as, for instance, the development of a serious physical defect.

illustrations and allusions involving the soldier, with his equipment and experience.

Only two matters of detail concerning the army need detain us here.

1. It is well that we should consider its *composition.* The Roman army consisted of two classes of troops: the legions and the auxiliaries. The legions were recruited from Roman citizens, or provincials who were so thoroughly Romanized as to be practically eligible for citizenship. The auxiliaries were recruited entirely from the provinces, but when an auxiliary had served his full term of twenty-five years, and had received an honorable discharge, he was thereafter recognized as a Roman citizen. It was the custom not to use auxiliary troops in their native province, which was doubtless a precautionary measure in case of rebellion—such being, however, a very remote possibility through most of the Roman Empire. The auxiliaries were under the command of officers selected from the legionnaires. Each legion was composed of ten cohorts, and a cohort of six companies, or *centuries,* of one hundred men each. Thus a legion had approximately six thousand soldiers in it. The auxiliary troops were organized into regiments, differing considerably in number. Connected with each legion there was a small cavalry of one hundred twenty Roman horsemen. Cavalries of much larger number were recruited from the auxiliaries.

In addition to the regular legions and auxiliaries there were special units of varying size assigned to some special duty, such as the Imperial Guards and City Guards at Rome.

2. As to *support,* the salary of a private soldier was about forty dollars a year, which, in comparison with remuneration in other vocations of the time and considering other items of support which he received, was a reasonable wage. The food rationed out to the private soldiers was very plain and of small variety. We consider it true, however, that the Roman soldier was ade-

quately supported, though certainly what he received was never extravagant. He was subjected to harsh treatment and received little humane consideration until he was elevated to the position of an officer, if he might ever be so fortunate. Nevertheless, the romantic appeal of such a career, the extraordinary thrills which it held in prospect, and the high honor attaching to the position in the popular mind, made vast numbers enter upon the life of a soldier by voluntary choice.[8]

Rome and Religion

I. The National Religion

Rome recognized the value of religion, and fostered the worship of the national gods. The native religion of Rome was decidedly polytheistic. In fact, the tendency of the Romans was to take every quality of character and experience of life which could be abstractly conceived and deify it. This produced a great multitude of gods.

Rome recognized the value of religion, and fostered the state, to be promoted by state officials at public expense. However, the state worship was devoted primarily to the national deities. There were multitudes of divinities whose worship was confined to particular localities or trades or families. Practically every Roman family had its patrimonial deities, which were installed in a little shrine, and to which were offered food and garlands in return for their protection of the home. It was the gods of general interest, such as those that had to do with the weather, the harvest, or successes in battle, whose worship was promoted by the state.

There seems to have been no idea of individual relationship or contact with deity. The gods were worshiped only that they might be induced to bestow good fortune upon the nation or the home. Since the home was re-

[8]"Military service was the occupation most preferred by the people." Friedlaender, *Roman Life and Manners*, Vol. I, p. 191.

garded as primarily an instrument of the state, the fundamental religious incentive of the ancient Roman was patriotism. The gods were essentially gods of the state, and benefited the individual only as they bestowed favor upon the state, or upon the household as an element of the state. Hence religion was essentially a governmental concern, and the gods were but factors in the progress of the Empire.

Just prior to the dawn of the Christian Era, as a result of the influx of Greek culture and philosophy, and new religious influences, the popular interest in the old religion of Rome began to recede. When the native religion was seen to be declining, a diligent effort was made by the imperial government to restore its power over the imagination of the populace. Large sums out of the public treasury were spent in the promotion of the national worship. But this interest was purely utilitarian; in no sense moral or spiritual. There was not in the imperial circles any devotion to religion as such. In so far as the emperors believed in gods, their primary concern was to enlist the gods as allies of the Empire. This was a natural inference from the fundamental conception that religion was a national affair and the gods a national asset. Consequently, to the Roman, religion was but one of the servants of Rome. The supreme interest of the Roman Government was the progress and prosperity of the state, and religion was just one of the factors employed for that end. If any religion failed to serve that end, the emperor was indifferent toward it; for a religion to appear unfavorable to that end brought down the imperial wrath upon it, and was regarded as necessitating its extermination.

II. Policy Toward Foreign Religions

Rome was remarkably tolerant toward foreign religions, considering the state of enlightenment at that time. But the imperial policy toward religion was purely one of tolerance, and not of religious liberty. In his vigilance for the best interests of the state, the emperor guarded the developments in religion as he did every other phase of life. No religion could hope to attain large success and at the same time escape very long the notice of the government. "The State, in fact, claimed the right to decide what gods might be worshiped, and although it did not trouble itself about a man's private opinions, it prescribed the objects of public adoration, and from time to time insisted on due reverence being paid to them."[9] In execution of this policy, the religions of the Empire were placed under two classifications, known as *religio licita* (licensed worship) and *religio illicita* (unlicensed worship). A *religio licita* had the recognition and, if necessary, the protection of the government. On the other hand, the *religio illicita* was not granted state recognition or state protection. It must not be supposed, however, that such a religion was considered as illegal, or as outlawed by the state. It was not illegal, but "nonlegal": outside the province of Roman affairs. It might persist indefinitely, and its devotees might eagerly promote its worship, but so long as it gave no evidence of menacing in any way the unity or peace of the Empire, Roman officials made no effort to molest it. Christianity was a *religio illicita,* but at the beginning was regarded by Rome as merely a new development within Judaism, which was a *religio licita.* Hence through the early decades of its history Christianity escaped the notice of the Roman Government.[10] The earliest persecution, that by Nero in A.D. 64, was the personal whim of a capricious monarch rather than a settled imperial policy. But by the time of Domitian (81-96) Christianity had attained to such prominence and numerical strength that it was feared it would eventually imperil the integrity

[9]Foakes-Jackson, *History of the Christian Church to A.D. 461,* p. 45.

[10]Tertullian's reference (Apol. 5) to a proposal of Tiberius to the Senate that they recognize Christianity as among the *religiones licitae* cannot be accepted as authentic history.

and perpetuity of the Empire, so that what had been merely a non-legal religion came to be regarded as an outlaw religion.

III. Emperor Worship

While the old national religions of Greece and Rome had become entirely atrophied in the first century, there was a religious influence issuing from the imperial circles which made itself widely felt. This was the worship of the Roman emperor, promoted as a policy of political interest by the Roman Government. To decline to take part in this official worship of the emperor was to give evidence of disloyalty to the Empire, and might even, if stubbornly persisted in, be construed as treason. This fact made the worship of the emperor exceedingly embarrassing to the early Christians, and frequently the cause of severe persecution.

The basis of the appeal of emperor-worship differed in the West and in the East. In Rome itself, and so in the mind of the emperors, it was grounded in the old Roman idea of *genius*. The genius of a person, institution, or thing, was a representative guardian spirit which perpetuated the particular category to which its charge belonged. The genius of Roman imperial power presided over the destiny of each successive emperor. It was this imperial genius which elevated the emperor to the position of divinity.[11] Ordinarily the Roman emperor did not seriously regard himself as divine. "Doubtless Augustus, in giving sanction to the worship of his genius, had no thought of any deification of himself."[12] But in the East the case was different. The religious psychology of the Orient was quite susceptible to the appeal of a deified man. From the remote past kings had been regarded as divine beings, and looked upon with a reverence which is scarcely to be distinguished from worship.

[11]Cf. Friedlaender, *op. cit.*, Vol. III, pp. 114ff.

[12]Eakin, *Getting Acquainted with the New Testament*, p. 266.

Alexander had been looked upon as a god by his conquered peoples, and Pompey had made a similar impression. Thus the Asiatic mind had no difficulty in raising each individual emperor to the pedestal of deity, and the emperors did not hesitate to take advantage of this psychological trait. As a result Eastern Christianity had the most severe struggle with this form of opposition, particularly in Asia Minor.[13]

THE ROMAN EMPERORS

The design of this discussion makes us concerned here with only the character of the emperors in the first century, and their contact with the history of New Testament Christianity. We shall therefore mention them in chronological succession and note briefly their relation to the events of first century Christian history.

I. Augustus Cæsar (31 B.C. to A.D. 14)

After the establishment of the Republic, Augustus was the first Roman leader who succeeded in making secure for any length of time his place as ruler of the Roman people. Experience with their rulers in their early history had made the word king unbearably obnoxious to the Romans, so that they would not tolerate any intimation of an ambition for a crown on the part of any of their leaders. Even when Augustus did arrive at a secure position of supreme power, he was careful not to accept the odious title King, but insisted that he be known as "imperator," the Latin term which has been corrupted into our word emperor, and which denoted commander-in-chief of the military forces. We may observe by the date limits of his reign that Augustus was in the imperial office when our Lord was born in Bethlehem. His name is specifically mentioned in Luke 2: 1. It was he who

[13]Cf. Fowler, *Social Life at Rome*, pp. 319-352; Fisher, *Beginnings of Christianity*, pp. 74-139; Friedlaender, *Roman Life and Manners*, Vol. III, pp. 84-214; for a thorough discussion of emperor-worship, see Fowler, *Roman Ideas of Deity*, pp. 107-133.

appointed Herod as King of Judea. After the death of Herod, Augustus divided the Palestinian Kingdom between the three sons of Herod, though later he deposed and banished Archelaus, placing Judea in the hands of a procurator. Augustus was the greatest of the Roman emperors, and one of the greatest statesmen of all time. He secured in the Roman world the reign of peace, the renowned *Pax Romana,* and in a very significant sense prepared the way for the phenomenal spread of the Christian religion.

II. Tiberius (A.D. 14 to 37)

Tiberius gave promise in the beginning of his reign of becoming a ruler like unto his great predecessor, but after a few years he lapsed into a policy of cruelty and despotism. It was he who appointed Pontius Pilate as governor of Judea. The long administration of Pilate in Judea was due, not to his efficiency or popularity, but to a policy of Tiberius in dealing with his governors. He considered it better to permit a governor to retain a long term of office, on the ground that, under these circumstances, there would not be so great a temptation to plunder and rob his subjects in order to enrich himself during his brief tenure of office. Tiberius was to the time of his death the admiring patron and protector of Herod Antipas. Agrippa I incurred his displeasure and was banished by him at one time, and cast in prison in chains at another. Christianity had gained so little prominence during his reign that it is hardly possible it could have been noticed by him.

III. Caligula (A.D. 37 to 41)

This was one of the most cruel and profligate of the Roman emperors. He was a bigot and a despot. The Jews of Alexandria, suffering from an outbreak of the Gentile inhabitants against them, appealed to Caligula for redress, but received only insults in response. He took seriously the artificial ascription of deity to Roman emperors, and conceived a fanatical notion that he was in sober reality a god in human form, and determined to secure worship for himself throughout his realms. Emperor worship had begun with Augustus, but had never been promoted by any such extreme measures and fanatical demands as those adopted by Caligula, and never before nor after with such insane egotism. The pagan inhabitants of Jamnia in Judea built an altar and instituted, on Judean soil, the worship of the emperor. The Jews protested, and in reply to the protest Caligula ordered his image to be placed in the Temple at Jerusalem, and could be dissuaded from the rash act of sacrilege only by the importunate intercessions of Agrippa, who was in Rome at the time, and quite intimate with the emperor. It was Caligula who restored the fortunes of the long ill-fated Agrippa, and re-instated him in the imperial favor, granting him a kingdom. He banished Antipas, and added his realms to the domains of Agrippa. Caligula met death by assassination.

IV. Claudius (A.D. 41-54)

Claudius was a weakling in body and mind, but in spite of this his reign was one of prosperity, and in the earlier years one of peace. It embraced the greater part of Paul's missionary activities, and kept the world orderly while Paul preached to it. This was, of course, quite an unconscious contribution on the part of Claudius. He became the friend and patron of Agrippa I, conferring upon him the title of King, and granting him the control of most of the territory originally included in the domains of Antipas and Philip, as well as the former province of Judea. In the year 52, he became offended at the Jews of Rome, probably because of agitations among them over Christianity, and drove many of them from the city, among whom were Priscilla and Aquila.

V. Nero (A.D. 54 to 68)

This monarch holds the unenviable distinction of having been the most despotically cruel of all the Roman emperors. Prompted by motives of abject selfishness, he had a large portion of the city of Rome burned A.D. 64. So strong was the revulsion of popular feeling that Nero began to fear for his personal safety, and to turn suspicion away from himself he accused the Christians of the crime. A most cruel persecution broke out. "Nero lent his gardens for the purpose of exhibiting the tortures of the wretched victims, and at night he illuminated his grounds by the flames of the burning Christians."[14] This persecution was at first local, but later spread, in fitful outbreaks, to other parts of the Empire. It was during this persecution that Paul and Peter endured martyrdom. Nero was the emperor who first prosecuted the war for the suppression of the Jewish revolt in Palestine. He came to a tragic end. So unpopular did he become that he was condemned by the Roman Senate, and he knew their verdict could stand, for they had with them almost the unanimous sympathy of the people. In his disappointment and chagrin Nero took his own life.

VI. Galba, Otho, and Vitellius (A.D. 68 to 69)

After the death of Nero, confusion reigned in Rome for the space of two years. Three generals of the Roman armies in rapid succession seized the throne, each having it wrested from him by his successor, and forfeiting his own life as the price of his ambition.

VII. Vespasian (A.D. 69 to 79)

Finally Vespasian, commander of Roman legions in Syria and Judea, was proclaimed emperor by his army, the strongest in the Empire at that time, and succeeded in establishing himself in the imperial office. He had

[14] **Foakes-Jackson: *op. cit.*, p. 50.**

been for some time engaged in war with the Jews, and, after coming to the throne, sent his son Titus to put down the rebellion. Titus captured and destroyed Jerusalem A.D. 70.

VIII. Titus (A.D. 79 to 81)

The reign of this emperor, the son of Vespasian referred to above, was short and peaceful, and without any further connection of importance with Christian history.

IX. Domitian (A.D. 81 to 96)

In Domitian we have a combination of administrative ability with tyrannical cruelty. The early years of his reign were fairly mild and peaceful, but his unpopularity increased and augmented his thirst for blood. In the beginning he paid little attention to the Christian movement, but in later years, especially the last two of his reign, he pushed the persecution of the Christians with unrelenting ferocity. Early tradition reports that during this period John the Apostle was exiled on the Isle of Patmos and wrote Revelation. It is possible that near the beginning of his reign (85-90) the Book of Hebrews was written. Just after the close of the reign of Domitian, the Apostle John died in Ephesus, bringing to a close the period which we denominate the Apostolic Age.

CHAPTER IX

GREEK CULTURE

As one proceeds with a review of the history of New Testament times he cannot fail to be impressed with the frequent recurrence of Hellenism as a factor in so many phases of first century life. In fact, there does not appear a feature of the Mediterranean world in this period which was not affected by Greek influence. Even Judaism, with its rigid exclusiveness and fanatical loyalty to its own ideals and culture, was not able to escape the permeating effects of Hellenism. It appears quite evident that one fails utterly to grasp the situation in which New Testament life originated unless he discerns the presence and force of Greek culture. It had shaped and was dominating the intellectual life of the day.

The entire first century world went to school to Hellas —and the world has not yet quit going to school to Hellas. The greatest single intellectual influence which has ever been exercised over the thought life of mankind was Greek culture. The world has found it best to worship with the Jew, to govern with the Roman, and to think with the Greek; a threefold heritage which was combined and perpetuated by the unparalleled spiritual vitality and breadth of a movement which issued from the mind and heart of the Galilean Teacher. The Jewish worship has without doubt been the supreme benefit, but it failed to prove effective until it was universalized and rationalized by the effects of Greek culture. When the old wine-skin of Jewish legalism proved insufficient, the new wine-skin of Greek thought offered a ready receptacle for the spiritual gospel of Christ.

Without the vital force of this Greek intellectuality it is difficult to conceive of Christianity winning its signal and lasting victory over the religious life of the ancient Mediterranean world. To one who contemplates in broad perspective the historical situation at the beginning of the Christian Era, it appears that Greek culture was just waiting to become the willing servant of the new religion.[1]

Language and Literature

In the creation and dissemination of Greek culture, the language and literature were naturally the most conspicuous instrumentality, though not the most effective, for this distinction must be accorded to the Greek mind itself, with its superior qualities and its unrivaled philosophy. The Greek language was one of the truly great developments of antiquity. Its known history stretches far into the past, being fairly clear as far back as a thousand years before the Christian Era. The epic poems ascribed to Homer originated certainly not later than 800 B.C. From this point the stream of Greek literature gradually widens into the flood-tide of the classical period, the products of which are represented in an abundance of writings which have survived to our time. But what we call "classical" Greek literature represents but one dialect of the language, the Attic Greek. Though Attic was the only dialect which produced literature of any consequence, and was the most highly developed in linguistic finish, yet there were several other dialects of Greek, contemporary with the Attic, which were of importance because of their effects upon the subsequent developments of the Greek tongue.

As the several Greek tribes, who in earliest times lived quite separate lives behind the natural barriers which surrounded them, came into closer relationships through trade, religion, war, and other causes, there began the inevitable process of amalgamation between the different dialects. This blending process reached its culmination in the period of the Alexandrian conquest. In the armies of Alexander, Greeks from various tribes were brought together in intimate contact, which caused them to seek a common means of communication by modify-

[1]Cf. Glover, *The World of the New Testament*, pp. 29ff.

ing and combining dialectical variations to form a common language. The basis of this common, or *Koiné*, language was the Attic dialect, the ancient literary language of the Greeks.

This Koiné language was planted by the armies of Alexander wherever they extended their conquests. In a few generations the entire eastern Mediterranan world was using Greek as the chief means of communication. When the Romans conquered the Greeks, they carried the Greek language back to the west with them, as a result of which Greek became the literary, and to a large extent the spoken, language of the entire Græco-Roman world of the first century. It was the current tongue of Egypt, had penetrated as far east as the Mesopotamian valley, still held supreme sway on its native heath of Asia Minor, and the Achæan peninsula, and prevailed in Italy —even in Rome itself. In Western Europe and North Africa, though Latin was still widely used, Greek had been introduced and was the language of the cultured classes.

This universal language was waiting as a ready instrument of the Christian message when it began its westward progress. And a marvelously effective instrument it was. Koiné Greek is without doubt the most richly and accurately expressive language which human history has known. Its possibilities of subtle distinction in the expression of thought are vast, and the writers of the New Testament were remarkably adept at using the finer capacities of the language. It is certainly no exaggeration to maintain that the Greek New Testament is the most richly expressive text in all literature, and this fact is in no small measure due to the character of the language in which it is written.

It is important, however, that we understand that the New Testament is not, strictly speaking, a literary product. That is, it was not written as literature, but as a practical means of securing on a single given occasion certain religious and moral objectives. It is clear to the competent Greek student that the text of our Greek Testament is not in the class with the pedantic efforts at classical exactness exhibited by the Hellenistic writers of the time. There is another group of writings, which for the past century or more have been rapidly coming to light, to which the New Testament belongs. These are the papyri, ostraca, and inscriptions.

The papyri are fragmentary texts, found chiefly in the dry sands of Egypt, where they have been preserved for centuries. They consist of a material roughly similar to our paper, called papyrus. This writing material received its name from the substance out of which it was manufactured, for it was made from the papyrus-plant, a reed which grew by the water's edge in warm climates. Thin strips were cut from the pith of the papyrus-plant, these strips placed side by side in a layer, another layer placed on them at right angles, the whole dampened with a preparation similar to glue, and pressed into a thin sheet. This was placed in the sun to dry, after which it was smoothed off on the side where the strips ran horizontally. The papyrus sheet was then ready for use. It was customary to write on only the side where the fibres were horizontal, but in cases of emergency or poverty the rough side also was used. If one wished to write a document of considerable length, he purchased a sufficient number of papyrus sheets, pasted them together at the edges, making a long strip, and wrote along this strip in narrow columns. When his document was complete he rolled it into a scroll. In this way probably the great majority of our New Testament books were written. Remains of these papyri, from the first and adjoining centuries, have been found in vast abundance. They consist of letters, receipts, contracts, legal documents, and so forth, just those forms or written material which reflect the common habits and common language of the people in their everyday lives. There is none of the deception of literary artificiality here; they open the door right into the living-room of Græco-Roman society.

For an understanding of the life and language of the New Testament they are of incalculable value.

The ostraca are fragments of broken jugs or earthenware—potsherds, they are also called—upon which brief written texts have been scratched with a pointed instrument. They contain letters, receipts, memoranda, and so forth. The ostraca were used by those too poor to buy papyrus, or who did not regard the matter to be written as of sufficient moment to justify the expense of papyrus.

The inscriptions are epitaphs on tombstones, notices posted for civil purposes, or permanent markers of some description. Their evidential value has been found of great importance in historical criticism, but for a detailed study of the life and language of the New Testament they are much inferior in value to the papyri and ostraca. In fact, the order in which we have treated these three classes of ancient texts is the order of their importance in New Testament interpretation. They are commonly referred to as the "non-literary sources" of New Testament study.

It would be a serious mistake to leave the impression that the classical literature of the time is without value in New Testament interpretation, for this is far from true. The great writers of classical literature have preserved for us information which is indispensable. There are the ancient historians, such as Polybius, Strabo, and Plutarch among the Greek writers, and Sallust, Livy, Tacitus, and Suetonius among the Latin writers, from whom we get the general political and social picture of first century life. They give us the larger outlines of the world in which Christianity originated. From them we learn the general progress of events in the history of which the New Testament is a part. Then there are the Latin poets and essayists, including such names as Plautus, Cicero, Virgil, Horace, Ovid, Pliny, and Juvenal, who provide us with valuable evidence bearing upon the details of social and personal life, though not so valuable as that derived from the non-literary sources, because not so spontaneous and unaffected. Sometimes the picture is purposely drawn by the writer, where he colors it to suit his design in writing. It is where the life of the times is incidentally reflected that their evidence is of most value. Though not all this literature is directly the product of Greek culture, it all springs from a soil in which Greek culture was the chief component.[2]

EDUCATION

Not until the dawn of the eighteenth century do we find a higher state of intellectual activity and enlightenment than that presented in the Græco-Roman world at the beginning of the Christian Era. As fine a type of scholarly research and investigation was carried on in the first century world as we know today, the chief difference being that their facilities were not nearly so numerous or effective as those at the command of modern scholarship. Surely we may safely say that the intellectual competency was as great and the effort as eager and diligent. The age produced several whom we may justly call scholars.

I. Educational Progress

Scholarly effort had attained some really remarkable achievements. The development of Greek culture along scientific lines was far more advanced than the modern student has usually realized. Three centuries prior to the New Testament period, science had found in Aristotle one of the greatest exponents its history has ever known. He had emphasized the inductive method in reasoning, which is the basal principle of modern science. The geological theories of Strabo excite the admiration of moderns, the histories written by Tacitus and Livy are highly valued sources of modern historical science, and the pedagogical methods of Quintillian are being

[2]We have not mentioned the philosophical writers here, because they are reserved for a later connection. Cf. Glover, *op. cit.*, pp. 108-113.

applied in twentieth century education. The mathematicians of Alexandria were making astronomical calculations which varied but little from the standard results of modern astronomy. They had calculated with remarkable precision the distance of the sun and moon from the earth, and had posited the theory that the earth is round. Men had already discovered the power of steam, though unable to invent means for using it. However, machinery and mechanical engineering had reached a remarkably high state of development. "Hero of Alexandria is said to have constructed during the Apostolic age the first hydraulic engine."[3] Surgery and medicine were remarkably well advanced for the times. The surgical instruments found in the excavation of Pompeii excite the admiration of even the modern surgeon. Diagnosis was crude and inaccurate, and sanitation all but unknown, but remedies for ordinary maladies were quite effectively used. There were various branches in the practice of medicine, with specialists in each. A seal belonging to the first century has been found bearing the name and title of an oculist. As a necessary auxiliary to the practice of medicine, the science of pharmacy had been rather well developed. Art, though already on the decline, still excelled anything known to subsequent ages. This statement applies to painting, sculpture, and architecture, but these were not the only fine arts known to the first century. Music was also a well-known and highly developed art. A large variety of musical instruments was used, and a system of musical notes had been devised.

From the viewpoint of the Romans, decidedly the most important lines of culture were literature and oratory. Schools for special training in these subjects were maintained. Writing was extensively carried on in all the more enlightened centers, and books in vast number were produced. Scribes who had been specially trained for the task devoted themselves to the reproduction of

[3]Cobern: *op. cit.*, p. 636.

manuscripts as a profession. The professional scribe was one of the most familiar figures in first century Græco-Roman life. There were book-sellers—publishers we might call them—who employed several scribes at a time, either slaves or hirelings, to copy manuscripts for the market. Any home of means and culture had its own library. Wide research was a familiar exercise—in fact, with some, a pleasant pastime. Alongside literary interest there was a prevalent interest in public discourse. This interest, however, was in many instances practical or commercial, for it was in the schools of oratory that preparation was given for the practice of law. In fact, it is probable that chief interest in such schools was on training as a lawyer. The practice of law was a fairly well-developed and extensively pursued profession in the first century Roman world, hence special preparation must have been offered somewhere, and nowhere more likely than in the schools of oratory.

II. Educational Processes

In the Græco-Roman world teaching was a popular, honorable, and fairly profitable profession. Academic achievement was awarded recognition through distinctive titles, such as "philosopher," "doctor," or "sophist." The education of the day was dominantly Greek. The literature of culture was Greek, the teachers were usually Greek, the method and material were Greek. Greek was the standard language in the educational systems of the day, though in some localities Latin also was used. The universities in which the Romans sought their higher education were all Greek. Cicero and Horace were trained in the University of Athens. There were also Greek universities located at Rhodes, Tarsus, Antioch, Alexandria, and Marseilles. Alexandria was the chief center of learning, having a library and museum in addition to the university. These universities taught a variety of subjects, doubtless the most popular of which was philosophy. But instruction was also given in rhetoric or oratory, which included law, mathematics (including astronomy), medicine, geography and botany. As has been observed above, in these lines of scholarship the first century was remarkably well advanced.

Of course it would be natural to expect that education would be begun as early as reasonable in childhood. Evidences from the papyri indicate that the education of children was regarded as of exceeding importance. Actual practice, of course, varied in every household, as it does in our own time, but the standard of the time demanded that the child should be properly taught. The extent and effectiveness of a child's education depended entirely upon the means and disposition of his parents. There was no provision made for education by the state. Hence there was a great deal of illiteracy, and not many had more than the bare rudiments of education. The children were taught by a slave or a private tutor in the home, where the financial status admitted of it, or were sent to the elementary schools which were conducted according to the demands of the locality and supported from fees paid by the parents, or, in rare instances, provided through the benevolence of a wealthy benefactor. Large numbers of children were gathered together in the schools, and a sufficient number of teachers employed for their instruction. Most of the teaching was done by men, though women teachers were not unknown. It is certain that in at least a few instances women attained to a relatively high degree of scholarship. However, higher education was regarded primarily as a privilege of the male sex.

The children of a particular home were usually accompanied to school by a slave or servant called the *pedagogos.* This servant also had general guardianship of the child's conduct until he came to maturity. Though, as noted above, higher education was all but entirely confined to men, this was not true of elementary education, for it is certain that girls as well as boys were sent to school. The curriculum of such schools generally consisted of three subjects, reading, writing, and arithmetic. Books were used, and written exercises required, though no doubt the bulk of the instruction was oral.

For a child to become very far advanced in education required that the parents possess considerable wealth, which was not true of many parents. But any diligent and intelligent child who did have parents of sufficient means could attain to a degree of culture approximating our high school education. And while it is true that there was a great deal of illiteracy, yet, considering the fact that there was no system of public education provided by the state, culture was remarkably prevalent. In the light of all the evidence, our conclusion must be that, in the Græco-Roman world, the first century was an age of enlightenment.

Philosophy

By reason of its very nature, Christianity is especially susceptible to the influence of philosophy. This has been true from its earliest stages of development, for it arose as a product of reflection, as an interpretation of certain facts of history and experience. It began historically in the life and teaching of Jesus of Nazareth. Developments in the lives of his followers during his ministry and subsequent to it caused them to make extraordinary claims for his Person and work. That is, in its very incipiency Christianity consisted of an interpretation of Christ and his relation to Christian experience. Interpretation is essentially a rational process, a function of reason. Therefore the Apostolic message made its original appeal to the intellect. It called for reflective contemplation. Whenever the gospel was preached it provoked thought and challenged comparison with the results of thought which had already been achieved. This fact brought the Christian message into immediate and intimate contact with the current philosophy of the Græco-Roman world. Contact at such a vital point could not but have the most far-reaching and profound effects. The relation of Apostolic Christianity to its historical environment presents no feature of greater significance than its contact with Greek philosophy. Therefore it is highly important that the New Testament student should secure a comprehensive view, in historical perspective, of the philosophical developments which created the intellectual life of the first century.

The dawn of Greek philosophy appeared at Miletus, a Greek city in Asia Minor, at approximately 600 B.C. Crude in its beginnings, it made marvelous progress in the next three hundred years, reaching its zenith in Plato and Aristotle, two of the greatest thinkers humanity has ever produced. The history of Greek philosophy was marked by three phases of development—physical, ethical, and theological. As Angus correctly observes, this is "the natural order of man's progress, taking first the outward look, then the inner, and then the upward; or nature, man, God."[4] These cannot properly be termed stages of development, even though they do appear successively in the order mentioned, but no clearly marked chronological divisions can be pointed out, for the three phases overlap as to time. In fact, the theological interest came almost as early as the ethical, and the two developed side by side for several centuries. The physical interest was never entirely lost, but was subordinated in the more advanced stages of development.

I. The Physical Aspect of Greek Philosophy

In its ultimate origin philosophy arises from that faculty of the human mind which we denominate *wonder*. Man looks out upon his environment, upon the tangible world about him, and begins to ponder and question. Or, more technically stated, consciousness

[4]*Environment of Early Christianity*, p. 174.

through the senses perceives its environment, and reason seeks to construct rational judgments. This effort to form an intelligible and intelligent interpretation of environment is philosophy. In its simplest and most primitive form it naturally contemplates the physical order, the universe of tangible reality. The first world which the human mind discerns is the material world. So it is only normal that philosophy in its beginnings should be naturalistic.

As the primitive Greek philosopher looked out upon his physical environment, that which most impressed him was the fact of variety and change which was perpetually manifest, while at the same time there was an evident order, suggesting a permanent law of direction for this variety and change. Hence Change and Permanence in the natural world were the earliest problems of ancient Greek philosophy. The initial philosophic effort was to discover the underlying principle of Permanence, or the elemental basis of control in the natural order. Thus philosophy in its incipiency started straight toward God, and it seems strange to us, who bask in the full light of revelation, that it was more than two hundred years in arriving at anything approximating a clear conception of him.

Thales, the pioneer of Greek philosophy, who was living at Miletus at about 600 B.C., thought he found the ultimate substance in water. Anaximander and Anaximenes were the pre-eminent followers of Thales. The former considered matter as ultimately originating from water and fire, while the latter maintained that the essential substance was air. To Heracleitus (536-475 B.C.), the basis of reality was fire. This was because Heracleitus was most deeply impressed with the fact of perpetual change, and fire is obviously the most radical and expeditious agent of change. As expressed in his own words, "All things are exchanged for fire, and fire for all things, as wares are exchanged for gold, and gold for wares."[5] He did not, however, regard change as a chaotic process, but as governed by an ultimate Law. Thus we may say that for Heracleitus fire was the *essence* of permanence and law the *principle* of permanence. Already the Greek mind in its earnest quest is faintly discerning that somehow the universe is to be accounted for by fundamental Reality.

As to its bearing upon the interests of the present investigation, the most important forward movement of this naturalistic group of philosophers was represented by Anaxagoras (500-428 B.C.), who proposed the hypothesis that Mind was the permanent and controlling principle of the natural order. It was but a short step from this conception to the idea of one supreme intelligence, producing and governing the material universe. Thus even in its contemplation of nature, Greek thought began to perceive the image of the true God, whose incarnate revelation it was one day to have an important part in interpreting to the world.

II. The Ethical Aspect of Greek Philosophy

The strictly ethical interest of philosophy first appears in Pythagoras (580-500 B.C.), the originator of Pythagoreanism, a system of philosophy which endured for many centuries, and was still making its influence felt at the dawn of the Christian Era. Pythagoras founded and promoted a fraternity of ascetics, who bound themselves by rigid rules to a life of temperance. The pervading spirit of indolence and indulgence which characterized the age caused the ethical emphasis, when finally it did dawn, to take an extreme form. To Pythagoras all life took on a moral and religious aspect. He was keenly sensitive to the ceaseless conflict between good and evil, and recognized the spiritual element in human nature and experience.

[5] In the quotations and summaries used in this discussion, the author acknowledges his large indebtedness to Rogers, *Student's History of Philosophy*, and Zeller, *Outlines of Greek Philosophy*.

In his explanation of the natural order, Pythagoras made number the fundamental reality, and consequently his physical philosophy was a mathematical system. Between this and his ethical philosophy it is difficult for our modern minds to detect the connection.

An entire chapter in the history of ethical philosophy belongs to the Sophists, who flourished in Greece in the fifth century B.C. The movement was practical and utilitarian rather than metaphysical, and had a detrimental effect upon Greek life. Its chief interest to us is in its pre-eminent product, which was represented in the person and teaching of Socrates (470-399 B.C.). Only in the sense that he was one of the philosophical teachers of the day can Socrates be called a Sophist. His ethical viewpoint and system, while it appropriated the best that was in Sophism, differed widely from the typical Sophists of his day. It is true, however, that he was influenced by them in the fundamental principle upon which he built his philosophy, that whatever is right is right in its own nature, and not merely because it has upon it the traditional sanctions of society. But he greatly refined this principle, and modified its application in actual practice. Socrates believed firmly in the validity of the individual conscience, and the reality of final truth and justice, and urged that men live in accordance with their inner sense of right and impressions of God's will, rather than in mechanical conformity with arbitrary laws. He differed from the Sophists in that he would not allow that expediency or policy should ever determine one's conduct. He died a martyr to this conviction. His career was a pathetic groping after the final truth about life and the soul. Socrates inaugurated a search for the supreme expression of Good, which reached its beatific goal under the radiance of Bethlehem's Star.

The philosophy of Socrates may be said to have presented two aspects: a theory of conduct and a conception of reality. These two aspects of his thought produced two lines of philosophical development which eventually came to be rather widely separated. The former found its most prominent representatives in the Cynics and Cyrenaics, with their successors, the Stoics and Epicureans, respectively;[6] the latter phase issued in the splendid philosophical systems of Plato and Aristotle. It is with the developments (or rather perversions) of Socrates' theory of conduct that we are concerned in our consideration of ethical philosophy.

Socrates had regarded happiness and virtue as in some way clearly related. Just what that relation was either was vague in his own thinking, or has been vaguely reported to us by his followers—most probably the latter. At any rate, there existed confusion as to whether Socrates meant to teach that virtue is happiness or happiness is virtue.[7] The Cynics took the former position, the Cyrenaics the latter.

The Cynics taught that the supreme good lies in pure and rational conduct, and the suppression of all human desires. Their most familiar representative was Diogenes, who renounced all social ties, professed regard for nobody, had his only habitat in a tub, and even discarded his drinking cup as an unnecessary encumbrance.

An advanced and more refined development of Cynicism appeared in Stoicism, which we regard as having originated with Zeno, a philosopher who lived 342 to 270 B.C. The Stoics urged endurance and self-restraint, but did not, like the Cynics, repudiate the conventions of society. Obligations to others were regarded by them as exceedingly sacred. In fact, to the Stoic duty was his god, and practically the only expression of deity

[6]In commenting on these schools, Gilbert Murray says with obvious truth, "These schools belong properly . . . to the history of religion" (*Five Stages of Greek Religion*, p. 17). This fact makes them of special interest to our study.

[7]The difference between these two views can be more distinctly stated in Greek than it can in English. Hence if Socrates discerned the distinction clearly he was able to state it quite specifically. To put it in Greek idiom, if he said, "The happiness is virtue," he made happiness the supreme good, but if he said, "The virtue is happiness," he made virtue the supreme good.

with which he was concerned. Stoicism was a philosophy of conduct, with but slight religious aim or incentive. To them man must be and could be his own savior. Epictetus, one of their chief representatives (born about 60 A.D.), declares as a divinely ordained principle, "if you wish good, get it from yourself" (*D.* 1: 29). And again, the same writer says, "You must exercise the will, and the thing is done . . . for from within comes ruin, and from within comes help" (*D.* 4: 9). "What do you want with prayers?" inquires Seneca, a contemporary of Paul, "make yourself happy" (*Ep.* 31: 5). Yet there was in the Stoic a sense of the moral incompetency of human nature, and of man's need of grace, for Seneca said, "No man is good without God. Can any one rise superior to fortune save with God's help?" (*Ep.* 41: 2). Seneca is here reaching eagerly toward a personal God and a gracious God. But to the typical Stoic salvation consisted in the attainment of absolute virtue, which was regarded as the highest possible state of human life. It was to be accomplished by the gradual suppression of all desires and the extermination of affection and emotion. It is distinctly manifest that the Christian movement could not contact such philosophy without both positive and negative reactions.

According to the view of the Cyrenaics, pleasure is the only real good, and hence the supreme concern of life is to secure from each passing moment the maximum of enjoyment, subordinating all else to this aim. This form of philosophy was advanced to a rational and æsthetic form of treatment by Epicurus (341-270 B.C.), who founded a philosophical system known as Epicureanism. He rejected moral law as such, and urged pleasure as the chief good; but the pleasure which he proposed was not so grossly sensual as that contemplated by the Cyrenaics, and virtue was approved as an important means to pleasure—but only a means, never an end. A temperate and virtuous life would be found in the main the most pleasant life to live.

Epicurus thus outlines his own position: "When we say that pleasure is the end, we do not mean the pleasures of the libertine and the pleasures of mere enjoyment, as some critics either ignorant or antagonistic or unfriendly suppose, but the absence of pain in the body and trouble in the mind. For it is not drinkings and revellings . . . nor tables loaded with dainties which beget the happy life, but sober reasoning to discover what must be sought and avoided, and why, and to banish the fancies that have most power over men's souls."[8]

We need, however, to distinguish between theoretical Epicureanism and practical Epicureanism—the speculative views of the high-minded philosopher and the actual conduct of his self-indulgent follower. As accepted and applied by the rank and file of its adherents, Epicureanism was employed as a philosophical sanction for the grossest forms of sensuality. In the first century world it was justly regarded as a synonym for moral corruption.[9]

Thus pagan Greek philosophy, guided only by the uncertain instincts of conscience and the flickering light of reason, groped its way toward a state of life where true happiness might be found. Life as the fulfilment of a moral ideal was clearly seen by the best and purest minds, but the incentive and means for the attainment of that ideal remained an unsolved problem. Greek thought, though having no revealed moral law, became a law unto itself (Cf. Rom. 2: 14), but was forced to await the advent of the One who was himself the perfect fulfilment of law and the supreme moral ideal, and who could provide the heart of man with a sufficient incentive to realize in his own experience the spiritual application of law.

[8]Wenley, *op. cit.*, p. 64.

[9]Cf. Fowler, *Social Life at Rome*, pp. 121ff.

III. The Theological Aspect of Greek Philosophy

As we have seen, religion was not originally a concern of Greek philosophy. The ancient gods of the national religion were taken for granted, and philosophy concerned itself with man and nature. But theology was an inevitable outcome of philosophical advancement, for when the Greek mind began to penetrate the nature of reality it could but discover that the phenomena of the universe exhibit the presence of spirit as well as matter. The recognition of mind and matter as the two fundamental elements of reality brought a primitive theology in by the side of the primitive science and ethics.

Faint gleams of a rational theology were breaking through the haze of Greek polytheistic conceptions even before the dawn of philosophy, for Zeller informs us that, "among the poets of the seventh and sixth centuries, the traces are perceptible of a gradual purification of the idea of God, for Zeus as the uniform representative and protector of the moral order of the world begins to come forward more prominently from among the multiplicity of gods."[10] The earliest distinct traces of theological development in Greek philosophy appear in Xenophanes (572-480 B.C.). His distinctive contribution to the history of Greek religious thought was his protest against the polytheism and anthropomorphism of ancient Greek religion. Evidence of this advancement may be seen in his statement, "There is one God, the greatest among gods and men, comparable to mortals neither in form nor thought." It is to be observed how the striking approach toward monotheism apparent in this statement is modified by the phrase, "greatest among gods and men." But the monotheistic direction of the conception is obvious. Another approach toward the idea of one God appears in Heracleitus, one of the early naturalistic philosophers. He discerned a principle of order in a universe of fluctuation and change,

[10] *Op. cit.*, p. 25.

and this unifying principle of permanence and order he said was Law. The identification of this basal Law with God was an easy step. However, he was more of a pantheist than a monotheist, as may be seen in his observation: "God is day and night, winter and summer, war and peace, hunger and satiety; but he takes various shapes just as fire, when it is mingled with different incenses is named according to the savor of each."

The next step, that of finding unity and intelligence in the directing principle of the universe, was taken by Empedocles, who declared: "Mind is the spell which governs earth and heaven." Anaxagoras held practically the same view. The evidence of order in nature impressed him, and he was unable to account for order independent of intelligence. Therefore Anaxagoras posited Reason, or Mind, as the fundamental reality, whereby all else originates and is directed. A supreme volitional Reason is but another name for God; hence Anaxagoras was practically a monotheist.

Greek theology now awaited only one step in its development—that of ascribing moral and spiritual personality to God. This step was taken by Socrates and Plato. Socrates believed that there were universal principles of truth and right, and that these principles found their ultimate embodiment and personal expression in God, Whom he regarded as supreme in conduct and character. To his Athenian persecutors he declared, "I must obey God rather than you." The remarkable advancement of this statement toward a true theistic conception may be appreciated by comparing it with that strikingly similar statement of the Apostle Peter, when, standing in the clear light of redemptive revelation, he told the Jewish Sanhedrin, "We must obey God rather than men" (Acts 5: 29).

A still further step in the direction of pure monotheism was taken by Plato (427-347 B.C.). He believed that fundamental reality consisted in certain "Ideas," or Essences, of which tangible material objects are but the outline or form. The supreme Essence of the universe is Good, and this supreme Good he identified with God. At this point his thinking became vague and not well defined, but we at least may be sure that to Plato this supreme Good, which is God, was the apex of all being and the goal of all endeavor.

About the second century before the Christian Era there began a blending of elements from both Greek and Oriental sources which produced an eclectic form of philosophy known as Gnosticism.[11] This philosophical system—if system it may be called—resulted from selecting and combining elements from every current school of thought, and presented a confusing variety of views. It found fruitful soil in the doctrinal developments of early Christianity, and produced there its most familiar and characteristic results. The reaction of its thought tendencies on early Christian theology generated the first great heresies.

Another highly important form of eclectic philosophy in the background of the New Testament was presented in the teachings of Philo, the great Alexandrian Jew. Though a Jew, Philo was an enthusiastic admirer of the philosophic thought of Hellenism. True to the eclectic method of his day, he sought to set forth the teachings of Moses and the traditions of Israel in the terms of Greek philosophy and Jewish religion, but with chief emphasis on the latter.[12] Religion constituted the basis of his philosophy. He was an intense mystic, and endowed with a marvelous degree of spiritual discernment. Often his religious conceptions approached remarkably near to Christian ideas. However, we must beware of fitting Philo into the categories of Christian theology, and defining his views by means of distinctly Christian terms, which in reality have in their content of meaning much which was never within the borders of Philo's thinking.

[11]Cf. Angus, *The Religious Quests of the Græco-Roman World*, pp. 379ff.

[12]Cf. Kennedy, *Philo's Contribution to Religion*, p. 31.

One of his most intimate contacts with Christian teaching was in his view of mediation. This he expressed with the Greek term *Logos,* rendered "word" (John 1: 1). He held thoroughly and tenaciously to the Jewish conception of the utter transcendence of God, and yet his mystical nature and ideas called for contact between man and God. To reconcile this conflict he devised the mediatorial function of the Logos. Thus his formulation of the Logos doctrine was not a mere convenient theory of philosophical speculation, but a necessity growing out of his own religious experience. It was an effort to secure logical harmony between his own intensely mystical nature, and his belief in the transcendence of God, a view inherited from both Judaism and Platonism. His heart hungered for fellowship with God, whom he believed it impossible for his sinful soul to reach, so he seized upon the idea of the Logos, already formed in the religio-philosophical mind of his day, and found in it a satisfactory means of assuring himself of peace and fellowship with God.[13] Just here lies the crux of Philo's religious experience and conceptions, and the chief means for an accurate understanding of him.

Another potent impact of Philo upon Christian thought was his eclectic method, his combining of elements from various philosophical systems. His philosophy was not an independent product of his own mind, but the flowering of processes which were in operation in many minds before and during his day. He is a typical representative of the eclectic tendency, for he sought to form a syncretism of elements selected from Greek philosophy, Oriental mysticism, and Jewish theology. In the realm of Greek philosophy his conceptions bear genetic relations to Platonism, Pythagoreanism, and Stoicism. The effects of Oriental mysticism and dualism reached him through the inclinations of his own Semitic mind and the Persian and Babylonian elements of the

[13]Cf. C. H. Moore in Foakes-Jackson and Lake, *Beginnings of Christianity,* Vol. I, p. 253.

Gnostic currents in philosophy of the first century. The Old Testament and current Jewish theology furnished the basis for his philosophical speculations.

The effects of this eclectic philosophy of Philo are doubtless in the background of much of New Testament life and literature. Especially do the later New Testament epistles reflect its influence.

This discussion may properly close with a brief survey of the philosophical situation in the first century, that the student may see the whole in single perspective. The dominant philosophical system of the day was Stoicism.[14] But the eclectic tendency had exercised a strong influence over Stoicism, so that in it were many elements from other systems. Especially in the Roman mind was the eclectic tendency pronounced, for the art of selection and blending was characteristic of Roman genius. Stoicism as a philosophical basis appealed to the Roman because of its emphasis upon duty and loyalty. But the most indulgent and passionate natures of the Græco-Roman world were adverse to the restraints of Stoicism, and turned to Epicureanism as a more liberal form of philosophy, and at the same time offering the consolation of a rational plan of life. The eastern Mediterranean mind found greatest satisfaction in Gnosticism, with Platonic transcendentalism and Oriental dualism infiltrated with other contributions from Greek and Jewish sources. Gnosticism was really a philosophical method rather than a philosophical system. It found a distinct and quite individualistic representative in Philo.

The confusion and uncertainty of these varying systems convinced many that there could be no final and dependable knowledge; therefore they resorted to Scepticism, the philosophy of probability, which had as its slogan, "What is truth?"

Such were the varying and conflicting currents of thought into which flowed that mighty stream of Chris-

[14]For a comprehensive and carefully inductive discussion of first century Stoicism the student cannot do better than refer to Glover, *The Conflict of Religions in the Early Roman Empire,* Chapter II.

tianity's message of Redemption, destined at first to utilize and gather into a common channel the best of that with which it mingled, and combat the erroneous; but ultimately to be poisoned by the tributaries from which it found itself unable to escape.

CHAPTER X

GRÆCO-ROMAN SOCIETY

Life in the Roman world of the first century presented most of those features typical of the general average of civilized society. Those who could afford it were providing themselves with the luxuries and amusements which the world of their day offered, and seeking by every possible method to enhance the interest and pleasure of living. The poor were struggling to provide the bare necessities of life, and meet the excessive burden of taxation. Men were seeking intervention or promotion through the influence of friends in order to improve their lot in life; they were worrying over financial perplexities; they were manufacturing pretexts of religion or business to excuse themselves for absence from home and evasion of family obligations; they were practicing graft in places of public trust, and imposing upon their subordinates; they were fawning in servile homage before those in high official positions, and preparing for such high officers most extravagant entertainment. Young men drifted away from home, and squandered their substance in riotous living; or, remaining at home, overwhelmed their parents with debt by extravagance. On the other hand, love and loyalty, benevolence and service found abundant expression in many beautiful lives. Parents nourished and cherished their children, who, in turn, honored and respected their parents. Neighbors offered sympathy and help to one another in times of distress; or, on the contrary, quarreled and purloined, even assaulting one another in physical violence, and appealed to officers of the law for redress.

Such is the vivid picture thrust before us by the papyri and ostraca. We see there men toiling diligently for an honest support, and providing as best they can for the necessities of those dependent upon them; or, sad to say, far more frequently we see them cringing under the dread hand of the law, as it menaces them in some evil which they thought securely concealed; having recourse to courts of the law to settle their disputes, or defrauding one another in defiance of the law; buying and selling goods with due caution against being cheated; and reproving agents and employees for failure to discharge their duties.

Of wickedness there was a shocking excess, especially in the upper stratum of society; and abject poverty prevailed on every side. But in the better class of the common people the simple practices and pastimes of ordinary life, as universally common to humanity, were in vogue. There were love of amusement, indulgence in curiosity, fondness for display, enthusiastic interest in competition, pursuit of popularity, and desire for social contact: elements of life which spring from normal instincts of human nature. Yet, though these facts were basal, there were characteristics of Græco-Roman society which gave it a distinctiveness of its own. Our purpose here is to examine carefully its separate elements, that we may discern those distinctive characteristics.

THE HOME

Domestic conditions in the Græco-Roman world were so varied that one finds it difficult to paint a single consistent picture. It is doubtless best simply to reproduce the various views which the sources afford just as they come to us, so that the impression upon the mind of the student may carry with it the wide range of differences which the life of the day actually presented. By way of interpretation we may call attention to some features which we regard as typical. The evidences used have been derived from both the literary and non-literary sources, but the latter have been relied upon as giving the more accurate representation of the real facts.

Life in the Roman Empire was predominantly urban. To the sparse and despised rural population the term *pagani* was applied, and became a word of so much abhorrence that the Christians of later generations adopted it as the designation for the heathen population in general—whence our word "pagan." The residents of towns and cities were the recognized populace of the Roman world, and the larger the city, the more important and influential its inhabitants. It is interesting to observe how Paul adapted himself to this fact of Græco-Roman life in his propagation of the gospel in the Mediterranean world. It also makes it obvious that the great system of Roman roads, so vital to the progress of first century Christianity, was the imperial method of threading together into one gigantic whole this widespread expanse of city life.[1]

I. The Material Comforts

It is logical to contemplate first the material structure in which the home was domiciled. The description cannot be exhaustive, but only suggestive, for plans of house building differed widely then as now. There were a few minor differences between the style of home architecture in the East, where the Greek type prevailed, and the West, which followed the Roman style. Such differences, however, must have been but slight, for there was reaction of the one type upon the other, and many characteristics were possessed in common by both. In this brief description our effort will be to furnish an adequate general impression, suggesting the points at which distinction should probably be made between the Greek and the Roman types.[2]

Houses in the towns were ordinarily built of brick and concrete, of course with wooden fixtures and finish-

[1]Cf. Fowler, *Rome*, pp. 212ff.

[2]The houses of the better classes in the towns and cities of the western Roman world may be judged by those unearthed in Pompeii. Excavations on the site of some of the Greek cities furnish us evidence of the typical house in the East.

ings. Frame houses, or huts, would be found among the poor in the suburbs and the rural districts. Stucco and sun-dried brick were widely used among the provincials, particularly in the East. Unlike the typical house in Palestine, the Græco-Roman house had no windows opening on the street or highway. Commonly, the large front entrance, composed of double doors, furnished the only access to the interior of a home. Rarely there might be one or more side entrances. The doors turned upon pivots, inserted in sockets in the lintel and threshold. Bolts, bars, and props were used in making them secure against intrusion.[3] Sometimes the front door was equipped with a knocker. Before the door there was a small vestibule, open at the front, in which callers might wait for admittance.

Just within the main entrance was a large central court, ornamented and furnished as beautifully as the family could afford, and lighted from above by an uncovered skylight. This central court, called the atrium, served as a reception room. Passing on beyond the central court, one came into the peristyle, another large, unroofed court, with rooms on either side. Among the Romans the rooms were usually comfortably large, but the tendency in the East was to build them small. To the rear of the peristyle would usually be found the "garden," or a space used as a dining-room. In the Greek home the front court was confined largely to the use of the men, while the women would occupy the rear court. When there was a second story it rarely covered the entire dimensions occupied by the lower floor, but was arranged only on those parts which furnished the most convenient foundation. In homes of the better type the roof consisted of tile of practically the same composition as that which moderns use. The houses of peasants were probably covered with thatch, though of course no such remains could survive the passing of centuries and furnish

[3]There comes to light an interesting instance in the second century where the doors were nailed up during the absence of a family. Cf. P. Teb. II, 332. But this was probably exceptional.

their own evidence to modern investigators. The finish and ornamentation of the house would depend upon the means of the proprietor.

Houses of the middle class might consist of only one inner court, with rooms surrounding; or, in some cases, of two or three small adjoining rooms. Among the more humble residents, especially in the East, there were many houses into which were built work-shops and stores.[4] Among the poorer classes in the rural districts one would find only rudely constructed huts or cabins of one to three rooms. Of course the country homes of the wealthy were more elaborate, and were built according to any plan which suited the fancy of the owner. In metropolitan centers might be found numbers of tenement buildings, where one not able to own or rent a separate house might rent a room, or, infrequently, two or more rooms.

In the larger cities buildings sometimes arose to five or six stories in height. In Rome the limit on building altitude was set at seventy feet. But tall buildings were undoubtedly rare, because of the lack of material for construction and of the requisite knowledge in foundation laying. The great majority of the houses were one or two stories, more often one.

The furniture in a Græco-Roman home was simple and scanty, as compared with the modern home. In kind, however, it was very similar to ours. There were the chairs, tables, beds, carpets, and curtains, such as are familiar to us, but not nearly so many in number. It appears that the couch was the staple article of furniture in the first century household. It was the facilities for preparing and serving food which differed most from that which we know. The practice was to recline at meals on couches, usually arranged on three sides of the table, one side being left open for serving. The cooking was done on an open hearth, or in an earthen or stone oven. Lighting was secured from oil lamps, consisting of terra-

[4]Cf. Tucker, *Life in Ancient Athens*, p. 89.

cotta or metal urns, usually oblong in shape, with exposed wicks; or in poorer homes, from wax or tallow candles. The evidence from the ruins of Pompeii is that plumbing and heating systems were quite well developed, baths and fountains were to be found in many of the better homes, and ornamental finishing of extraordinary beauty was provided. The walls were decorated with paintings of real artistic merit, and other decorative effects were used which are commended by the best artistic judgment of modern times. It is probable that Paul, in his extensive travels and wide acquaintance, was sometimes entertained in homes of surpassing beauty, though, doubtless because of his lack of æsthetic interest, he mentions no such experience.

In the average home of the common people the ordinary fare consisted of such food as bread, porridge, lentil soup, goat's milk cheese, vegetables of several varieties, fruits and olives, and bacon or sausage. Fish could usually be had in abundance and at small cost. As a beverage they used cheap wine diluted with water. The meals were served in dishes of coarse earthenware, with usually a silver salt-cellar, which was regarded as an important article in the home.[5]

II. Marriage

The first century Mediterranean world had an unfortunate attitude toward marriage, an attitude which jeopardized the most sacred interests of life. There prevailed a flippant, though perhaps considerably feigned, scorn of marriage and its resultant responsibilities. We are not able to accept at face value the statement that "married happiness and the virtues upon which it is based, were no more uncommon than with us."[6] We must recognize that the customs pertaining to marriage were far

[5]Cf. Friedlaender, *op. cit.*, Vol. II, pp. 146-173.

[6]Halliday, *The Pagan Background of Early Christianity*, p. 113.

from conducive to either domestic happiness or moral integrity, and quite naturally resulted in this sacred institution falling into disrepute and degeneration.

Marriage was regularly preceded by betrothal; but such an engagement was not the plighted troth of mutual love between a man and a maiden, but an arrangement between the parents of the young people, or between the girl's parents and the prospective husband. The betrothal was regarded as a serious obligation, but was never viewed by the Greek or Roman in so solemn a light as by the Jew. The marriage was supposed to be arranged by the parents of the contracting parties, though the consent of the latter was regarded as highly desirable, and was usually sought. But such a thing as spontaneous love and courtship were all but unknown—or at least were unknown as a necessary preparation for happy marriage. It is significant that the ancient Latin language had no terms for such prenuptial relations. The dominating considerations in betrothal and marriage were wealth, lineage, and social standing.

The average age of marriage was younger than that to which we are accustomed, especially in the case of the bride. Men were supposed to have attained maturity before assuming the responsibilities of wedlock, but the average age of the bride was about sixteen. It was nothing uncommon for a girl to wed at fourteen or fifteen, and was clearly not a shocking affair for her to marry as early as thirteen.

The bride was granted a dowry by her father or guardian. This dowry, however, was never committed absolutely into the possession of the husband. The wife's property remained in her possession, and could be disposed of as she chose.

As seems to have been the custom as far back as civilization extends, the bride was adorned in the most attractive attire which the means of those concerned would permit. A "bride adorned for her husband" (Rev. 21:

2) was a vivid picture to both Jewish and Gentile imagination. The groom likewise was attired in his best, and decorations were lavished upon the homes of both parties.

Even in the pagan world marriage had a religious as well as a civil and social significance. In the light of strictly Roman ideals it was primarily a service to the state, while in the Greek world it was the means of securing a legitimate progeny and the guarantee of a respectable burial. Every Greek desired sons who could lay him honorably to rest. Thus religion, society, and the state were interested in the union of male and female in the bonds of matrimony.

The chief ceremonies were at the home of the bride, consisting of solemn vows by the principals, a religious sacrifice or ritual, and a wedding feast. The vows taken were more in the form of a business contract than a religious ritual. The religious element of the occasion was in the form of sacrifices to patrimonial deities. The marriage procession to the home of the groom was an essential and important part of the proceeding. Music, torches, and hilarity marked the progress of the nuptial procession. Upon reaching the home of the bridegroom, the bride was inducted with due formality into his home by being lifted bodily across the threshold by her attendants. She immediately assumed her responsibility as director of his household affairs—that is, that was the theoretical requirement of custom, though likely applied in consideration of the age of the bride. In cases where the bride was a mere girl, as often happened, we must suppose that her husband's mother or some mature relative assumed actual direction of affairs until the wife attained to more mature years.

In a manner which conformed in general to the practices here described, the first century pagan home became an accomplished fact. Its close similarity to the customs of marriage among the Jews is manifest and natural. Probably the forms of marriage among the Hellenistic

Jews were practically identical with those described here, except for the religious aspect.[7]

III. The Family

The average family of the Græco-Roman world was not large. The birth-rate in the Empire had decreased to such an extent that it became a matter of imperial policy to offer special concessions to parents of three or more children, and it is probable that there was a tax on bachelors. The law regulating inheritance is said to have discriminated against bachelors and married men without children. Such laws, however, were probably not rigidly enforced. A comprehensive review of the domestic life of the first century, with all its features from various sources of evidence, convinces one that tragic abuse of these sacred relations was widely prevalent, and yet beneath the neglect and disregard was that deeper human impulse which sometimes asserted itself in tender and beautiful manifestation, awaiting the empowering touch of that inspiring and enlightening influence which should flow out to the Græco-Roman world from him who should reveal to mankind the deeper divine meaning of Home.

That the society of the day was sensitive to the obligation of the husband and father to love and support his family is evident, but it is equally evident that this ethical standard was lightly regarded in many individual cases. It was certainly not at all uncommon for a man to squander his wife's dowry and forsake his home, abandoning it to the horrors of abject poverty in an uncharitable world, while he sought additional opportunities of gain and indulgence in some large city, or fought his deserted wife's efforts at redress in the courts of the land. Nor was the man always the offending

[7]Cf. Fowler, *Social Life at Rome*, pp. 135ff.; Tucker, *Life in the Roman World of Nero and St. Paul*, pp. 289ff.; *Life in Ancient Athens*, pp. 158ff.; Friedlaender, *Roman Life and Manners*, Vol. I, pp. 232ff. The accounts given by these historians are based upon the literary sources, but an abundance of inferential evidence from the papyri confirms their description.

party, for the documentary remains reveal instances of the wife deserting the home and defrauding the husband.

On the other hand, the ancient records also present instances of touching parental and conjugal loyalty and affection. There was the doting father, who lavished his affection upon his son so excessively that the youth became unbearably spoiled, and manifested an attitude of swaggering impudence, and was consequently a problem to his father and the despair of his mother. But there was also the father who could speak to his son with a tone of authority and confidently warn him not to disobey. The records exhibit instances of genuine solicitude for the future welfare and moral rectitude of the child. Genuine conjugal affection is also revealed. In an inscription of the early second century, a husband refers to his companion as "his sweetest wife." She is commended for living with her family for thirty years in affectionate devotion to her husband and children. This is but one example from a number of similar epitaphs dating back to the times of primitive Christianity.[8] A husband whose wife has for some reason departed for a season, reports to her his great grief at her prolonged absence, and his loss of interest in the routine of life. Another husband who is away from home at work assures his wife that when his wages are received they shall be sent promptly to her. A devoted wife writes to her husband about the sleepless nights she is spending in her anxiety for him, and insisting that he protect himself in every way possible as he confronts some imminent danger.

The love of the child for home and loved ones finds unmistakable expression in the non-literary sources. Beautiful domestic sentiment is expressed in the letter of a daughter addressed "to her sweetest father," telling him that the reception of his letter conveying the information that he is well and safe has made her "very glad." A young man who is absent from home as a soldier writes

[8]Deissmann, *Light from the Ancient East*, p. 315.

in affectionate terms to his father, also expressing loving interest in other members of the household. Many years later the same soldier writes to a sister who still lives, exhibiting a beautiful tenderness of attitude toward the old home circle, and an admirable domestic situation in his own home. Then another interesting, if pathetic, angle of human life appears when a prodigal son, who has left his mother as the result of an unfortunate estrangement, finally becomes penitent, and writes to his mother for forgiveness, telling her of his tragic plight of poverty and privation. Quite different is another son's letter, of approximately the same period, expressing abounding appreciation and affection for his mother, reproaching his brother for neglect of her, and insistently though tactfully urging him to greater filial devotion. However, the same letter discloses a reckless disregard of maternal love and authority on the part of other sons in the same home.[9] In another situation an ungrateful son refuses to come home, or even to write, leaving his old father to take care of the work of his farm alone, and his mother to grieve in despair. In the ideals of the time there was a high sense of the sacred significance of motherhood, but this ideal was all too often ignored.

In general, the position of woman in the Græco-Roman world was relatively low. This was especially true among the Greeks and Orientals. We have already noted that in the Jewish home the wife and mother held a place of honor and respect. It is also true that in the Roman home she was accorded high consideration, though the relation between the Roman and his wife lacked that element of genuine affection and mutual sympathy which distinguished the Jewish home. But the typical Jewish or Roman home was exceptional in the world at large. The average man of the first century world looked upon his wife as little more than a necessary possession in life. She was expected to yield uncompromisingly to his will, to serve his pleasures, to stay

[9]Cf. Deissmann: *op. cit.*, pp. 179ff.

in the home and rear his children, while he moved about the circles of society with some "mistress" of physical and intellectual charms, whom he had chosen as his real companion. It has become clear, however, from evidences given above, that such was not the status of the wife in every home, though we may be sure that it is correctly presented as the average. But it is refreshing to find the numerous exceptions, where tender devotion and constant faithfulness exist between husband and wife. This, however, is to be expected as the inevitable result of the normal impulses of human nature when rightly adjusted. In such homes Christianity must have found its most susceptible prospects. Divorce occurred with shocking frequency, but in divorce we find that the woman's rights were carefully safeguarded.

The child was very lightly regarded in the first century world. The infant was not considered as having any rights at all. Parents were allowed to destroy a new-born babe, or cast it out to die of exposure, or be picked up by a chance passer-by and brought up in slavery. The child was the chattel property of the father and might be sold by him into slavery. Nevertheless, it is extremely probable that the humane sensibilities of society and the natural impulses of parental love prevented any very prevalent exercise of such prerogatives. But that there were all too many instances of such unnatural treatment of children is beyond any possible question.[10] The authority of the father over the child theoretically continued after the child was grown and married, though in practical fact, especially in the case of the male child, this authority certainly ceased to be exercised in most cases after he was grown. Usually there was a "day appointed of the father" (Gal. 4: 2) when the son reached his majority and came into

[10]In Oxyrhynchus Papyrus 744 is this instruction from a husband to his wife: "If you bear a child, if it is a boy, let it live; if it is a girl, throw it away." In the same collection, No. 37, we find this item in a court record: "Pesouris, my client, . . . picked up from the gutter a boy foundling." The picture behind these papyrus fragments is only too terribly obvious.

independent possession and control of his own affairs. This would normally be around twenty to twenty-one years of age, though in exceptional cases it might be younger. This policy of unlimited parental control was likely the residue of a primitive patriarchal system among the ancient Romans. When left to anything like its normal freedom of development, the life of the child was just such as has been typical of all children as far back as history knows the human race.

Economic Conditions

The Græco-Roman world of the first century was slowly recovering from a state of serious economic depletion.[11] Most of the countries embraced by the Empire had for generations been suffering from frequently recurring wars of conquest or rebellion. Armies had overrun them and lived off their meager resources. Then there had been exacted of them the inevitable booty of the victor. This process had left their material resources exhausted. The toll of life offered in hard-fought battles had diminished the man-power, leaving fewer who were able to labor at the tedious task of reconstruction. The returning soldiers, accustomed as they were to the thrills of military life and to governmental support, were ill-disposed toward the monotonous drudgery of earning a scant livelihood by poorly rewarded labor.[12]

Employment was scarce and slave labor plentiful, which meant long hours and small returns for the free workman. This offered scant inducement for aggressive effort, and fatally obstructed economic progress. Much idleness was forced upon the people, and, be it confessed, was not unwelcome, for the Greek or Roman, unlike his Jewish contemporary, placed no premium on honest toil.

[11]A splendid brief discussion of economic conditions in Asia Minor is given by Samuel Dickey, "Some Economic and Social Conditions of Asia Minor Affecting the Expansion of Christianity," in Case, *Studies in Early Christianity*.

[12]The social and economic effects of the wars, especially the civil strife, upon the Roman public is presented in considerable detail by Rostovtzeff, *Social and Economic History of the Roman Empire*, Chapter I.

He regarded it as a thing to be avoided as far as possible. To do work of any kind placed one on a very low plane socially. Conversely, idleness was a badge of aristocracy. Many who had no wealth of their own contrived ways to secure the patronage and support of those who were possessed of large means. Luxury and idleness marked the pinnacle of social achievement; to toil for one's material support was regarded as a very unfortunate lot in life.

As a result of these conditions, the rich grew richer and the poor became poorer. The wealthy capitalists organized into syndicates, comparable to our modern trusts, and gorged themselves with riches, while the poor had scarcely the means of bare physical support. Of course this represents conditions in general. In spite of these difficulties there were many who struggled on and attained to some measure of economic success, even though they had but little capital to operate on. These, however, were unquestionably exceptions. But it is also true that the Roman world was slowly moving toward a better material status, due to the reign of peace ushered in by Augustus, and a fairly complete economic system was in operation.

I. Commerce

Commercial enterprise was almost as extensively pursued in the Græco-Roman world of the first century as in our own modern world. Buying and selling were carried on in practically every commodity incident to human life. Roman coinage was the standard medium of exchange. Shops lined the streets of every town and city. Products of the soil were everywhere on the market. Agriculture was extensively pursued, the land being sometimes owned by the one cultivating it, sometimes rented or leased. The rental was paid in either money or kind. Stock-raising for commercial purposes was dealt in to a considerable extent. The fuller, the miller, the baker, the smith, the wine-seller, all appear in the commercial life of the time. Syndicates offered commodities in wholesale quantities, and retailers dispersed them to consumers, often using rented quarters for their business. The principle of agency was a familiar commonplace, and was applied in a variety of ways. Systems of accounting and commercial records were employed,[13] and a careful check was kept of property committed to the hands of an agent.

The transfer of land from one party to another, either in rental or sale, was certified and recorded in writing. Personal property could also be registered as a matter of permanent record, with legal protection of property rights. From evidence of the papyri it appears that transactions of every kind were made matters of record. There were special officials whose duty it was to receive and preserve such records.

Lending of money was a commonplace and widely prevalent enterprise. Small loans were made on property held in pawn, large loans were made from private capital, and much money lending was done through banks, comparable to those of modern times. The evidence of the documentary sources is that the banking business was well advanced. Not only money lending, but the refunding of loans, purchases, payments of leases or rentals, of dowries, taxes, and other financial transactions, were made through the banks. "The bronze bust of Cæcilius Jucundus, the banker of Pompeii, whose receipts and legal documents, carefully signed by nine witnesses, have come down to us from A.D. 15, A.D. 27, A.D. 52-62, shows a typical capitalist's face and would not look out of place in the office of any modern captain of industry."[14] Of course, as in our day, banking was necessarily promoted by members of the aristocratic class. Many Roman knights supported themselves in

[13]Cf. P. Teb. II, 401-406. These are fragments of commercial accounts recorded in the first, second, and third centuries. They appear quite clumsy as compared with present-day systems of bookkeeping, but at least they reveal care in recording business transactions. The general practice of giving receipts is abundantly attested by payri and ostraca.

[14]Cobern, *New Archeological Discoveries*, p. 377.

this way. Those able to promote a banking business usually reaped large returns, lending money at a high rate of interest and well secured by notes and mortgages. These mortgages, or deeds of trust, were very specific and rigid in their terms, and usually required a full description of the property mortgaged, so that there might be no fraud as to identification. Notes and mortgages were negotiable, for there are extant records of instances where they were transferred from one individual to another. Such securities were protected by law, and collection could be effected by legal processes. Failure to meet the terms of a loan or provide the stipulated security was punishable by forfeit of property or imprisonment.

The Roman government sought to regulate the interest charged on loans, but with little success. The standard rate was supposed to be about eight per cent, but was sometimes lower, or far more often higher. Twelve per cent was a common charge for the use of money. Provisions were made for checking accounts and for savings deposits bearing interest. In some banks a service charge was made on deposits.

The traveler who did not care to bear the inconvenience and risk of a large sum of money on his person could secure letters of credit or certificates of exchange.

Thus it may be seen that banking in the first century was developed to a degree of efficiency approximating that of modern times. It is to be observed, however, that the banking system was not sufficiently developed to take care of the enormous wealth which had poured into the purses of the wealthy Romans, a condition which left a great deal of surplus capital to be spent in luxuries and corrupt indulgence.

II. Labor

When we come to consider the question of labor in the first century, we meet with both the slave and the wage-earner. Menial tasks about home or business were performed almost exclusively by slave labor, where one was able to afford slaves. The poorer classes, who could not keep slaves, performed the servile labor for themselves. Nearly all the paid labor was engaged in agriculture or the trades, though the wide use of slave labor in these capacities reduced wages to the minimum, and made living exceedingly difficult for the free workman. The average wage-earner received from thirty to forty cents a day, which, at prices paid for food, would purchase not more than one moderate meal for a family of five. This made living conditions among the laboring classes exceedingly stressful, and resulted in the wide prevalence of extreme poverty. Economic destitution was a familiar fact confronting the early Christian missionaries, which called for organized provision for the poor on the part of the churches. However, many private enterprises were carried on in which the proprietor did his own work and lived off the products of his own toil, or employed help from the cheap labor which was always at hand. In such situations living conditions were far more satisfactory than for the wage-earner.

Those who worked at a common trade frequently organized themselves into trade-guilds, comparable to our modern labor unions. Thus there were guilds of bakers, of smiths, of fullers, and of practically every trade known to the period. The Roman genius for co-operation and organization facilitated and accelerated the development of trade-guilds, as well as the organization of capital.[15] It is probable that there was a tent-makers' guild, and it may be reasonably assumed that Paul was a member of it. Of course the purpose of the guild was the co-operative promotion of the trade, and the mutual benefit of the member. Religion likewise played a part, for most guilds had a special patron deity; for example, Vesta was goddess of the bakers and Minerva of the fullers. Some effort was undoubtedly made

[15]Abbott, *The Common People of Ancient Rome*, p. 208.

to secure fair returns for labor, but this was not a recognized purpose of the trade-guild. Such an effort as a strike would have been necessarily futile, because of the ever-present competition of slave labor. The evidence of inscriptions shows that they took a considerable share in local politics. One distinct advantage was that a member might find favor from another of his guild when traveling, or seeking employment in a new place. Again, a convenience Paul might have enjoyed suggests itself to our minds. Mutual aid to members in poverty or distress was a quite natural feature of the guild system. Death-benefits were provided for in the case of widows and orphans and the burial of the members.

In preparation for a trade, one was expected to serve for a season as an apprentice. The terms of such an apprenticeship are fully described in several extant papyrus documents.[16] First the parties entering the contract were given full descriptive identification, as was the custom in all business or legal proceedings of the time. If the apprentice was a minor, the father or guardian assumed responsibility for him in the contract. The period of apprenticeship in the contract before us (P. Oxy. 275) is one year, but we may infer from other evidences that it varied. During this period the apprentice was to be entirely subject to the orders of his employer. In some instances the apprentice or his sponsor assumed his support, while the employer paid a small stipend for his services; at other times the employer agreed to assume support of the apprentice, and pay wages in addition. The apprentice was bound by the contract to his employer for the full period agreed on, and penalties were imposed upon either party for violation of the contract. Of course we are not to regard these papyrus texts as furnishing exhaustive evidence of all

[16] P. Oxy. 275, 322, 725; P. Grenf. II, 59; B.G.U. 1021; P. Flor. 44; P. Teb. II, 384, 385.

features and forms of practice, but they may certainly be accepted as representative.[17]

There were in the first century Roman world several of what we now know as the higher or liberal professions: artists, physicians, surgeons, attorneys, teachers, professional scribes, and so forth. Though not having the social standing that such occupations hold in our world, yet it is probable that, outside Rome where aristocratic exclusiveness debarred them from higher society, these professions were highly respected—in proportion, of course, to the degree of individual merit. As far as facilities within their knowledge or reach would allow, these professions attained in many instances to a high degree of proficiency.

Medical science, though crude as compared with modern achievements, had nevertheless made advancement which commands our respect.[18] In Ephesus there were at one time ten public physicians supported by the city. In the fourth century there were public physicians in Oxyrhynchus, and the custom, apparently so well established at that time, must have originated much earlier.[19] There were drug stores to dispense medicine, the

[17]Practically all the trades of the day were represented among the members of the Christian churches. This is one item of the much valuable information which comes to us from the Catacombs, a vast labyrinth of subterranean corridors built by the early Christians under the city of Rome, to be used primarily for burial purposes, but also to some extent serving as places of refuge from persecution.

[18]Among the extant papyri we find physicians' prescriptions (e.g., P. Teb. II, 273), and an interesting medical fragment deals with the methods of handling a particular disease, treating of its symptoms and offering advice relative to an apparent complication: "If during the paroxysms the patient is also attacked by severe and unbearable thirst, not because of the malignity or complication of the diseases but owing to some peculiarity of the affection, this must of necessity be taken as a mischance and relieved even if such a treatment is not required by the stage of the illness. Such will be judged to be the case if the increase of thirst is out of proportion to the height of the fever" (P. Teb. II, 272). This fragment is quite evidently part of a considerable treatise on medicine. A very interesting group of prescriptions is given in P. Oxy. 234; e.g., "Pound some calices of pomegranates, drop on saffron water, and when it becomes discolored draw the liquid off. When required, dilute as much as the bulk of a pea with raisin water, warm, and drop in." There is extant a remarkably thorough medical treatise by Claudius Galen. Cf. Friedlaender, *op. cit.*, Vol. I, p. 170, also Goodspeed, *Chicago Literary Papyri*, pp. 28ff.

[19]Cf. P. Oxy. 51, 52.

good quality of which was guarded by the law.[20] In the ruins of Pompeii there were discovered evidences of the effective practice of surgery. In an excavated tomb there has been found a pair of forceps, undoubtedly buried with a dentist.

We have seen how the practice of law was provided for by a definite course of training. It was an honorable and popular profession. In general it may be said that all the existing professions had attained to a worthy degree of proficiency. The extreme probability is that "Luke, the beloved physician" (Col. 4: 14) was a highly cultured and well-trained individual. This probability stands independent of the tradition relative to the authorship of the third Gospel and Acts.

III. Travel

The first century was an exceedingly restless age. People of all classes traveled much, in spite of the fact that there was much inconvenience from lack of facilities and considerable danger from outlaws. However, in provisions for travel the first century was considerably beyond many subsequent centuries. "Facilities of communication were more abundant than at any time prior to the invention of steam and the era of railway construction."[21]

The civilized world was threaded in every direction by the Roman roads, which were relatively straight, frequently paved, and well kept. Many travelers walked, while some rode on horse or mule. The wealthy rode in carriages or were borne by slaves on a litter. There were horse-drawn vehicles, carriages, and carts, let out

[20] An interesting papyrus fragment contains an order for drugs, with an emphatic caution that they be not stale. See P. Brit. Mus. 356, 1st cent.

[21] Angus, *Env. of Early Christianity*, p. 13. A similar but more emphatic statement is made by Wenley (*op. cit.*, p. 128): "Till the invention of the locomotive and the marine engine, travel was never so rapid over long distances as it had been under the Cæsars. We hear of a high Roman official who was able to pass from southern Spain to Rome in a week; and, speaking more generally, we know that the feats accomplished by what might be termed the imperial post were little short of marvellous." Cf. Friedlaender, *op. cit.*, Vol. I, p. 268.

for rent. A common mode of conveyance was the two-wheeled cart.

In all the larger towns and cities there were inns, but the accomodations in these were usually meager and unpleasant. Many travelers obtained lodging in private dwellings, or carried with them tents or other provisions for taking care of their own lodging. The prevalent use of tents made the tent-making trade a lucrative occupation. One belonging to the same trade-guild, religious cult, or having any other personal relationship to any resident of the locality where he was stopping for a period, could nearly always find welcome more or less genuine in a private home. But "there is evidence that (as we should expect) they generally requited their hosts with some form of payment."[22] This was the prevailing manner in which the first Christian missionaries were provided for, though likely the entertainment was tendered them without cost (Cf. 2 John 10, 11; 3 John 5-8).

In some districts travel was seriously menaced by bandits, but organized efforts were made by the Roman Government to eradicate this danger wherever it existed; and, as the papyri bear testimony,[23] appeal could be made to the Roman officials for redress and relief from banditry. It is true, however, that in most of the territory under the control of the Roman Empire travel was relatively safe and convenient.

A great deal of travel was done by way of the Mediterranean Sea, for passage by water offered accomodations much superior to those which could be obtained by land. There was the inevitable risk of storms, and slight danger still from pirates, but of the latter the Roman Government had succeeded in almost entirely ridding the Mediterranean. Hundreds of ships, capable of carrying several hundred passengers each, were constantly plying the larger waters of the Mediterranean world,

[22]Haverfield, Peake's *Commentary on the Bible*, p. 615.

[23]P. Fay. 108; P. Teb. II, 332.

except through the winter season, when maritime navigation was considered impracticable. By this means of transportation the gospel of Christ frequently made its way into vast new fields of opportunity.[24]

This brief sketch of economic conditions should enable the student to visualize the ordinary man of the first century as he pursued the inevitable routine of supplying the temporal demands of life. It was into this busy, restless world that the messengers of the Cross went. They must of necessity submit themselves to this same temporal status in life. Those who made up the constituency of the first churches were partakers of these living conditions. For these reasons this briefly sketched economic picture will help greatly in a true conception of the life which lies in the background of the New Testament.

Social Life

We now pass out beyond the confines of home and business, and enter the circles of society where the people are mingling in social contacts. Again we are confronted with typical human life. The barriers of social distinction are found, the social instinct of human nature is manifest, the eager search for pleasure is in full sway, and common human experiences are being enacted.

I. Social Classes

Here there is the possibility of considerable difference in view between different authorities. Lines of distinction between social classes are never absolutely exact or unalterably rigid, except where there is an accepted caste system, and this was not true of Græco-Roman society. The nearest approach to caste was in the imperial and senatorial circles, or high official classes of the government, but even these mingled freely with the extremely rich, even if the latter had no high office in

[24]Cf. Tucker, *Life in the Roman World of Nero and St. Paul*, pp. 16ff.

the state. Thus there was an upper stratum of society consisting of aristocrats and plutocrats.

There are among the most competent authorities those who consider that first century Græco-Roman society had no middle class. This is because there was such a wide breach between the higher circles of official distinction and wealth and the common masses of the people. But there was that vast multitude of ordinary humanity, who pursued the average ways of life, sought to secure by honest toil a competent support for themselves and those dependent upon them, and conformed their conduct to the better instincts of human nature. It is this vast social class that we look upon when we read the papyri, and we see clearly there that they were not of a common level of social attainment, but present varying grades of culture and refinement.[25]

There were social standards arising from the economic organization of the time. Business relations divided society into two great classes: proprietors and hirelings. This distinction, of course, ran throughout the social life of the Mediterranean world, including the masses. No difference was recognized between the manual trades and the "higher professions," such as is common in the modern world. The proprietor operated his own enterprise; any one who received from him remuneration in return for services rendered, regardless of the nature of such services, was simply a hireling. The tentmaker from Tarsus, though to us he may be Paul the great Apostle, was to the upper stratum of Corinthian society but a laboring man, and therefore among his converts there were "not many wise after the flesh, not many mighty, not many noble" (1 Cor. 1: 26). This basis of social discrimination was without doubt to some extent a handicap to Paul in reaching the upper classes with his gospel. However, it is not to be supposed that no respect was accorded to superior native gifts or highly

[25]For a similar analysis of Roman society, see Fowler, *Social Life at Rome*, p. 26.

developed proficiency. There was a premium on ability then as now. Thus a Roman prisoner on a Roman ship, ordinarily despised and ignored as unworthy of notice, could be treated with cordial consideration and even heard in the offer of timely counsel for no other reason than that his own personal powers were obviously manifest (Acts 27: 3, 9-11).

Beneath the masses was another social class which we may call the rabble. This was that great horde of idlers, scattered throughout the empire, but congregating especially in the larger cities. They lived shiftless and grossly indulgent lives, depending for support upon charity, gambling, and theft. In Rome the emperors fed many thousands of them out of the public treasury, thus encouraging their indolence. The majority of this class were doubtless idle from choice, yet there were certainly many who were unable to secure employment. As a rule they lived in a wretched state of poverty. We cannot escape the conviction that the early Christian missionaries rescued many of them from their dismal plight, and that the apostolic churches had a large representation from this class in their membership (Cf. 1 Cor. 1: 26ff.). As is always true of such people, they were easily excitable, and therefore could be readily incited against the missionary efforts of Paul in Thessalonica when the Jews "took unto themselves certain lewd fellows of the baser sort, and gathered a company, and set all the city on an uproar" (Acts 17: 5).

Below the rabble in popular esteem, but far above them in average character and culture, were the slaves. Of these there were many hundreds of thousands. Their social standing was *nil*, and their influence upon society indirect, yet they had an effect upon Græco-Roman society which their contemporaries little realized.

II. Social Intercourse

The instinctive human fondness for social contact was, of course, found in first century life. Ties of friendship were often warm and genuine, and tender sympathy was manifested toward friends in trial or sorrow. People mingled with one another in the common relationships of life. Dinner parties and social entertainments were given, to which guests were formally invited by written invitation, and visits paid between homes, just as in modern society. There were places of social resort, such as public baths, colonnades of the great public buildings, open squares, shops, eating houses, taverns, and beaches. Loitering about public places was a pastime of the idle then as now. A familiar sight was a group of gossipers gathered about a shop or any other place of public patronage. The social impulse was strong, so that every opportunity for social contact was utilized.

As a natural concomitant of the highly developed social life, we find first century society interested in the matter of dress. Of course this matter was automatically regulated by the means in possession of the individual. The representative of the common people would be found ordinarily dressed simply in a tunic (Greek *chitoon*), a garment falling skirt-like from the shoulders to the knees and girt about the waist with a belt. On his feet he would wear coarse shoes or sandals, and on his head a conical cap. The more formal dress of the higher classes consisted usually of the same garments, though of finer texture, more elaborate head-dress, shoes of better material, and frequently short hose. Under-garments were worn in accordance with the demands of comfort. When the weather was cold a mantle or heavy cloak was worn, such as that which Paul requests Timothy to bring from Troas (2 Tim. 4: 13). Those who were traveling might wear a hat with a broad brim, though frequently they went without anything on the head. The distinctive garb of the Roman citizen, and allowed to none other, was the toga, a long blanket-like garment which was worn draped about the shoulders and body. The wearing of it was much more a matter of formal distinction than of comfort. Though

Paul was a Roman citizen, and as such had a perfect right to don this distinctive dress, it is highly improbable that he ever availed himself of the privilege. Instead, it is probable that as his more formal attire he wore a light mantle or *himation.* In imperial circles at Rome garments were trimmed in royal purple to denote high official rank.

A woman of reasonable means wore two principal garments. There was an under tunic, short and sleeveless, and bound high about the bust. The outer tunic, of linen or silken texture, was fastened above the shoulders with broaches, and encircled by a girdle just under the arms. It was equipped with sleeves and flounces, and extended to the feet. These garments were commonly white, but might be trimmed with colors. Sandals were worn in the home, but shoes out of doors. A mantle was thrown about the shoulders when the woman was out of doors. The arrangement of the hair varied according to vacillating styles, which were as unstable as are the modern styles of feminine attire. Hats were not worn by the women of the first century. Cosmetics and other artificial means for heightening physical charm were used lavishly. Jewelry, in form and use similar to that of our own time, was worn in accordance with the lady's means.[26]

III. Amusements

The society of the Græco-Roman world found many forms of diversion and pastime; some harmless, most of them demoralizing, and the more demoralizing the more popular. There were a number of Roman holidays, some such occasions covering a week at a time. Tucker places the total number at approximately one hundred days during a year.[27] These holidays were times of great merry-making, and frequently of riotous demonstrations. In Rome the government or individual officials

[26]Cf. Friedlaender, *op. cit.*, Vol. II, pp. 173-185.

[27]*Roman World of Nero and St. Paul,* p. 260.

spent large sums in promoting such celebrations. Favorite forms of public entertainment were the games and theatrical exhibitions, the latter generally very degrading in moral effects. But most popular of all were the chariot races and the bloody spectacles of the amphitheatre. These were to be found in most of the principal cities of the Empire, particularly where Roman influence was dominant. To the Jew and the Greek gladiatorial combats were unendurably repulsive, and were aggressively opposed by them wherever their influence had weight. It was to the utter horror and intense abhorrence of the native inhabitants that Herod established an amphitheatre just outside Jerusalem. In these gruesome spectacles there were exhibitions of bloodshed and cruelty too horrible to describe: men torn by wild beasts, slain or mangled by an opponent's deadly weapon, the arena literally soaked in human blood.

Strange to say, gladiatorial combats began as exhibitions in honor of the dead. But in the first century their original significance had been utterly lost sight of, and they were put on display in horrible excess and in unblushing gratification of a brutal delight in the thrill of witnessing agony and bloodshed. On some occasions as high as ten thousand combatants took part in the ghastly performance.[28] So profuse was the flow of blood that the sand in the arena had to be changed several times in the course of a single exhibition. The greater the amount of bloodshed the more popular was the performance. One of the highest achievements of the gospel was the abolition of this brutal pastime.

The standard view of enjoyment in first century society is probably reflected in the following inscription found upon a gaming table in Timgad: *Venari, lavare, ludere, ridere—hoc est vivere* (to hunt, to bathe, to gamble, to laugh—this is to live).[29] There were the pleasure resorts of the more respectable type, with their numerous lights

[28]Cf. Fisher, *Beginnings of Christianity*, p. 214.

[29]It appears that we have here a popular application of Epicurean philosophy.

and various devices for amusement. Then there were the haunts reeking with filth and iniquity, which served as a chosen rendezvous for the debauched and a resort of desperation for the destitue or the fugitive. To these base resorts there frequently came representatives of the higher grades of society, seeking the gross pleasures to be found there. This fact is sadly typical of human nature—in the first century and in all other centuries. In Pompeii "the barroom, . . . with marble counter and with glasses and decanters in place, was almost exactly like a modern barroom, even to the hot lunches offered with drinks."[30]

IV. At the Exit of Life

Before Christianity had come, to shed the glory of its redemptive interpretation about the grave, death was a dread ordeal, the expiration of all that was of known value to man, the uncertain passing into an uncertain domain beyond the gates of the tomb. Comfort and hope were sought in philosophy and religion, but only scant returns were obtained. Quite naturally ignorance and fear had surrounded death with superstition, and intensified its dread. The chief preparation for death was temporal and commercial. One exercised exceeding care to secure proper burial rites and interment, for not to be properly buried was a dishonor and calamity. Those wishing to bequeath their property to any individual or interest made wills, which were quite similar in form to those with which we are familiar in modern times, and which could be revoked at the will of the testator. To this practice the papyri bear abundant testimony.

When death had come the body was turned over to the professional undertaker, who provided all the accessories and attendants for the funeral. The corpse was borne to the place of interment upon a bier or, in cases of extreme poverty, in a rude box, preceded by

[30]Cobern: *op. cit.*, p. 377. Cf. Friedlaender, *op. cit.*, Vol. II, pp. 1-130.

mourners and, if the means of the family would allow, a band of musicians, and followed by a procession of relatives and friends. Among the wealthy Romans cremation was extensively practiced, but among the masses in the Empire burial took place in tombs or graves. Many monuments or other markers were used, bearing epitaphs which were usually expressive of great affection and honor, but sometimes were crudely incongruous.

Thus the Greek and Roman stumbled into the night at the end of life's brief journey, where remained the unbroken shadows of darkness until the appearing of that One "who hath abolished death, and hath brought life and immortality to light through the gospel" (2 Tim. 1: 10).

Morals

Conditions in the Roman Empire for the last two centuries before the Christian Era were far from conducive to the improvement of morals. Indeed the very opposite was true. The almost perpetual warfare by which Rome extended her conquests and settled internal disputes gave dominance to the spirit of militarism, which is always destructive of moral fiber. Economic and industrial life was greatly interfered with, which resulted in the prevalence of extreme poverty, with its attendant evils. A few people acquired wealth and oppressed the poor. The love of luxury and ease increased among the rich, and the recklessness of despair degraded the poor. Petty thefts were being constantly perpetrated, men defrauded one another in business transactions, and graft in public office was so common as to be a matter taken for granted.[31]

In their conquests the Roman legions took multitudes of prisoners, who were sold into slavery. Strabo reports that on the island of Delos, which had become a center

[31] A government inspector of the second century makes the following report: "On examining the accounts of the money revenue, I discovered that certain of the magistrates and imperial clerks had paid themselves salaries for a certain period on their own responsibility, in defiance rather than obedience to the proclamation." Cf. P. Oxy. 474. How remarkably modern this report sounds!

of slave trade, as many as ten thousand slaves were sometimes sold in one day.[32] Kidnapping and enslaving for debt, along with natural reproduction, added to the enormous number of slaves.[33] By these means the number of slaves became enormous, inevitably giving rise to much idleness on the part of their masters; and idleness is always productive of evil. A further result of slavery was the increased indulgence of lust and the production of a progeny without moral training or responsibility. The spirit of unrest which prevailed caused much moving about in the Empire, and destroyed the charms of quiet, domestic life. Family ties were entirely too lightly regarded. Thus the sanctity of the home and the marriage vow were not properly respected. Common-law mating was a prevalent, and apparently a legalized, practice. The evils of the stage and the amphitheatre agitated sensuality and lust for excitement.

Many of the rites of pagan worship were extremely coarse and sensual, thereby lending to immorality the sanction of religion. In the worship of Aphrodite at Corinth a thousand priestesses devoted themselves to prostitution in the name of religion. There has been found in Antioch of Pisidia remains of a "holy bed" which was "used for the mystic marriage ceremony between the god and his goddess—in which service, according to immemorial traditions, Anatolian ladies, even of the highest rank, were expected to take part."[34] A prominent feature of the worship of Artemis at Ephesus was the dedication to prostitution of a group of priestesses who came to the temple as chaste virgins. In Phrygia the worship of Cybele required of women in general that they sacrifice their virtue to the goddess, and if a husband should protest against his wife performing this service it was regarded as a grave offense, meriting the wrath of the goddess. Sexual vice was the

[32]*Geog.*, p. 668.

[33]Fowler, *Social Life at Rome*, pp. 206ff.

[34]Cobern: *op. cit.*, p. 585.

chief corruption of pagan worship, but not its only vice, for drunkenness and gluttony also abounded.

In general, philosophy offered a check upon vice, but, as observed above, Epicureanism furnished a cloak of philosophy for degraded conduct.

As a result of these various demoralizing tendencies the Græco-Roman world of the first century reeked with the most revolting forms of vice. In higher society, though morality was still nominally identified with respectability, yet there was a light-hearted spirit of tolerance toward vice, a willingness to condone human weakness and indulgence, based upon the prevalent conviction that such conduct is the inevitable result of normal human desires. Among the rabble, as in our "under-world," moral restraint was an unknown factor. The upper and nether strata of society being saturated with corruption, it was inevitable that much immorality should invade the middle classes as well. In the light of all the evidence we can but conclude that society of the first century was frightfully corrupt. Indulgence was taken for granted, license was condoned, and greed was the accepted rule of life. The birth-rate decreased, marriage became infrequent, and the home became the instrument or occasion of lust. Divorce was undoubtedly very prevalent, for, among the papyrus remains, one of the most abundant classes of documents is the divorce certificates, and their evidence is supported by the literary sources.

Sensual corruption abounded in its most degraded forms. In the ruins of Pompeii are, on the walls of what were recognized as respectable homes in the first century, pictures which are painted "engaged in such evil actions, with such devilish ingenuity of imagination, that ordinary visitors to the ruined city are not allowed to see them. When the present writer was taken, in 1913, through the new street which had just been discovered, he found that the walls of the houses fronting the street were covered with such abominable pictures that the excavator had covered them with sheets so that his working men might not be debauched by them."[35] In their original situation these pictures were scanned daily by the children growing up in a Græco-Roman home! The result of such constant and degrading influence could be nothing short of debauchery. Archæologists tell us that many of the scribblings on the walls and other surfaces in Rome and Pompeii are too obscene to appear in print. And there is no evident reason for considering these cities as exceptional; such conditions may be taken as typical of urban life in the first century. Paul's arraignment of the Græco-Roman world in Romans 1: 24-32 is a true representation of the real conditions as they existed in the great centers of population. When apostolic Christianity faced out toward the world of its day it was confronted with one of the darkest pictures ever presented in human history.

But our sketch of moral conditions in the Græco-Roman world is certainly incomplete if we fail to give notice to that brighter side of the picture, the presence of many factors which were operating for the betterment of human life, and many instances of genuine moral excellence. Corruption did not reign unopposed and without exception. Throughout first century paganism there were noble spirits who were raising the most forcible protest within their power against the abounding immorality. The voice of the sincere moralist was heard in opposition to practically every vice of the day. Philosophers and rulers joined in protest against cruelty to slaves. Seneca denounced the gladiatorial combats of the amphitheatre. Plutarch pleaded for more just and equitable principles governing marriage. Musonius interceded with society on behalf of the child, and eloquently portrayed the charms of a happy home. Ovid inveighed bitterly against the crime of murdering the unborn infant. Tacitus, Epictetus, Seneca, and many others heartily condemned the horrible practice of exposing infants.

[35]Cobern: *op. cit.*, p. 376.

Vice in every form found bitter antagonists among the better minds of the day.

Nor was the higher moral tone confined to leading thinkers and writers. Among the common people there were many instances of wholesome moral and domestic conditions. Here the picture is brightened by light from the papyri. It is exceedingly dark as we see it in the literature of the day—in the verdict of the essayist, the poet, or the philosopher, or as painted by the Christian apologists, or in the remains of an ancient Roman city; but the brighter side of the picture appears in the background of the non-literary witnesses of the age, the inscriptions, ostraca, and papyri. These reveal the moral life of the masses. In the formal literature we meet in the main the vices of the aristocracy, the profligacy of wealth, the indulgence of luxury and idleness; but "when we descend into the great masses and listen to them at their work, in the fields, in the workshop, on the Nile boat and the Roman cornships, in the army and at the money-changer's table,—he must be blind who cannot see that many were leading useful, hardworking, dependable lives, that family feeling and friendship bound poor people together and strengthened them, that the blessings of an old and comparatively established civilization were felt in the smallest villages, and, chiefly, that a deeply religious strain went through that entire world."[36]

However, it is undoubtedly true that even the better side of the picture of first century moral life is none too bright—it is not without its dark spots. Even in the papyri we find "only too abundant evidence to support the statements of the Roman satirists, for example, regarding the wickedness, the unblushing wickedness, of the times, and the gloom and misery with which it was accompanied."[37] Human nature then was as lustful and vicious as it is now, with far less restraint and inferior culture. It is certain that even the best life of the age

[36]Deissmann: *Light From the Ancient East,* p. 284.

[37]Milligan: *Here and There Among the Papyri,* p. 84.

had in it a considerable admixture of the current forms of indulgence and corruption. We should beware of permitting the discovery that the better features of Græco-Roman life have sometimes been overlooked, to create the equally mistaken impression, at the opposite extreme, that moral conditions were approaching the ideal. The important fact to recognize is that the first century knew how to live well, and did in some instances succeed in living well, but lacked the motivation for permanent moral excellence. The moral sense and ethical ideals of the age had reached a high state of development, even if practice did fall far below theory. Some of the reasons for this fact have appeared above in tracing the development of ethical philosophy. Then moral standards no doubt arose spontaneously from human conscience, under the influence of civilized conditions. Thus the noble ethical message of Christianity, though decidedly superior to its pagan counterpart, at least found a ready point of contact with the first century mind and conscience. The first Christian missionaries found, even among the Gentiles, a nucleus of characters who were highly susceptible to the ethical appeal of the gospel, and were already trained to a considerable extent in the art of moral living. Paul's ethical instructions were not utterly strange to readers but recently converted from paganism. But the very nature of those instructions is convincing evidence that Paul had a severe conflict with a state of extreme corruption in undertaking to establish and stabilize his converts in moral rectitude. Frequently he cautions his readers against such sins as theft, drunkenness, and lying. In writing to the Ephesian "saints" (1: 1) he exhorts them in 4: 28 to desist from stealing. The extended warning against unchastity in 1 Thessalonians 4: 3-7 strongly suggests that this bestial sin was invading the Christian congregation there. From 1 Corinthians 5: 1-8 we learn that a Christian church was ignoring the sin of a member who had violated his own step-mother. A close study of Paul's moral instructions compels the conclusion that his converts were in the main won from a wretchedly immoral state.

In the light of all the evidence, we would conclude that first century Græco-Roman life was generally and mainly bad, with much good interspersed here and there, and with a moral ideal considerably superior to moral conduct. The need of the age was a refinement of the moral ideal by association with the principle of unselfish love, and an impulse for its attainment. With what sublime adequacy the Christian message met this need!

CHAPTER XI

GRÆCO-ORIENTAL RELIGION

The religious condition of the Græco-Roman world at the dawn of the first century was characterized by two very pronounced features; namely, dissatisfaction with the old national religions, and the demand for a religion of practical moral and spiritual value to the individual. It is an age marked in a special way by the growth of individualism. Man was no longer merely a cog in the machinery of tribe or city or state, but a distinct entity within himself, with an independent significance and prerogative of his own. This development deeply affected the religious consciousness of the period, producing the two characteristics to which we have referred.

The religion of ancient Greece may be described as anthropomorphic polytheism. The Greek gods were but superior human beings, with the cravings and weaknesses of human nature, transcending the common plane of humanity only in power—never in character. The religious conceptions of the Greeks found their most elaborate, if not their highest, literary expression in the Homeric poems. Therefore, Homer is sometimes called the "Bible" of the ancient Greeks, though with doubtful appropriateness. The ancient Greek religion, like the Roman, was distinctively national, but was not so much a concern of the state as was the Roman religion. However, the Athenian state considered that it was its duty and prerogative to promote and safeguard the religion of the commonwealth. The Greek gods were far more personal and realistic than those of Rome, though the contact of Rome with Greek religion after the Romans conquered the Greeks brought a change in the Roman view of religion in the direction of a more personal worship of the gods. However, worship with the Greeks was nothing more than adulation of a national hero, and the gods were national rather than universal. Though the gods themselves were contemplated as persons, there was no general conception of personal relations of the worshiper with the gods.

Religious Decadence

The gods of Greece and Rome were unequal to the conditions which prevailed in the first century. In fact, for several previous centuries they had been declining in influence. The intellectual advance of the Greeks rendered them superior to the crude religious conceptions of Homer and his age, and as a result there came two developments. Those who were still inclined to cling to the primitive worship took refuge in the allegorical method in interpreting Homer, construing his myths as symbolic representations of philosophical conceptions. Those who were more coldly intellectual and speculative utterly abandoned faith in the primitive gods. This religious attitude spread with the advance of Greek culture. Then came the Roman legions, to break down all the barriers of race and nationality and throw the religions of the civilized world into one vast, confused, contending mass of rival deities. These developments inevitably ushered the Græco-Roman world into a serious religious crisis. As the cultural effects of Greek philosophy and the universalizing effects of Roman conquest pervaded the Mediterranean world the old religious conceptions and forms inevitably collapsed.

Since the pagan deities of the former age had been local, belonging to a single nation, city, or household, when people began to move from place to place they confronted a serious religious difficulty. If one left his native locality he thereby severed his connection with his national or family gods. It was difficult to become accustomed to the peculiarities and worship of the new god or gods in the locality to which he moved. On the other hand, as new neighbors moved in from other localities, bringing new gods with them, perhaps with more attractive qualities and inducements, one of a pronounced religious temperament felt inclined to take in the new gods alongside the old ones. As a result, the common people became confused as to the character and limits of the realms of deity, and credulously put their trust in all gods, but without intense devotion to any. This attitude of the masses is abundantly reflected in the papyri. Then as the effects of Greek culture increased its sway over the first century mind, the better intellects began to think and to question, and soon perceived the obvious fact that one who was really a god could not consistently be subject to local and racial limitations, or possess the character in which the gods were popularly conceived. Hence the more cultured minds lost faith in the gods which their fathers had worshiped. The old national and local religions were threatened with dissolution, but for obvious political reasons the Roman officials wished to keep alive the gods of Rome. Therefore, the state sought to perpetuate the old forms of the Roman religion, even when it was currently admitted that they were but empty forms.

Provincial Religions

There was one form of the ancient localized worship which still survived, and maintained itself with greater or less vigor and effectiveness. This is what we call the provincial religions. In certain districts, usually consisting of a city or group of cities with the adjacent territory, there was still to be found the worship of a local deity. Prior to the Roman conquest of Asia Minor the organization of many of these provincial religions had been identical with the civil administration, the officers of the law being at the same time the functionaries of the religion, but under Roman control the civil and religious government in most localities were separated. The civil government was reorganized, while the religious government was allowed to maintain itself along former lines. In Asia Minor these community religions were numerous.[1] In several cases they united with one another in politico-religious federations.

Of special interest to the New Testament student was the local religion of first century Ephesus, the worship of the Greek goddess Artemis; or, as she is known in Latin, Diana (Cf. Acts 19: 23ff.). This goddess had been known and worshiped throughout the Greek world, but her religion became specialized in Ephesus, where it was provided with elaborate equipment. The image of the goddess, which was believed to have fallen from heaven, was housed in a beautiful temple, and elevated upon a pedestal constructed from jewels and treasures contributed by her devotees. The temple was a vast edifice, so remarkable for its magnificence that it was reckoned among the seven wonders of the world. The worship was more elaborate than that of the Temple at Jerusalem, but consisted in some particulars of disgracefully lewd practices. In distinctively Greek mythology Artemis was the goddess of chastity, but through Oriental influence the Ephesian deity was regarded as representative of the productive forces of nature, and was probably a localized appropriation and adaptation of the Phrygian goddess of nature Cybele. The worship of Artemis held a large place in the public affairs of Ephesus. Officials of the city government were expected to enforce respect for this patron deity. This place of the ancient goddess in the life of the city was recognized and protected by Rome. One chief means in the propagation of the religion of Artemis was the manufacture and sale of small images of the goddess, which became, for those promoting it, a very lucrative trade. It was the curtailing of this enterprise which got Paul and his companions into trouble.

At the dawn of the Christian Era the city of Corinth was celebrated for the worship of Aphrodite, the Greek goddess of beauty and love. Her temple was located on the Acrocorinthus, the most prominent point in the

[1]For a full discussion cf. Foakes-Jackson and Lake, *Beginnings of Christianity*, Vol. I, pp. 199ff.

city, and a very elaborate ritual was performed in her honor. Aphrodite had been worshiped in other Greek cities, but her worship persisted longest in Corinth, and was characterized by many Oriental excesses which would not have been tolerated in the more conservative Greek communities. More than a thousand women were used as prostitutes in the ceremonies devoted to the goddess. The gross immorality of this religion doubtless aggravated the desperate corruption of Corinth in Paul's day.

The worship of Artemis in Ephesus and Aphrodite in Corinth, instances which are of special interest to the New Testament student, were conspicuous cases from among the localized forms of the ancient worship which still survived in the first century. But even these provincial religions were passing, for they were out of accord with the dominant religious demands of the age. They belonged to a stage of development which had been abandoned to the past, and were of necessity receding before the advance of a new world of thought and activity. Those which survived were in the nature of remnants rather than progressive developments.

Religious Longings

The old gods were gone—whither should the world turn for other gods? Some doubting souls gave up the quest in despair, and lapsed into a sort of passive atheism. Many adopted a pessimistic view of life, and resigned themselves to a dismal fatalism. Multitudes were wandering in the darkness, having no religion which they could consider as satisfactory or reliable. Gilbert Murray, adopting the suggestion of another, describes this religious destitution as a "failure of nerve." He considers that it resulted from the breaking up of the old beliefs and traditions, and a desperate grasping after a new religious hope.[2]

[2]Cf. *Five Stages of Greek Religion*, pp. 8, 9, 155ff.

Yet one is far from correct if he supposes that religious interest and activity had been stifled. Never was there in the world's history a situation in which the human heart cried out more insistently for religious satisfaction, sought more diligently for religious benefits, or engaged more heartily in religious privileges. To their gods they went with the everyday problems of life and their physical afflictions, and believed that by miraculous methods aid was rendered or cures effected. Intercessory prayer was offered for friends, and thanksgiving for the safety of relatives. Dreams were ascribed to the influence of the gods, and were believed to forecast coming events. The devout made pilgrimages to their favorite temples, where they offered rich gifts, doubtless often at great sacrifice, expecting from the god or goddess some kind of favor in return, usually a temporal or physical benefit. Oracles were consulted relative to the commonplace details of life.[3] Nor was the interest in religion confined to its application to this life. It turned with deep yearning to the other world. Men were grasping blindly at the hope of a peaceful future beyond the grave, longing for some one who could "bring life and immortality to light."

Hearts were sincerely burdened with a crushing sense of sin and spiritual deficiency, and yearned for an experience of fellowship with the one true God. The philosophic mind of the Græco-Roman world had caught an enthralling glimpse of the reality of the one God of all the earth, and hungered intensely for a greater knowledge of him. There was a prevailing demand for a word of certainty to answer the theoretical questionings of philosophical speculation, an authoritative revelation of the real truth about God.[4] The Word must become flesh and dwell among men, before the passionate longing of the first century heart could be satisfied. The world had grown weary of philosophical abstrac-

[3]For every religious reaction mentioned here there may be found clear testimony in the papyri.

[4]Angus, *op. cit.*, pp. 70f.

tions. The yearning was for a God who was sensitive to human need and suffering, to whom one could pray with the hope of being heard, and with whom he might enjoy personal communion. The spirit of the age cried out for a God who was a loving, sympathetic Redeemer. All the Mediterranean world was asking, "Sirs, what must we do to be saved?"

Many serious minds had devoted themselves to an effort to solve the religious problems of the age. Philosophy gave itself primarily to a ministry of religion.[5] "As a matter of fact, the whole tendency of Greek philosophy after Plato, with some illustrious exceptions, especially among the Romanizing Stoics, was away from the outer world toward the world of the soul. We find in the religious writing of this period that the real Saviour of men is not he who protects them against earthquakes and famine, but he who in some sense saves their souls."[6] For this problem of the soul's salvation many solutions were offered. It was no novel occurrence to find some earnest soul undertaking to tell the world of a plan of salvation. Various systems of religion and theories of life were being offered to the hungry hearts of the age.

Preaching became a familiar practice in the propagation of these religio-philosophical systems. It was particularly characteristic of the Stoics and Cynics. A common incident of the day was the sight of a Stoic or Cynic preacher, standing on a street corner or in an open square, preaching his message of moral philosophy to the wayfarer who might linger to hear him—and usually the audience was considerable in numbers and largely sympathetic. Much good was undoubtedly accomplished by these missionaries of philosophy. In important respects they were precursors of the missionaries of the Cross. They created a deeper interest in morality and a more intense craving for a sufficient

[5]"Die Philosophie des hellenistischen Zeitalters will dem Gebildeten Zugleich Religion sein." Wendland, *Die Hellenistisch-Roemische Kultur*, p. 106.

[6]Gilbert Murray, *op. cit.*, p. 194.

moral dynamic, and made preaching familiar and effective as a method for the propagation of doctrine. Angus significantly says of them, "they were voices crying in the wilderness of Paganism, preparing the way of the Lord."[7]

The Mystery Religions

To sum up the situation in a word, the old national and local deities no longer satisfied the religious necessities of the time, for there had come a prevalent craving for a spiritual, personal, universal religion. To some extent this demand was met by the Greek and Oriental mystery religions. These religions gathered about weird and wonderful legends of gods and goddesses, and usually the chief features of the legends were portrayed in symbolic rites. These rites, both as to their manner and significance, were largely kept secret, supposed to be known only by those devotees who had been initiated as full participants in the privileges of the cult. These secret doctrines and rites were called the "mysteries" of the religion. Whenever the peculiar rites of a given religion were observed in any part of the world, they were expected to secure for the participants the benefits of that religion and favor and fellowship of the deity. Usually the gods of these mystery religions were represented as concerned in the welfare of the individual votary, and as having the power to confer personal salvation. Thus these mystery cults met the demand for a universal and personal religion. In a real and significant manner they prepared the way for Christianity. They constitute one of the most important features of the New Testament world.

I. The Greek Mystery Religions

The Greeks had developed mystery religions, but with much borrowed material from Oriental sources.

1. A prominent instance is that known as the *Dionysian cult*. Dionysos was originally a nature god, adopted

[7]*Op. cit.*, p. 78.

by the Greeks from the Thracians. The vague legendary basis of the religion belonged to remote antiquity, and had doubtless undergone great modification in the course of its transition to the first century Greek world. Its ceremonies consisted of frenzied performances, eating the raw flesh of a bull or other sacrificial animal, and orgies too revolting to bear detailed description. The religious objectives of the cult were mystic union with the god and personal immortality. It was therefore individual in interest and application.[8]

2. Arising as a sort of reform movement in the Dionysian worship was the religion known as *Orphism.* It became a widely popular religion in the Græco-Roman world. Its basis was a legend about a priest named Orpheus who had been slaughtered by the frenzied devotees of Dionysos. It made a great moral improvement on the Dionysian worship, and a decided advance in doctrine, particularly in eschatology. Not only was immortality anticipated, but along with it judgment and eternal reward or retribution. Such views give striking evidence of the fundamental instincts of religion which are inherent in human nature, implanted there by the beneficent purposes of God.[9]

3. The most popular religion at Athens for six centuries before the Christian Era was the *Eleusinian* mysteries. In fact, it was adopted as the state religion of Athens. This religion originated as an agrarian cult, designed to secure the fertility of the soil and greater fruits in the harvest, a prevalent objective in primitive religion. The myth on which it was based is contained in the Homeric hymn to Demeter. This goddess Demeter appears to have been a modification and adaptation of the Corn-goddess of ancient Eleusis. According to the legend Persephone, daughter of Demeter, is carried away by Pluto and made queen of the Underworld. Demeter, goddess of the grain harvest, forsakes her agrarian func-

[8]Cf. Percy Gardner, Hastings' *Ency. of Rel. and Ethics,* art. "Mysteries."

[9]Kennedy, *St. Paul and the Mystery-Religions,* pp. 9-17.

tions and descends to the Underworld in pursuit of Persephone and her captor, in consequence of which the earth is left barren and famine prevails. Zeus interferes and orders that Persephone be returned to her mother eight months in the year. As a result the god-mother celebrates her daughter's return by granting the earth eight months of fruitfulness. The ceremonies of this mystery cult were quite elaborate, including first a fast, then sacrifices and the immersion of the initiates, followed by a pilgrimage from Athens to Eleusis, where the rites were completed. These ceremonies seem to have been originally a celebration of the harvest, but came later to be regarded as a means of securing immortality. It contained at least some moral emphasis, but this was not a prominent feature, and it is thought probable that some of the rites involved gross immorality.[10]

II. The Oriental Mystery Religions

The pagan religions of primary interest to the New Testament student are the Oriental mystery cults. This is because, in the first place, they were most closely associated with primitive Christianity, and, secondly, they exercised the greatest influence upon the environment into which Christianity advanced from its Palestinian home.

No other element of Orientalism permeated the Græco-Roman world quite so completely as did its religion. The imperial government frowned with disfavor upon the steady encroachments of eastern cults, but was unable to stem the advancing tide. By the dawn of the Christian Era the mystery religions were an accepted fact in the Roman world.[11] Cybele and Isis were unwittingly opening the door of the West to Jesus!

1. In Egypt was found the worship of *Isis* and *Osiris*. Osiris was a mythical king of Egypt, of divine lineage,

[10]Cf. Percy Gardner, *ibid.*

[11]Cf. Halliday, *Pagan Background of Early Christianity*, p. 235.

who lived in conjugal relations with his sister Isis, and co-operated with her in the promotion of agriculture and arts. Osiris incurred the jealousy of his brother, Typhon, who secured his death by strategy, and having cut his body into pieces scattered it throughout Egypt. The grief-stricken Isis set out in search of the dismembered corpse and finally succeeded in gathering it together and restoring it to life. Osiris became ruler of the Underworld, but was avenged against Typhon by his posthumous son Horus. The elaborate ceremonies of this religion represented the death and restoration of Osiris and purported to impart immortality to the worshiper. Beyond this the religion was without moral or theological significance. In the third century B.C. the Greek god Serapis became identified with Osiris, and the worship of Serapis and Isis was thereby instituted, but with only slight modifications of the original religion. From both literary and non-literary sources we learn that the worship of Serapis was a very popular religion in Egypt at the dawn of the Christian Era.[12]

2. A very important religion of the Græco-Roman world was the worship of *Attis* and *Cybele*. It was transported to Rome from Phrygia in the third century B.C., but because of its wild and orgiastic nature was forbidden to Roman citizens until the time of Claudius. Exactly what the rites of this worship were in the first century we do not know, since our definite information comes from a much later date. The general features of the worship, though, we may ascertain with fair certainty. The ceremonies took place during the latter part of March, beginning on the fifteenth. It was accompanied by the most frenzied expressions of grief and excitement, even to the extent of physical mutilation. An important feature of the ceremonies was the cutting of a pine tree, which was made sacred by the myth concerning Attis. The trunk of this tree was carried, swathed in black garments like a corpse, and with great

[12]Cf. Frazer, *Golden Bough: Adonis, Attis, Osiris*, pp. 267-400; also P. Brit. Mus. 42; P. Par. 26, 47, 51.

pomp and solemnity, to the temple of the goddess Cybele. This was intended to represent the death of the god Attis. The following day his resurrection was celebrated. Then followed other festivities and processions, the ceremonies being concluded at the temple of Cybele. The details of the underlying myth are vague and uncertain, but appear to be the primitive nature-religion conception of the goddess of fertility mourning for her beloved, and eventually restoring him to life again. In its native Asia Minor home the religion was one of extreme sexual excesses. "As late as the second century, women of the higher circles in Lydia lived as courtezans before the goddess. . . . Even after civilization stopped this as a general custom, a class of priestesses kept it up."[13] To what extent this characteristic persisted in other localities we cannot tell, but its sensual and sensational appeal were its chief attractions.[14]

3. A religion of Babylonian origin was based upon the myth of *Ishtar* and *Tammuz*. It was another of the many forms of nature-worship. Tammuz was a god who departed each autumn to the nether world, whither he was followed by Ishtar, the goddess of love and reproduction. After a few months of absence the goddess returns, bringing Tammuz with her, whence comes spring with its renewal of life and inspiration of love. The methods of worship in this religion were crude and revoltingly sensual. Its emphasis upon sexual love and fecundity lent to it ritual practices which are indescribable.[15]

4. An approximate parallel to the Tammuz and Ishtar worship is found in that of the Phœnician deities *Adonis* and *Aphrodite*, with its centers at Paphos in Cyprus and Byblos in Syria. In fact, it is probable that it is historically related to the Tammuz-Ishtar religion, for Frazer, a leading authority on ancient religions, consid-

[13]Cobern, *op. cit.*, p. 418.

[14]Cf. Frazer, *op. cit.*, pp. 217-265.

[15]Cf. S. Langdon, Hastings' *Ency. of Rel. and Ethics*, art. "Mysteries."

ers that the name Adonis is doubtless a development from the Semitic title *adoni*, "my lord," the god having been called "my lord Tammuz."[16] The worship of Adonis was originally and essentially a nature-religion. The withering of vegetation in the autumn and its reappearance in the spring constituted its chief basis. Out of this recurrence of the seasons grew the myth which gave form to the worship.

In the mythical basis of the Adonis worship we again find features strongly suggestive of historical connection with the Tammuz cult. In his Græco-Oriental garb Adonis is a charming youth beloved by the goddess Aphrodite, another Græco-Oriental deity. While Adonis was an infant Aphrodite concealed him in a chest and placed him in charge of Persephone, the queen of the Underworld. So completely was Persephone captivated by the beauty of the handsome babe that she declined to return him to Aphrodite. A bitter conflict followed, and was not settled until Zeus interfered as arbiter and decreed that Adonis should remain with Persephone, the goddess of death, in the Underworld a part of the year, and with the goddess of love, Aphrodite, in the upper world during the other part. In a fit of jealousy the god Ares disguised himself as a wild boar and slew the fair Adonis, to the unbounded grief of Aphrodite. The ritual of the religion consisted in the dramatizing of the death of the god, and his resurrection on the following day. It was assumed that on the day of his resurrection he ascended to heaven. There developed, probably as a late addition, the idea of the marriage of the god to the goddess. Originally the relations between them contemplated no thought of formal wedlock, the result of which was a degraded ritual. We are told that in the ceremonies at Byblos, "The disconsolate believers, left behind on earth, shaved their heads; . . . women who could not bring themselves to sacrifice their beautiful

[16] *Op. cit.*, p. 6.

tresses had to give themselves up to strangers on the day of the festival, and to dedicate to Astarte the wages of their shame."[17]

The devotees of this religion found in the Christian faith striking analogy to their beliefs, but an incomparably superior moral tone. It was like passing out of the dim glow of a tallow candle into the full light of the noonday sun. Yet the analogy of the Christian views with those of Adonism might have furnished a helpful point of contact.[18]

5. Among the Oriental mystery religions that which presents the highest ethical and religious character, and approaches most nearly to Christianity in forms, views, and ideals, was *Mithraism.* It was of extremely ancient origin, and had probably passed through several stages of modification. It is thought probable that in remote antiquity Mithra was an Iranian tribal god. Later he came to figure in Zoroastrianism as the mediator or manifestation of Ahura Mazda, the supreme Persian god. In the Chaldean form of the religion Mithra is a sun-god. As the worship appears in the Græco-Roman period, Mithra is again a supreme god rather than a subordinate or mediating deity.

Mithraism was probably present in Asia Minor for a century or more before the Christian Era, but it did not spread widely until the second century and after. Thus it had exceedingly doubtful opportunity for any genetic contribution to Christianity. But its parallels to Christian doctrine and ceremony, and its place in history as the outstanding rival of early Christianity in the Roman Empire, make it worthy of extended notice. In fact, its strong resemblance to Christianity has caused some scholars to assume, in spite of the lack of definite historical evidence, that there must have been some genetic dependence of Christianity upon Mithraism. This po-

[17]Frazer, *op. cit.*, p. 184.

[18]Cf. Frazer, *op. cit.*, pp. 1-216.

sition. however, can never be more than a very doubtful hypothesis, with all the probabilities being favorable to the dependence of Mithraism on Christianity, if there be any genetic relation existing.

Mithraism was fundamentally dualistic. This was its Iranian heritage. The rites of initiation were divided into seven stages, consisting of ablutions, sacrifices, and sacred meals, and designed to impart to the candidate a rebirth into fellowship with the god. In the "doctrine" of the religion Mithra is the creator of the world, and through several conflicts saves it from being destroyed by Ahriman, the prince of darkness. In these conflicts there is a flood story similar to the record in Genesis. When the earth was finally made secure against the evil one, Mithra returned to his heavenly abode. The initiates were promised that he would return again to endow them with immortality. A conspicuous feature of the ceremonial was the sacrifice of the sacred bull. It is probable that in an extremely ancient form of the religion the god was identified with a bull.

Mithraism held out the anticipation of a blessed immortality and of peace with the god. It held to the doctrines of a final judgment, resurrection, and the ultimate destruction of the present world order. These ideas came from Persian and Babylonian sources. The moral tone of Mithraism was much superior to most of the other mystery religions—a Semitic trait and probably traceable to an original Sumerian heritage. It made quite an effective appeal to the Græco-Roman world, and from the second through the third century was a formidable competitor for Christianity, but declined rapidly thereafter, so that by the dawn of the fifth century it was practically a matter of history. One of its most serious disadvantages as a rival of Christianity was the fact that women were not accepted as communicants of the religion. Here again is a trace of Semitic influence.[19]

[19]Cf. Halliday, *op. cit.*, pp. 281-311; Cumont, *The Mysteries of Mithra.*

III. Characteristics of the Mystery Religions

Based upon the foregoing review, we may present a summary of those general features which characterized to a greater or less extent all the mystery cults. Such a survey will enable us to form a more accurate estimate of these religions in comparison with Christianity, and visualize correctly the essential attitude of Christianity toward these cults as it moved into their midst from its cradle in Palestine.

1. They were based upon myths descending from remote antiquity and undoubtedly conceived by their devotees as supra-human—outside the course of common history. It was not a conception of God active in history, but of a god acting outside history.

2. Their benefits were secured by the magical effects of some physical process. It was in the actual mechanics of the ritual, and from the priestly agent performing the ritual, that the worshiper received benefit. Their ceremonies were not symbols of spiritual operations, but were magical processes having an essential efficacy of their own.

3. Salvation consisted for the most part in securing desirable human ends. The mystery religions seldom presented any conception of a new ethical and spiritual sphere of experience. Morality was frequently ignored, and when recognized the evidence is clear that it was a secondary consideration. It was morality in order to a religious experience, and not religious experience as a basis of morality.

4. The mystery cults were all essentially polytheistic, for if the religion itself did not have two or more deities, it was tolerant toward the deities of other religions. That is, at best the mystery religions were only henotheistic—having a supreme god in the particular religion itself, but not excluding the possibility of valid gods in other religions.

5. The higher religious features which they did possess were crude manifestations of basal religious instincts,

native to the moral nature of man, such as the communion of humanity with deity, attainment of the soul to a higher sphere of experience, triumph of life over death, religion as a source of relief in human distress, and so forth. The religious nature of man has in many instances given expression to these inherent instincts where there could not conceivably have been any process of divine revelation involved. It is a fact worthy of remark though that these instinctive reactions were so concentrated and pronounced in the Græco-Roman world at the advent of Christianity's redemptive message.

6. The mystery religions were characterized by extreme sensuality, especially sexualism. Many of the basal myths unblushingly represent a male and female deity as consorting in sexual relations upon a plain basis of free love—that is, with no thought of any sanction from legitimate union or issue. Roman and Greek influence brought considerable alteration in this sordid view, but never succeeded in eliminating it. The ritual of paganism appealed primarily to the sensual instincts. The high spiritual, moral, and ethical idealism of Judaism and Christianity were all but unknown to them. Their standards of purity offered little restraint to man's natural appetites; on the contrary, in several instances they provided for the indulgence of these appetites. Hence gluttony, drunkenness, and unchastity mar the picture of pagan religion.

The student is at first startled by the obvious points of similarity between Christianity and the mystery religions. They have in common teachings on death and resurrection, the idea of redemption through mystical union with deity, at least a slight parallel in the thought of religion as a challenge to purity of life, an experience of satisfaction in this world issuing in immortality and happiness in the world to come. Some of the pagan religions had a doctrine of regeneration, practiced a ceremonial bath or baptism, and a sacred meal, sometimes of memorial significance. However, when rightly viewed there is nothing here necessarily to disturb Christian faith. These historical facts but manifest the broad religious basis which is inherent in human nature, and show how remarkably well adapted Christianity was to that inherent religious basis. If one will only presuppose a merciful God providing that religious basis, and preparing a glorious historical religion which was admirably well fitted to that religious basis, the difficulty vanishes. The reason Christianity has satisfied representatives from all races of humanity is because it has been satisfactory to all races of humanity. It is adapted to the fundamental religious nature of man.

It is clearly certain that these religions were utterly inferior to Christianity, and could have made only the most incidental contribution to its outward form and expression, and none to its essential content. Halliday has well said that "the concentration of Christian doctrine around the character, life, and teaching of a concrete and historical personality gave to it a convincing reality which all its rivals lacked."[20] The essential historical facts of the Christian religion are authenticated beyond any reasonable doubt, and the fundamental benefits of the Christian religion are matters of conscious experience rather than theory or tradition. By its own inherent merits Christianity won its victory over the rival religions of the ancient world, so we need not be alarmed at any dangers which may seem to threaten from these religions as revamped by modern criticism.

The Jewish Diaspora

When the first Christian missionaries faced their world-encompassing task, the Jews were spread over almost the entire Mediterranean world. This distribution of the Jews, known as the *Diaspora,* or "Dispersion," began in Egypt as early as the time of Jeremiah (Cf. Jer. 41: 16, 17; Isa. 11: 11). Alexander colonized

[20] *Op. cit.,* p. 310. On the essential differences between Christianity and the pagan religions, a splendid brief statement may be found in Halliday, *op. cit.,* pp. 320ff.

a number of Jews in Egypt, and his policy was continued by the Ptolemies. The disturbances which were attendant upon the conquests and struggles of the Greek age threw the eastern world into a very unsettled state, in consequence of which the Jews joined many other peoples of that religion in wandering from place to place. Many Jews remained in Babylonia after the Restoration, and from there it is quite probable that colonies were formed in various parts of the Syrian empire by the Seleucidæ. Antiochus the Great transported a large colony of Jews from Mesopotamia into Lydia and Phrygia in Asia Minor, in an effort to stabilize conditions among the seditious inhabitants of that region. Many of them for purposes of trade or other advantages migrated into the Greek cities. Hence by the beginning of the Roman period the Jews were distributed through the greater part of the eastern world, and were still maintaining tenaciously their racial identity and religious heritage.

When Pompey captured Jerusalem he carried back to Rome as captives many hundreds of Jews, thus extending the Diaspora into the western world. A reference in Strabo seems to indicate that there were Jews in Rome even before the time of Pompey.[21] This may be regarded as highly probable. During New Testament times there were Jews in practically every part of the Roman Empire.

The majority of the Roman emperors were very tolerant of Judaism, and so permitted the religion to become well established in their domains. The Jews had a synagogue in nearly every city of any considerable size or importance. Consequently, we find that as Paul proceeds on his missionary tours he visits only one place in which he fails to find a synagogue, namely, Philippi. Services were held in these synagogues regularly, at least on the sabbath, so that it could be said in literal truth, "Moses from generations of old hath in every city them

[21] Cf. Schuerer, *op. cit.*, II, ii, p. 221.

that preach him, being read in the synagogues every sabbath" (Acts 15: 22). At the sabbath exercises of the synagogue three classes of people usually assembled.

1. There were the Jews, chiefly born and reared in the Hellenistic world, but nevertheless loyal, pure-blooded Jews.

2. There were the Gentile proselytes; that is, Gentiles who had submitted to the rite of circumcision and proselyte baptism, and had accepted the obligations of the other ceremonies and traditions of Judaism. They were regarded as regular members of the Jewish community, with all the privileges of a Jew.

3. The third class were the "Godfearers"; Gentiles who had accepted Jehovah as the true God, and respected the Old Testament Scriptures, but had never received the full rites of induction into Judaism. They appear frequently in Acts under such descriptive designations as, "a devout man, and one that feared God" (10: 2); "ye that fear God" (13: 16); "those among you that fear God" (13: 26); "the devout (and) proselytes" (13: 43), and so forth. There were many Gentile women in this class. Of such were the "devout women of honorable estate" of Acts 13: 50, and Lydia, who is described as "one that worshiped God" (Acts 16: 14).

The spiritual nature of the Jewish religion made it popular in the first century, though the bigoted exclusiveness of many Jews prejudiced the majority of the Gentiles against them. Converts from the Jews and proselytes and God-fearers always formed the nucleus around which Paul built his churches. It is hardly possible to exaggerate the service of the Diaspora to the initial propagation of the Christian religion.

In very brief review we have scanned the religious situation of the Græco-Roman world. We have seen in it the fact which has faced us in every other phase of this investigation. There appear in each successive feature as it passes in review abundant reasons for believing that an All-wise Providence was molding the situation in such way as to make it best adapted to welcome and effectively appropriate the redemptive message of the Christ. God has not only been active in redemption, but in the world which he purposed to redeem.

APPENDIX

The Herods

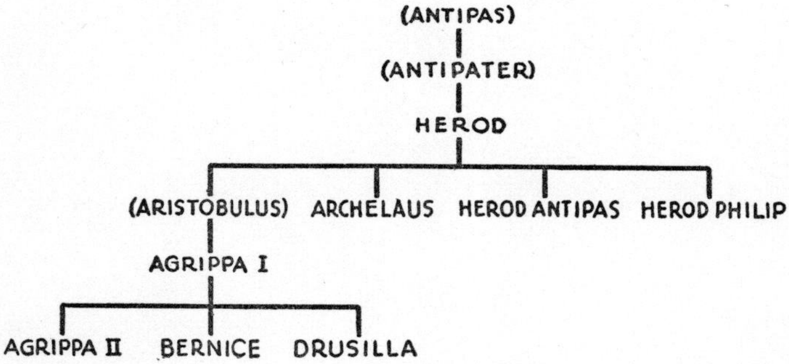

This graph is designed to show the family relationship between those members of the Herodian family which appear in the New Testament. The names in brackets do not occur in the New Testament, but are placed here because necessary to complete the family connection.

BIBLIOGRAPHY

A vast number of books in English, German, and French are related to the field of investigation to which the present work has been devoted. It would be impracticable, not to say impossible, to list every work in the field. An exhaustive bibliography would make a large volume in itself. Our object here has been only to list enough of the works dealing with the New Testament background to cover all the important aspects involved, offering a bibliography from which the scholar may derive helpful suggestions and the average student may make selections for equipping his library.

GENERAL WORKS

Adams, *Biblical Backgrounds.*

Breed, *The Preparation of the World for Christ.*

Fiebig, *Die Umwelt des Neuen Testaments.*

Fisher, *Beginnings of Christianity.*

Foakes-Jackson and Lake, *Beginnings of Christianity,* Part I, Vol. I.

Glover, *The World of the New Testament.*

Hausrath, *New Testament Times* (4 vols.).

Holtzmann, *Neuen Testament Zeitgeschichte.*

Krueger, *Hellenismus und Judentum in Neutestamentliche Zeitalter.*

Moulton, *Social Life and Religion of New Testament Times.*

Purdy-Macgregor, *Jew and Greek: Tutors unto Christ.*

Scott, *The Gospel and Its Tributaries.*

Wenley, *The Preparation for Christianity.*

JEWISH BACKGROUND

Adeney, *The Hebrew Utopia.*

Baron, *A Social and Religious History of the Jews.*

Bentwich, *Josephus.*
Philo-Judæus of Alexandria.
Hellenism.

Bloch, *Israel und die Voelker.*

Booth, *The Bridge Between the Testaments.*
The World of Jesus.

Box, *Judaism in the Greek Period.*

Braley, *A Neglected Period.*

Charles, *Between the Old and New Testament.*

Daiches, *Jews in Babylonia.*

Delitzsch, *Jewish Artizan Life.*

Dembitz, *Services in Synagogue and Home.*

Doubnow, *Outline of Jewish History* (3 vols.).

Drummond, *The Jewish Messiah.*

Edersheim, *In the Days of Christ* (Sketches of Jewish Social Life).
Life and Times of Jesus the Messiah (2 vols.).

Emmett, art. "Messiah" in Hastings' *Encyclopedia of Religion and Ethics.*

Ewald, *History of Israel* (8 vols.).

Fairweather, *Background of the Gospels.*
Exile to Advent.

Foakes-Jackson, *Josephus and the Jews.*

Gavin, *The Jewish Antecedents of the Christian Sacraments.*

Graetz, *History of the Jews* (6 vols.).

Grant, C. M., *Between the Testaments.*

Grant, F. C., *Economic Background of the Gospels.*

Gregg, *Between the Testaments.*

Herford, *The Pharisees.*
Judaism in the New Testament Period.

Hollmann, *Jewish Religion in the Time of Jesus.*

Huffman, *Progressive Unfolding of the Messianic Hope.*

Keith, *The Social Life of the Jew in the Time of Christ.*

Kennedy, *Philo's Contribution to Religion.*

Mathews, *A History of New Testament Times in Palestine.*

Moore, *Judaism in the First Three Centuries of the Christian Era* (3 vols.)

Muirhead, *The Times of Christ.*

Myers, *Story of the Jewish People.*

McGinty, *Babylon to Bethlehem.*
Oesterly, *Evolution of the Messianic Idea.*
Radin, *The Jews Among the Greeks and Romans.*
Riggs, *History of the Jewish People.*
Robertson, A. T., *The Pharisees and Jews.*
Schwalm, *La Vie Privée du peuple Juif à l'Epoque de Jésus-Christ.*
Schuerer, *The Jewish People in the Time of Jesus Christ* (5 vols.).
Simkhovitch, *Toward the Understanding of Jesus.*
Smith, G. A., *Historical Geography of the Holy Land.*
Smith, W. W., *Students' Historical Geography of the Holy Land.*
Stanley, *History of the Jewish Church* (3 vols.).

GENTILE BACKGROUND

Angus, *Environment of Early Christianity.*
Christianity and the Mystery Religions.
Religious Quests of the Græco-Roman World.
Abbott, *Common People of Ancient Rome.*
Arnold, *Roman Systems of Provincial Administration.*
Barrow, *Slavery in the Roman Empire.*
Baur, *Christian History of the First Three Centuries,* Vol. I.
Bevan, *Hellenism and Christianity.*
Case, *Evolution of Early Christianity.*
Clemens, *Christianity and Its Non-Jewish Sources.*
Cobern, *New Archæological Discoveries.*
Cumont, *Oriental Religions in the Roman Empire*
Deissmann, *Light From the Ancient East.*
Fairweather, *Background of the Epistles.*
Firebaugh, *Inns of Greece and Rome.*
Foakes-Jackson, *Rise of Gentile Christianity.*
Fowler, *Rome.*
Roman Ideas of Deity.
"Roman Religion" in Hastings' *Encyclopedia of Religion and Ethics.*
Social Life at Rome in the Age of Cicero.
Frazer, *The Golden Bough.*
Friedlaender, *Roman Life and Manners Under the Early Empire* (4 vols.).
Gilbert, *Greek Thought in the New Testament.*

Glover, *Conflict of Religions in the Roman Empire.*
Halliday, *Pagan Background of Early Christianity.*
Kennedy, *St. Paul and the Mystery-Religions.*
Kimball, *Bury's Students' History of Greece.*
Milligan, *Here and There Among the Papyri.*
Murray, *Five Stages of Greek Religion.*
Myers, *History of Rome.*
Neander, "Relation of Grecian to Christian Ethics," Bibliotheca-Sacra, Vol. 10.
Ramsay, *Cities of St. Paul.*
Paul the Traveller and Roman Citizen.
Pauline and Other Studies.
"Roads and Travel in the New Testament," Hastings *Dictionary of the Bible.*
Reitzenstein, *Die Hellenistische Mysterien-religionen.*
Rostovtzeff, *Social and Economic History of the Roman Empire*
Tucker, *Life in Ancient Athens.*
Life in the Roman World of Nero and St. Paul.
Wendland, *Die Hellenistisch-Roemische Kultur.*
Zeller, *Outlines of Greek Philosophy.*

SOURCE MATERIALS

Charles, *Apocrypha and Pseudepigrapha of the Old Testament.*
Cohen, *Babylonian Talmud.*
Colson-Whitaker, *Philo-Judæus* (Greek text with English translation.)
Danby, *The Mishna.*
Davis, *Greek Papyri of the First Century.*
Goodspeed and Colwell, *A Greek Papyrus Reader.*
Grenfell, Hunt, and Hogarth, *Fayum Towns and Their Papyri.*
Grenfell and Hunt, *The Hibeh Papyri.*
The Oxyrhynchus Papyri.
Grenfell, Hunt, and Goodspeed, *The Tebtunis Papyri.*
Hicks and Hill, *Greek Historical Inscriptions.*
Johnson, Martin, and Hunt, *Catalogue of the Greek Papyri in the John Rylands Library.*
Lamm, *Jerusalemikische Talmud.*
Lindsay, *Handbook of Latin Inscriptions.*

Milligan, *Selections From the Papyri.*

Newton, Hicks, and Hirschfeld, *Ancient Greek Inscriptions in the British Museum.*

Report of Harvard Excavations at Samaria.

Rodkinson, *Babylonian Talmud* (new ed.).

Schwab, *Le Talmud de Jerusalem.*

Thackeray, *Josephus* (Greek text with English translation).

Whiston, *The Works of Josephus.*

Winter, *Life and Letters in the Papyri.*

INDEX